Alexander's Journey

Dum spiro spero

Love   from

Alex   ☺x

Alexander's Journey: Dum Spiro Spero
ISBN Number 978-0-9991164-0-1

Jeff W Goodwin asserts the moral right to be identified as the author of this work.

A copy of this book has been deposited at both the Library of Congress in the United States of America and the British Library in the United Kingdom of Great Britain and Northern Ireland.

Arcanum Press LLC is registered in the State of Kansas, United States of America, entity number 8681348.
Arcanum Press Ltd is registered in England & Wales, company number 10704825

This book and the DVD of the same name complement each other and tell the story together. Enjoying both will allow you to best appreciate Alexander's Journey.

A message from me and the rest of the Goodwin Family:

Thank you to everyone who made a positive contribution to Alexander's Journey in his battle against cancer and in his rehabilitation as a cancer survivor.

Thank you to Dr. Lou Wetzel, Chief Terry Zeigler and the main benefactor and their family without whom none of this would have been possible. Your kindness will never be forgotten and saved Alex's life!

Thank you to Damian and all those working at and with Into Productions for making this a reality and for all the effort that was involved. Thank you to TJ and KJO Media for the backup and for collaborating to make this even more amazing than it already was! Thank you to Arcanum Press, Rainy Day Books, Warwick Books, Richard from Streamline Press and especially Allison and the rest of AlphaGraphics KC for that extra help and believing.

Thank you, Warwickshire & West Mercia Police and Kansas City, Kansas Police and all the great and good who serve with them who went above and beyond. Thank you to the Police Firearms Officer Association and the Police Federation of England & Wales. Thank you to Kate and the rest of the team in Corporate Comms. Special thanks to Warwickshire Police Chief Constable Martin Jelley and Police & Crime Commissioner Philip Seccombe.

Thank you Dr. Massimiliano Pinarello and to Anita Morris & Kim Hess, our Bird of Prey ladies at Hack Back and Lakeside Nature Center, you three brought light and hope into Alex's life during the darkest times. Thank you also to Jessica of F.L. Schlagle Environmental Library and Cheshire Falconry who also made things a little brighter for him.

Thank you to Dr. Rosenthal, Dr. Chastain and Dr. Massey for their skills, dedication and care. You made the difference.

Thank you to my brothers and sisters in the thin blue line across the world that have stood with us. Thank you to the police forces of the UK, US, Canada, Australia, Gibraltar and Bermuda that rallied to our banner especially for the Horizon on my Mind recording on that rainy day in Leek Wootton and the escort when we arrived in Kansas City on that freezing night. Thank you too, to the Officers of the Thin Green, Red and Orange lines that did the same. We salute you all.

Thank you to the good folk at Kansas University Hospital and Children's Mercy Hospital who played their part especially Lindsey, David, Kendra, Pam, Jill, Becca, Haley, Scott, Chris and the rest (you know who you are!).

Thank you Dr. Visser and those Nurses and other healthcare professionals who did their best and cared when treating Alex at Leicester Royal Infirmary, Royal Orthopedic Hospital in Birmingham and the Children's Hospital in Sheffield. Special thanks to Marie, Rohila, Lucy, Rachel, Jen from the LRI and Jo, Sue, Claire and the rest of the Thin Purple Line at Diana's Children's Community Services.

Thank you to Jane and the rest of the family Wetzel. You made us feel welcome and at home: every single one of you, every single time.

Thank you to David Jones Senior & Junior for the song Horizon on my Mind and to Stephen Walters & Ross Owen for the song Hold On. Thank you to Judy, Simon, Mandy and everyone else who we first met at Bruntingthorpe. Thank you to the 9th Earl Bathurst and Countess Bathurst.

Thank you to the people who made sure the day at Leek Wootton filming Horizon On My Mind worked through sheer hard work managing the unmanageable: Peter, Lucy, Carl, Mark to name a few. Thank you also to the women of our village school and village who came and made tea and coffee and braved the weather (everything seems better after a cup of tea).

Thank you to KCTV5, KMBC9, Fox 4, WIBW, BBC Midlands, BBC Coventry & Warwickshire, Harborough & Lutterworth Mail, Leicester Mercury, Coventry Telegraph and the Kansas City Star and all the good people associated with them: special thanks to Amy, Donna, Joan, Antonia, Alex, Shawn and Keleigh.

Thank you to Congressman Kevin Yoder, Congressman Cory Booker, Sir Alan Duncan MP, Alberto Costa MP, The Secretary of State for Kansas Kris Kobach, Michelle from U.S. Customs & Immigration Service in KCMO and Nicola & Eileen from The Foreign & Commonwealth Office.

Thank you to The Roasterie, Black Sky Radio, The Kansas City Chiefs, Kansas City Royals, Mr. Block, The Ernie Miller Park & Nature Center, Kansas City Zoo, Residence Inn Marriott at the Legends in KC, Sombrero's, Salty Iguana, First Watch at Fairway, Cosentino's Price Chopper in Gardner, The Mystery Fishing Tackle Shop and the amazing Bass Pro Shop in Olathe. Thank you Forbidden Planet in Leicester and a special thank you to Craig and Esther at Blink-print.

Thank you to Joy at Red Arc and Hannah and the team at The Bone Cancer Research Trust. Thank you to Unify Health Services of Jacksonville, Florida & Modern Mobility at Fosse Park, Sarcoma UK, The Sarcoma Alliance and Macmillan Cancer Support. Thank you to the Natural History Museum in London.

Thank you to Dunton Bassett Primary School and its Parent Teacher Association. Thank you also to the villagers of Dunton Basset and the congregation of All Saints Church, Dunton Bassett. Thank you to the British Takemusu Aikido Federation and the British Aikido Board. Thank you to those members of The United Grand Lodge of England who supported and donated.

Thank you to Make A Wish Missouri, Give Kids The World, CLIC Sargent, The Round Table Children's Wish Charity, Helping Hands Charity, Guns n'Hoses, Ronald McDonald House Charities and the Rotary Club of Lutterworth.

Thank you to our supporters on Twitter and Facebook for wishing us good mornings every day and putting a smile on Alex's face. Special thanks to @ghostmagic48 for the magic of course!

Thank you Mariette for helping, proofreading, editing and assisting so very much! You did a much better job than Jon, Eddard, Tyrion and Tywin!

Thank you Shona for the steer, direction and motivation.

Thank you Liz for the editing, comments and proofreading.

Thank you so much Mark Hamill, William Shatner, Diana Gabaldon, Adam Baker, Eric Idle, Boy George, Mark King, Bo Derek, Ian Royce and Tim Peake: you didn't have to... but you did.

They say that friends are the family you choose so an extra special thank you goes to the old friends that cared and new friends who came into our life. You are loved and we will not forget. Thank you to our family members who have been there for us.

A final extra special thank you to the officers on the Firearms and Traffic OPU and the Wheel Unit in KCK for all that you did and continue to do. #PoliceFamily

Prologue

Like untold millions, I have a very special place in my heart for Alex. Visiting hospitals, I have been so touched & inspired by the children who persevere in the face of such profound challenges. I love Alex for his optimism & bravery more than I can say. It does such a positive service to the world to see what children with adversities deal with on a daily basis and Alex's video-diary is a treasure!

From one of his many, many fans: ME!

All the best.

Mark Hamill
California, 21 August 2017

FOREWORD 1

'One day, I want to be a scientist like you'—anyone could make you feel cool saying that. But then, there is Alex, and if he is the one telling you that, you fly. As it surprises you, your muscles tighten; you have to swallow your emotion, because there is no space for fears, no time for thinking how powerful that is, and Alex's energy has already overwhelmed you anyway. He is unstoppable.

That's how he spoke to me the first time we met in person on 1st September last year, one week after my myxoid liposarcoma had been resected from my left calf. I was trotting on my crutches, Alex was rocking his wheels already with mastery. His Ewing sarcoma had already required several chemotherapy and radiotherapy sessions and would have claimed more.

I met him and his family to take them for a quick tour of the London Natural History Museum. Alex and I had been Twitter friends for about three months by then. He first found me. I tweeted to Sarcoma UK and to The Royal Marsden Hospital in London about my first day of radiotherapy treatment there, in June, mentioning '#cancertreatment', '#awareness', and 'please #donate'. He tweeted back to me: 'Hi Max. Be brave. I'm at Leicestershire Royal Infirmary having my Hickman Line put in today, so I have a feeling on how you must feel. I shall message you tomorrow x'.

Posting publicly about my sarcoma was a sort of self-exorcism for me, because when you have cancer you are scared, and you want to get at least that demon out of your system. That is how I saw it. But Alex immediately proved to be special. With a simple message of solidarity, he spoke to me. Directly, as a friend, because we shared the same distress, he just wanted to cheer me up. And he did more than that. He inspired me.

When I looked at his profile, I saw the story of a nine-year-old child who was having his chemo drip put in his torso on that very day. I thought that if *he* could pass on to me energy, courage, strength, and comfort of not being alone, then *I* could do something for the others as well. That is when I saw for the first time how incredible he is. His superpower, as I see it. I used to love Batman and that is one point in common I have with Alex, but now Alex is my favourite superhero. Hands down. Sorry, Bruce.

The story of Alex and his family—Jeff, Maruška, and little Sophia—is a story of love and determination; it is a superhero story after all. There is tension, worry, sadness, but also joy, friendship, and generosity. Alex's superpower of empowering people is strong and it is a great gift. He has been through countless sessions of chemotherapy, radiotherapy, hospital tests, medical examinations, operations, but he is still throwing his thumb up and his portentous smile, every day, to everyone. He truly is unstoppable.

Alex and I had a chance to return to the museum together in November, for a special visit I organised with some friends, and we all had a great day. He then went with his family to the US for treatment and shall be back to the UK soon. We talk to each other whenever we want and tell how are things. The roughest part of one challenge is done and we are both dealing with its demanding aftermath. But we are aware of what happened and we know we can count on each other and the support of so many other people. Alex is always excited, kind, and dear. You can never feel lost when you are with him and he moves us all.

Alexander's journey is an expression for great endeavours done by great people, just like this one. You can only be amazed, considering how much has been asked of Alex and how much more he gives unconditionally. His story should be held as an example of simplicity and bravery, power and life. And Alex will also be a great scientist one day. But he knows this already, I am sure. *Dum Spiro, Spero.*

Dr. Max S. Pinarello, Doctor of Archaeology
Petrie Museum (University College London)
London, 4th June 2017

FOREWORD 2

Dear Alex, thank you for this book for us to read
The true story of a very courageous boy indeed
'Alexander's Journey' is a very special book. Be amazed at
the giant steps that Alex took Find a comfy chair to sit for
awhile With perhaps a teardrop but with many a smile

In June 2016 when PC Jeff Goodwin stood at my office door,
he didn't need to say anything, I knew it was bad news. He
sat down and told me that Alex's test results had confirmed a
diagnosis of Ewing Sarcoma.

Alex is an ordinary 9-year-old boy who likes dinosaurs,
nature and the great outdoors. He was no longer an
ordinary boy, but his way of dealing with the road ahead to
defeat his cancer was anything but ordinary. When meeting
Alex for the first time, we sat together and played with some
of his Ultraman toys, and it was then that Alex himself told
me about his cancer and the treatment he would be
receiving and he said to me " I'm going to defeat the nasty
cancer". I left Alex in awe of his positivity and determination.
Jeff, his dad, a police officer in my team was soon to find out
how the Police Family reaches out and supports each other
and would walk alongside him and his family every step of
the way. Soon various events began to be planned officers
supporting Alex when his hair fell out, by shaving their heads

too, cake making, tuck shop, sponsored events, and many, many more to begin raising funds to get Alex to America for his much-needed treatment.

By the team, Alex is fondly known as Constable Alex and we tweet daily with followers about Alex's progress, all who admire him for his positivity and physical courage.

Horizon on my Mind was a song given to Alex by Dave Jones, a police staff member on Jeff's team. It is a very rare occasion to see police officers singing their hearts out rocking with blow up colourful guitars, this song was the launch pad for many other fund-raising events and helped spread the word about Alexander's Journey.

Police Inspector Lucy Sewell
Warwickshire Police
1st July, 2017

FOREWORD 3

What can I tell you about Alex Goodwin that you don't already know? That he is a 10-year-old little boy involved in the battle of his life, fighting Ewing Sarcoma cancer. That he loves science and birds of prey. That he has a smile that will melt the hardest of hearts and a personality that is gentle and kind. You know all of that, but I can share with you what Alex has given to me and the Kansas City, Kansas Police Department.

On May 9, 2016, Detective Brad Lancaster of the Kansas City, KS Police Department (KCKPD) was shot and killed in the line of duty while assisting uniformed officers who were in foot pursuit of a subject near the Hollywood Casino. Detective Lancaster was the first line of duty death our Department had experienced in 19 years, but the KCKPD was in for a very difficult summer. About ten weeks later, on July 19, 2016, Captain Robert "Dave" Melton was shot and killed while assisting officers in apprehending a drive-by-shooting suspect. Both men were phenomenal police officers, dedicated to duty, and left behind devastated families.

It is difficult to describe the mood in the organization, shocked and overwhelmed with grief are the first two words that come to mind. As the Chief of Police, there was nothing I could say or do to take away the pain our officers and staff were feeling. I could only offer a hug, a weak word of encouragement like, "We are going to be okay." And, on numerous occasions I told an officer or staff member that I loved them. I was at a total loss on how to handle the situation and I was trying to deal with my own emotions. There is no instruction book to go to for an answer and you are left to muddle your way through the best you can, thank God I have some amazing team members!

The outpouring of support from our community, the law enforcement community, and the entire nation was amazing and at times overwhelming. Twitter and our other social media outlets provided additional platforms for people to express their condolences for our losses and show support. It was comforting to our Department to know we had so much support during our great loss. Now you are probably wondering what does two KCKPD officers being killed in the line of duty have to do with Alexander's Journey, they have everything to do with it!

In August, I took some time off to collect my thoughts and reflect on what had happened. One evening, I sat on my back deck watching the cows, drinking a beer, and searching Twitter for people with positive and uplifting messages. That evening I found @alex_journey. I was immediately drawn in to Alex Goodwin's story and felt a connection to him because his dad is a police officer in the UK. I started following Alex and interacting with him on Twitter. Everyday Alex would post a video updating his followers about his battle and he would always close with a word of encouragement and a big thumbs up! His innocence and sincerity just captivated my heart. I found the positive message of hope and inspiration I was looking for encapsulated in a 9-year-old little boy, half way around the world. Here is a little boy fighting his own Goliath and in the middle of the battle he takes time to focus on other people and I thought, "That's the SECRET!" Alex understands that we cannot always control what happens to us, but we can control how we react to what happens to us. Alex took a negative in his life and turned it into a positive by being an ambassador of inspiration and hope to his 20k+ followers on Twitter.

Eventually, we got to meet Alex, Jeff, Maruška, and Sophia in December when they arrived in Kansas City for Alex's cancer treatment at KU Medical Center. They are a very strong, loving family and it has been our honor to help them. Helping Alex and his family was a way for us to pay back all of the support and help we received when Brad Lancaster and Robert Melton were killed.

I believe Alexander's Journey will have a profound, if not life changing, impact on anyone who reads it. It is a message of love, hope, and courage! Everyone can learn a valuable lesson from Alex – We cannot always control what happens to us, but we can control how we react to what happens to us.

Terry Zeigler, Chief of Police
Kansas City Police Department, Kansas
2nd July, 2017.

FOREWORD 4

I first learned about Alexander's journey when Terry Zeigler, the Kansas City, Kansas, chief of police, called to ask if there was anything The University of Kansas Hospital could do to help the family of a police officer in Warwickshire, England. Terry had been following the story on social media and resulting heartfelt support from police all over the world. Jeff and Maruška Goodwin's 9-year-old son, Alex, was facing an advanced case of Ewing sarcoma, a malignant bone tumor in his leg. The initial diagnosis had been delayed, making an already difficult case that much more urgent. I promised Terry we'd take a look and do whatever we could to help Alex.

The critical point of my role in this journey came one month later in late November 2016. After hundreds of emails, dozens of professional consultations and daily phone calls with Jeff, we finally both broke down and cried. He had just been told that the surgery to potentially cure his son's cancer was no longer an option. "Jeff," I said. "I can't look at this medically anymore. I can only approach this as though Alex were my own son." I had no idea then how truly close we would grow to be in the months ahead.

Alex had first complained of pain in the leg and an unexplained fever in November of 2015. As is all too often the case with Ewing sarcoma, the symptoms were non-specific and initial X-rays were misleading. Finally, an MRI in May of 2016 showed a large, aggressive tumor arising in the right thigh bone with early invasion of the hip socket. After consultation with colleagues in our sarcoma program and several other major pediatric cancer centers in the U.S., I presented Jeff with 3 options. He had done extensive research of his own and simply responded: "I am very impressed with Dr. Rosenthal, and I feel such strong support from you and Terry," he said, "We would like to come to Kansas if you'll have us."

On a cold night in December, Jeff, Maruška, Alex and his 4-year-old sister, Sophia, arrived in Kansas City to a welcome befitting a head of state. From the start, the outpouring of support from law enforcement and the community was incredible. At the airport, police and fire departments from across the greater Kansas City area provided a 60-vehicle escort. When we arrived in our small neighborhood half an hour later, one hundred people lined the sidewalks to greet Alex with cheers and Christmas songs. When their planned accommodations fell through, my wife, Jane, and I were privileged to share the holidays and our home with the Goodwin's until Alex was through his first tumor surgery 6 weeks later. During this time we came to know and love Alex and his family, and they became an enriching addition to our own family.

The courage and warm personality of Alex and his family did more than touch those of us who had the privilege of being with them up close — it touched countless individuals and organizations across the city, the nation and the world. They embraced Alex and his family, providing calls and letters of encouragement, invitations to tour city attractions, and other gestures of support. Although gravely ill, Alex gamely returned the enthusiasm shown by his supporters, sending frequent tweets and video messages thanking everyone and asking for their continued support and prayers, always ending with a "thumbs up" sign and a smile.

Another landmark in Alexander's journey was his first appointment with Dr. Howard Rosenthal, the director of our sarcoma center at The University of Kansas Health System. In just 10 days, Dr. Rosenthal and Dr. Kate Chastain of Children's Mercy Hospital across town completed Alex's chemotherapy, restaged the tumor and laid out a treatment plan and timetable. After all the months of delay and uncertainty leading up to their visit to Kansas, Jeff and Maruška could hardly believe this expedience was possible. While talking them through each of Alex's X-rays and imaging studies later that night, I could tell they felt a new sense of encouragement and understanding of the challenges ahead, and how to best overcome them.

The best medical care has to go beyond just the science and technology involved. It takes insight, faith and compassion. Caring for a patient like Alex required not only doctors, nurses and medical support staff, but also willing administrators, international advisors, financial advisors, and media relations. I am humbly indebted to the hundreds of professionals at Children's Mercy Hospital and The University of Kansas Hospital who provided such outstanding care and compassion for Alex and his family.

At face value, this story is about an amazing young man's battle with cancer. But the lessons and experiences shared in this story hold value for all who face great adversity in their lives. It is the story of the indomitable drive of a father and mother to save their son's life, and of their constant questioning and refusal to accept the status quo. It is also about the incredible support and love of a professional brotherhood, a Midwestern community, and thousands of people all over the world. Without these, Alexander's journey — as yet unfinished — would not be possible.

Lou Wetzel, M.D.
Professor of Radiology, The University of Kansas School of Medicine
Chief of Staff, The University of Kansas Hospital

One

"Cancer is a thief. It steals your dignity. It steals you from your family. It steals your family from you".

This quote sticks with me and I thank Kim who said it to me. It has got to be one of the hardest things to go through for any person of any age. I had always thought, naively, that cancer, strangely for such an evil and deadly disease, was usually a compromising thing: it usually claimed people who are older, whose bodies have passed their growth period in many ways and are in decline. It could be said it is a natural thing that is simply a product of when natural cell division goes wrong. Cells need to divide, to grow and build, to regenerate. Sometimes they go a little wrong.

It could be said that cancer is one of the few ways we have left to control the population, today we live longer and have all means of medicine at our disposal to make us better again.

The problem is, however, that cancer affects children too. Children who have yet to taste the world and all the bittersweet experience that it offers. Children who need to be cared for, nurtured and cherished. Children who need to grow, fall in love, experience fulfilment, achievement, belonging and a sense of purpose.

It is when this evil and despicable disease takes children, steals them from their parents and families that it feels so wrong. Cancer in children seems to have no meaning, no place in this world. It shakes you to your very foundation, any sense or appreciation of natural order is destroyed. It is the very stuff to shake faith: in either God or in nature.

Everyone has been touched by cancer but for me until now it was on the periphery of my world. I lost my Grandfather to cancer and he was much loved by me. I felt his loss and still do. I miss him every day but despite this loss I accepted his death and never thought that cancer and I would become so intimate. I had never crossed paths with childhood cancer until now.

The language we use when it involves cancer seems to be martial: we battle it, we fight it, we strive to beat it, defeat it, as warriors. It is only when it stares you in the face as an enemy, wanting to take something that is yours that the fight is truly real.

It is true also to say that we spend our lives distracted. We look to our future: our goals, our hopes, the end of the week, the next pay day, the next year. Then we will do things differently. We also look to the past: we worry and ponder on what has been, what was said, what wasn't said, how it went, what we regret and what was wrong. We never look at where we are. What that day holds for us. What is happening, what needs to be said, done, managed, tended to at that moment. It is sad that this only becomes our focus when we are dealing with something that halts us in our tracks. Usually it is something distressing, destructive or depressing. Some trauma that stops us right there and then. A life-threatening illness or incident.

This is the story of my son. He was eight years old when it began and ten years old when this part of his journey drew to a close. That's twenty percent of his life spent locked in a battle. Whilst it is from my perspective, it is by no means my biography. It is a story about my son's journey, a diary and record of events and thoughts. It is a memoir. I have tried to include his direct thoughts and feelings where I can and keep the peripherals to a minimum. Alexander will surely write about his own journey in his own words one day and I hope to read it with much pride, love and admiration.

Alex had always been a reasonably healthy boy, we have been fortunate in that we didn't seem to have a child that had a permanent cold and sniffle. He had his knocks and bangs from falls which were usually from play and he has the scars to show for it. I recall he had a urinary tract infection when he was just a small baby and had to have a lumbar puncture. I recollect being stood, with his mum Maruška, in a side room in the Sheffield Children's Hospital listening to his

25

distress. He was only six weeks old when he underwent that procedure. The doctors wouldn't allow us to be with him in the treatment room. We waited outside and could hear his anguish. After all, every parent can recognize their own baby's cries. It stays with me, clear in my mind's eye. I felt his pain and struggled to accept that something so painful and disturbing should be happening to this little baby I had sworn to protect. Ironically, we would find ourselves in the same hospital and I would have those same feelings just a handful of years later.

I joined the police service as a constable in January 2002. Maruška and I had been married a few years before that and she naturally expressed surprise and dissent when I left my well paid and comfortable Local Government Monday to Friday job to become one of the United Kingdom's finest in South Yorkshire Police. I felt it as a calling and had always wanted to join the police or at least be a public servant. Ironically, for someone who studied Accountancy at University I really disliked commerce and the drive to work to create profit (mainly for someone else!). The police and everything that surrounded it was where I wanted to be.

That change in career had its impact on us financially and emotionally. We weathered many storms and managed financial difficulties due to me taking a huge pay cut to join the Service as well as other poor financial decisions. We had many family tragedies including one of my siblings being diagnosed with a life threating illness and wrestling with their mental health ever since.

Despite this I was so very proud to serve and continue to be. I would like to think, despite my foibles, failings and errors of judgment, that I was and remain well respected as a cop by my peers and I play my part in the thin blue line. I have served primarily in a uniform role on patrol and response and achieved Acting Sergeant rank in 2007 and Acting Inspector in 2015. I am now an Authorised Firearms Officer (A.F.O) and have been for the last 6 years. Alex was born as a Yorkshireman like his dad into this policing environment in May 2007. We were joined by his little sister Sophia, a Cumbrian, in 2012.

I served in South Yorkshire Police until 2011 and then joined the Civil Nuclear Constabulary (C.N.C) stationed in Cumbria where I gained promotion to Sergeant and then Acting Inspector. We stayed in Cumbria until I joined Warwickshire Police reverting back to the rank of constable in 2015.

I also studied martial arts including Japanese and European disciplines from college and this travelled with me too. I think this assisted me so much. The mind, body and spirit need to be as one. Without one, the other two will never be enough.

Maruška and I made the decision to have Alex and he was planned and highly sought after! When Maruška fell pregnant I remember keeping his baby scans with me and proudly showing them like medals to anyone who was unfortunate enough to be double crewing a patrol car or otherwise working on my duty group with me for that tour of duty.

We had a home birth with Alex and as the time Maruška spent in labour with him lengthened, the midwife expressed concern that he was becoming distressed and fatigued. Unless he arrived very soon we would have to be transported to hospital. Maruška resolved that matter very rapidly and he was delivered at home at 15.08 hours after some 13 hours of labour. When you're under pressure and it involves someone you love you can move mountains! That, you will find, is a recurring theme in this short book.

My changes in location entailed us moving house several times. We decided when Alex was very young that we wanted to live somewhere peaceful, rural and a little out of the way. As I look back now I see that I uprooted Alex and indeed Maruška from homes and villages they loved for my own career. I took them both from circles of friends they have cultivated and that must have been difficult for them both. I know it impacted on him, as I had spent hours and hours over the years comforting and consoling him with promises of new exploits and new fresh starts. As Alexander's journey continues it was made clear that these moves were vitally important for how we could get Alex the care and reduce the pressure of that delivery when he was ill. But the guilt still stays with me.

I transferred from the C.N.C in Cumbria to Warwickshire Police at the end of 2015. The decision to move was made in a very short time span and Maruška and my children reeled from that blow. It was a decision I had deliberated upon but to my shame, that deliberation was for my own selfish reasons only. I had made some strong bonds of friendship in Cumbria and the aikido dojo I had set up there was thriving. I was thriving at work as well obtaining Acting Inspector rank and undertaking an Operational Firearms Commander role. Still nevertheless I decided to move.

I had sold it to Maruška as a professional move which was about work satisfaction and allowed me to return to core policing roles. The reduction in rank came as a surprise and was puzzling to her. Maruška was self-employed but worked wholly for the National Health Service as an interpreter and translator. Her work base had been in Sheffield and remained there as that's where the work was and where her clients were. This involved her travelling and staying with family for periods of time. The trip to Sheffield from Cumbria was a long one due to their being no direct route and the fact that St. Bees, the small seaside village where we lived was somewhat isolated from the motorway network. Ironically the reality was that my reduction in rank and associated overtime would probably take a thousand pounds a month from my pay packet. I didn't dwell on this fact and skimmed over it as best I could. We would manage, we always did.

I further justified the decision to move to myself on a practical level by explaining that Maruška's work would be more accessible and would mean less time away from home. Our new home on the border of Leicestershire and Warwickshire was only some 80 miles and 90 minutes from Sheffield when compared to the previous 185 miles from St. Bees along country roads which would take a minimum of 4 hours usually.

I started in my new job at the end of October 2015 and had moved a week earlier than the rest of the family. Maruška and the children moved down on the 1st November and Alex had started school that following day on Monday 2nd November. As a baby just coming up to three years old Sophia was fine and took it all in her stride. Alex however had been unsettled again. I recall how we had moved houses twice in the short amount of time he had been in full time schooling: Ridgeway in Derbyshire to St. Bees in Cumbria and then to Dunton Bassett in Leicestershire. Alex was just starting at school; he made friends and then seemed to have to make new ones. He still has enduring friendships with children whose mothers are friends with Maruška from both Ridgeway and St. Bees. He seems to have started anew too many times in such a short space of time; I have the photos of him in his different uniforms. This must have impacted on his development and learning but that would be a mere shadow of what was to come.

The transfer to Warwickshire had happened quickly and we had just managed to sell the house before we had to move. We planned to find a new home once we had settled. One of my closest friends, Jonny, a Detective Chief Inspector now Superintendent in Leicestershire Police had offered for us to move in with him into his home at Dunton Bassett, a village on the Leicestershire and Warwickshire border which was just 20 minutes' drive away from my new police station at Rugby (yes, the sport is named after the city as it was invented there). This would be the case for a few months until we could find a place of our own.

I had known Jonny for many years and we had maintained contact through many life changes on either side. He was a constable when we had first met through martial arts training and now he sat many ranks above me. We didn't talk often but maintained some regularity. It seemed, throughout the time we had known each other, that we migrated to each other when we were in need. Jonny didn't have any kids but he always gave Alex and Sophia time when he was with them. He was Alex's godfather and it was a role he fitted rather well. Jonny was a very intelligent and astute man who had risen rapidly through the ranks in the Police Service. I sought his advice several times about the matters that would create so much frustration for me in the months to come.

We had lived in villages for the past eight years and that way of life suited us. Close to nature and to open spaces is always handy for exercising the dog and for enjoying rest days with the children. Village life can be very fickle though; you generally either fit right in or not. St. Bees consisted of families that were either farming stock that had lived there for generations or families that had moved into the area because of their employment as executives, scientists or technicians at the local Nuclear power plant. We didn't really fit in there with a police officer's wage. Ridgeway was like St. Bees in that were both small villages with a lot of wealthy families that lived in grand houses. Despite this we were blessed in that the friendships we did make were valued to all concerned.

Dunton Bassett seemed a little different. A few other police officers and emergency services personnel lived in or around the village and I genuinely felt that we were made to feel welcome by pretty much everyone.

In this positive environment Alex began at Dunton Bassett Primary School at the beginning of November and seemed to enjoy it there. I had just started in my new role and was undertaking intensive 'upskill' training on further firearms training and associated tactics. The physical demands were greater too and had required me to increase my fitness level and exercise regime. I felt fitter and stronger but was totally absorbed in work. I had left Maruška to manage the kids and the house. On reflection, this was something I had done often in the past and escaped in work and my hobbies (which I justified as a 'de-stress' from work).

I recall that Alex seemed to take an interest in the exercises I was doing at home and wanted to do more aikido with me and swim. I was surprised by his new-found passion for fitness and he would continuously tell me about wanting to get strong and lose his big belly. I didn't think anything of it at the time because I was so engrossed in my own development and desire to succeed in my new environment. I hadn't picked up on his sensitivity about his weight. I reassured him with words and told him not to worry as he was a healthy boy.

I would describe him as a broad or stocky boy and probably someone less kind may have called him chubby; he ate well and enjoyed his food and his treats but he was active. He enjoyed aikido and swimming and had started cycling.

Week commencing 16th November Alex fell ill with a fever. I was on residential training at this time and spent the working week away returning home at weekends. Maruška told me via one of our daily telephone conversations that Alex was ill and had a fever that had spiked at 40 degrees Celsius (104 degrees Fahrenheit). Whilst it wasn't usual for Alex to be ill it wasn't unheard of, all children got fevers from time to time. The timing was awful though; I was away from home and Alex had just started at a new school. It was week three and he was absent from school already. It couldn't be helped and he would be back at school as quickly as Maruška could get him there. She managed these things very well, used Ibuprofen to take the temperature and discomfort down. The usual recipe of hot soup, Maruška's natural remedies of honey and elderflower and lots of rest would do the trick in no time. I offered words of comfort and promised to spend time with him when I got home. Words of comfort, but just words.

Alex recovered and was back at school the following week. I continued to do exercise and would often drag myself through the Insanity fitness programme at weekends or on evenings when I was at home. Alex and Sophia wanted to get involved as I sweated and heaved my frame around the front room. They would do their versions of the exercise which were generally amusing and endearing. It was actually nice to have them with me and excited to be part of it because we spent precious time together. Alex continued to express his desire to be strong, always mentioning how he wanted to get fitter. Unknown to me at the time he was being mocked at school for his tummy. One of the children in the village, in the same class at school was making fun of him for having a big belly, which had been seen by his classmates during changing times for Physical Education. I remember he once grabbed his stomach and said he wanted to cut it off. I didn't really pay it the attention it needed at the time, in hindsight I should have sat with him and got to the bottom of it. Naively, I didn't think that he was at an age where he would be so self-conscious of his appearance or at the age where someone would bully him for it. He told me about this many months later when he was so thin and frail when our world had changed so much in such a short time.

It was at this time that he started with the aches and pains. It started with him having aches in the morning or after sitting or lying in the same position. Like pins and needles in his leg or soreness in his knee. He hobbled as he got up but rarely complained during the day. The nights were different. He would wake up once or twice in the night complaining of pain at first, he would fall back to sleep after he repositioned himself, but then after a few weeks he would need pain relief to send him back to sleep. Maruška gave me a debrief on the day's events, usually by telephone as I was away often. She would mention Alex's pains. He was swimming at school at that time and doing his exercises so I put it down to muscle soreness, maybe he was doing too much and he needed to take it easier on his growing bones and muscles. We both agreed that it was likely to be growing pains or perhaps too much exercise. Or did I think that because it was easier and did I press my opinions on Maruška? Many months later I learned that she had anxieties about what was wrong with Alex but didn't share them because life was hectic at that time.

Over exercise on growing limbs - did that serve as an easy answer for me? The thing is, we live in boxes and thrive on structure. I had pressure at this time and we were trying to stabilise things in a new place, with new challenges and priorities. I missed friendships that I had forged whilst in Cumbria, we had financial hardships that necessitated that Maruška would need to work more often. I questioned if I had made the right decision. My moments of self-doubt were always hidden and never visible to her. She missed the old house and worried about our situation. As soon as I had completed my training and was operational with a shift pattern of duties, she would recommence her work and begin the trips to Sheffield to stop us drawing on the limited savings we had.

Alex's pain continued.

He was waking up at night and getting up awkwardly after staying in the same position for so long. The moments of pain were fleeting because pain relief solved the problem and he went back to sleep momentarily feeling better. It was an immediate fix and one that allowed me to remain focussed on other things that at the time seemed so vital.

Two

I began operational duties in November. Now we could plan and get more of the structure and routine that we yearned for. Maruška was travelling to Sheffield earning money that we desperately needed. November became December and Alex's condition remained. The pain in the lower part of his leg around the knee and shin became more prevalent. He was waking up in the night in discomfort and we managed it with small doses of pain relief. I am ashamed now as I realise that this had become routine, it is amazing how you can be entirely distracted by what seems important and ignore something that is screaming in your face.

In December Alex began to have time off. His periods of waking in the night became longer and more regular. He was waking after poor broken sleep and was exhausted. He began to miss school: a day here, a day there. These single days combined with the whole week he had been absent within the first month of him starting at the school triggered concerns from them about his absence. We received a letter from the school about his attendance: they would no longer accept absence without a doctor's note.

I look back and wonder why we didn't take him to the doctors or hospital at this time. Both Maruška and I were raised to brush yourself off after falling down and get on with it. Alex didn't appear ill; he wasn't coughing or vomiting or showing physical symptoms like swelling, a cut or a bruise. He had these brief pains in the night or fleeting discomfort during the day. Sometimes he slept through the discomfort and other times we gave him medicine that quickly brought sleep on again. The pain passed and the problem was resolved: until perhaps the following day or the day after that. I was working for six days and then Maruška would take the baton and run the rest of the race for the next four days and hand it back to me again. That was the routine and Sophia and Alex were fitting into that. The first delays in Alexander's Journey were my own fault and I shall have to live with that.

I had settled into a new team and was enjoying the camaraderie and sense of purpose that being back on the front of the thin blue line had given me. It was the start of the festive season and we enjoyed our first Christmas in a new home. Christmas didn't go without its incidents, Sophia fell and banged her nose on one of the only four steps in our bungalow barn conversion and Bojar, our dog, managed to escape from the courtyard and was hit by a car. But we were together and our families visited over Christmas. My friend Jonny had practically relinquished the house to us and spent most of his time at his girlfriend's but she, also in the job, became closer to us and visited Alex often in hospital as his health worsened.

Maruška's mum, sister, brother and his fiancée spent Christmas with us, which was especially nice for Alex as he and his Uncle Paul were very close. Paul had stayed with us in Sheffield many years previously after he came out of the military until he could sort new employment and a home of his own. Alex was born at this time so Paul was often with him in those formative years.

Christmas came and went and we entered 2016. I can honestly say that without a shadow of doubt it would prove to be the most difficult year I have ever endured. Alex's first visit to a hospital Accident & Emergency department was at the beginning of January. My experience of visiting the doctor and visiting hospital Accident & Emergency had been limited but in truth, like many other people with whom I knew, the experience had been an unpleasant one every time.

It is, in my humble opinion, apparent throughout this journey that medical provision in the United Kingdom is outstripped by demand. It has been eroded over the years because as a nation we are living longer and the public purse is getting smaller. It is a plain and simple fact that too many people are drawing on the resources that are available. There are reasons and they vary depending on who you ask: budget cuts and significant increases in demand due to population etc are voiced as the main reasons. Maybe the truth lies somewhere in the middle. Whether I agree or not is irrelevant at this juncture, what is relevant is that regardless of when and where you go for medical treatment the wait is ridiculously long. It is something you avoid with small children and hectic and demanding lifestyles at almost all cost.

On Wednesday 6th January Alex went to bed as normal and woke up just after midnight in excruciating pain. He was in agony and it was the worst it had been. He was very vocal and the pain seemed different almost. It was localised at his knee and shin. Maruška took him to the hospital, at that time and before he was fighting this awful disease he migrated to his mum for comfort. Mum and Alex went to our local Accident & Emergency department at the Leicester Royal Infirmary for the first time of what would be hundreds of visits to that hospital. They say that first impressions last, what was certain is that our relationship with that hospital changed so much over the time that Alex was going there.

The Leicester Royal Infirmary is part of the NHS in the United Kingdom. The National Health Service or NHS as it is known is a strange animal. It has tremendous pressure placed upon it like all public services. It has undergone rapid and radical change over the past decade that is certain. As Britons, we tend to be proud of the NHS for what it is and the fact that it is free. The truth is, it isn't really. In the U.K. people pay National Insurance. British nationals automatically have this payment deducted from their salary to pay for the NHS. I have had many discussions with people from all walks of life about the NHS and medical provision in the United States over the past 18 months. I am not a wealthy man and my salary as a police officer with over 15 years' service can only be identified as an average salary but I still pay 40% in tax: compared with a cop in the United States who pays just over half that.

The NHS was started just after the second world war for all the right reasons but has been eroded over the years. Just like the police service. As resources dwindle, as the numbers of staff on the ground diminishes you just make do, push on, do more, take more because you joined to help people. As a police officer I had experienced the same. Things had changed so radically from when I started in January 2002 to just six or seven years later. I remember over 20 officers parading at our district when I was a probationer constable, now that number, I am told from previous colleagues, is usually less than ten. It was gradual and you accepted it because of your desire to make it work or because you had to make it work. Ultimately the end user took the hit and received a poorer service. It has happened in the NHS too. I had empathy and sympathy for them and maybe that was why it took so long for me to speak up about what was (or wasn't) happening to Alex.

Maruška and my eight-year-old son arrived at 1am on a Thursday morning at the Leicester Royal Infirmary. He had been given pain relief prior to leaving the house because of the pain he was experiencing. After five hours of sitting and waiting Alex was finally seen by an overworked and under-appreciated junior doctor. Maruška insisted upon an X-ray and described the symptoms in detail, explaining that this had been occurring for the last two months. Alex was a healthy active boy and it wasn't normal for him.

Based on the pain that seemed to be coming from his knee the doctor considered that he may have something called Osgood Shlatters Syndrome. I was waiting at home and I remember receiving the SMS text message from Maruška as I waited eager for news. It was named after two physicians in 1903 Dr. Robert Osgood and Dr. Carl Shlatter and is a condition that occurs through overuse or injury of the knee, or more specifically the patellar tendon and surrounding soft tissues. Apparently, it affects growing children and adolescents and is described as a very common cause of knee pain in children between the ages of 10 and 15 years of age. Basically, bones grow quickly and it can take time for the muscles and tendons to catch up. Ironically, this principle will affect Alex again many months later but in a totally different way for totally different reasons.

They took an X-ray but only of the area that Alex said hurt - his knee and lower leg. Maruška never thought to question this at the time. Why would she? We assume that professionals are making the right decisions because we don't know any better. We placed our faith and confidence in these people because we assume they know best and we didn't know any better.

After the X-rays were conducted Osgood Shlatter's syndrome was discounted. After some deliberation Maruška was told that it was "probably growing pains". She asked specifically for blood tests to be conducted and was told that they "did not do blood tests routinely, it wasn't something they would do". The doctor at Accident & Emergency said that if it persists over the next two to three months then we should go to our local family doctor and ask for a referral for blood tests and scans. We were advised to continue to give Alex the pain relief when the growing pains flared up.

It has been said that it was unusual for Maruška to be asking for a blood test at this stage: that is true. I would never have thought to ask for a blood test. It was something that was unusual in the United Kingdom. Maruška was born and raised in the Slovak Republic where it was common practice for you to undergo a blood examination when seeking to diagnose an illness.

Throughout January and February Alex continued to experience his "growing pains" and we continued to treat the issue with pain relief that was simply masking the problem. It seemed to have got worse and caused him more broken sleep. That broken sleep caused him more fatigue and he often struggled to get up for school and participate there. It was then that he also began complaining of the pain when sitting on wooden chairs at school. He was sent home on several occasions due to him being in too much pain to remain at his desk. It was a difficult time that was gradually getting worse. He was often too drained to go to school but we would make him. We felt we had no choice because of how the school had reacted to his absence previously. We desperately wanted Alex to fit in at the new school. He needed to be there. The school was in the village and was a short walk for him from where we lived. It was probably no more than a few hundred yards.

Alex had begun to develop an awkward gait and at times a limp, which was clearly his way of managing the pain and discomfort. The problem was manifesting itself more regularly now and seemed to be getting worse and showing no signs of abating. I remember taking him to school one morning in March and he was hobbling. I explained to the other parents that were walking with us about the hospitals diagnosis. I felt almost like I had to explain why he was walking the way he was. I felt very protective of him and was very distressed that everyone was staring. He just continued walking, without any complaint. I had endured the diagnosis for many weeks but it was clearly not growing pains. We had waited until the end of March and now he had to go to see his local doctor in the hope that it would be resolved.

The pain had continued over the months and had gotten worse. It was clearly grinding him down. The pain, usually manifested itself during the night and caused a lack of sleep. His limp became more pronounced. He had lost weight and didn't eat as much. He would come home from school and would go straight to bedroom to watch TV. The reality was that he was laying down on his bed and falling to sleep. Unbeknown to me, at the time, this was when we started to lose him. He was tired, drained and became more of a recluse. His absenteeism rocketed and he was sent home from school very often. From the month of March he couldn't stay at school for full days anymore. We sent pain relief to school and the school administered this during the day on occasion.

At this time, I knew something other than growing pains was affecting him, but even then, I never even considered cancer. That may seem strange now but at the time it didn't even occur to me. I also remember Maruška mentioning that Alex's eye sight seemed to have deteriorated rapidly in such a short space of time, but again, it did not ring any alarm bells. I had begun to dabble in internet searches then but frankly found them worrying and creating more confusion for me than actually helping me find a rational diagnosis. What was difficult to reconcile was that at times Alex would act like nothing was wrong and he was perfectly fine and at other times he was very depressed and clearly in pain.

Maruška's mother had, many years earlier, worked in an administrative role at an oncology clinic in Slovakia before coming over to the United Kingdom. She had friends and colleagues that Maruška had contacted seeking advice. Maruška had made the decision to take Alex to our local doctor and spoke to a paediatric haematologist in Slovakia and discussed the case with her. Alex's symptoms were relayed to her and the doctor told Maruška what tests to ask for. The Slovakian doctor was naturally reluctant to make a diagnosis but did advise us to seek several blood tests and scans. I suspect she had her suspicions about what it was but didn't share those with us at the time.

At the end of March Maruška took Alex to see our local family doctor, explained his symptoms and requested the blood tests and scans we have been advised to seek. Our practice was in Lutterworth, a market town just a few miles from our village. The head of the practice had come recommended to us by my friend Jonny when we moved into the village. Maruška and Alex were seen by one of the other doctors at the practice to whom she explained his symptoms and the length of time we had been dealing with them. I was not there so I cannot recount the events directly but from what I was told the encounter was not a favourable one. Maruška felt like her concerns were discounted and dismissed. Her requests for certain blood tests and scans to take place, as advised by the Paediatric Haematologist in Slovakia were declined.

The doctor would not provide any diagnosis on Alex's predicament and said that she would get back to us when she had spoken to her associates at the practice. Maruška tried to get a commitment as to when that would be, but she was not given a date or time.

Maruška had found this doctor incredibly condescending and felt she had been regarded as another overreacting parent. The doctor had apparently examined Alex by observing him walk from one end of the room to the other and back. Maruška left that meeting totally disheartened and we were no further forward now some three months after he began to experience his problems.

I only learned more about the actual situation with regards to action taken by our local doctors practice after another two weeks and then in reality only obtained any detailed disclosure that filled in some gaps in our analysis of the Journey much further down the line in July and August 2017: that's over a year later when life was so very different and I had returned from the United States. I shall elaborate on this later.

Life continued. We remained in this cycle of work and child care. The next morning following on from the visit to our local doctor, Maruška was scheduled to work in Sheffield. It was the school Easter break and the fact that the children could go with her and stay with grandparents had allowed her to take on the extra few days of work despite me being on my working days.

They all left for Sheffield that day and Maruška worked during the day. That night Alex was in excruciating pain and while Sophia was tucked up asleep at her mother's home, Maruška took him to the Accident & Emergency at the Sheffield Children's Hospital with my mother. Maruška often worked at the Sheffield Children's Hospital translating and interpreting for patients. She had built up a rapport with some of the staff there and felt more comfortable and confident that she may finally get some of the answers we were desperately seeking.

They arrived at Sheffield Children's Hospital at around 9.15 pm and after waiting a couple of hours to actually be seen he was examined by another junior doctor. This first doctor believed that something wasn't right and Alex had another X-ray. His weight loss, fatigue and pain was also explained. Maruška stressed her concerns without wanting to sound like an overreacting parent. She passed updates to me via SMS text message. We hoped and we both waited.

Alex finally had the X-ray at 2.30 am. Fortunately, this time, the X-ray also covered the upper part of his leg. We waited for news, but at least they seemed to be listening. The first doctor consulted a second and it was agreed that it was more than growing pains. The smallest of victories and the tiniest step forward, or so we thought. The case would go to a specialist Orthopaedic Paediatrician and Maruška was told someone would be in touch in a few days.

Maruška and Alex were back at my mum's apartment at 3.20 am and that afternoon they travelled home to Dunton Bassett. The travelling was hard for Alex; any period of time sitting down was very uncomfortable for him. The slightest jolt or bump in the car was difficult for him unless he had taken pain relief. The situation grew more and more unbearable. But we clung to the hope of a diagnosis and waited for news. We were to become adept at waiting for news, for updates, for any progress. At that time, I still unwisely, did not even consider cancer. Maruška was beginning to fear the worse, but for now kept these opinions to herself.

The following morning after just a handful of hours at home Maruška was on the motorway heading North again back to Sheffield. She had driven backwards and forwards numerous times over the past few days and this time she travelled alone for a training course that would give her the continuous professional development evidence she required for her accreditation. She was preoccupied with the situation as was I but she had little choice but to go. I remained at home with the kids.

Maruška recollected to me later that day that she received a call at 10am from the Children's Hospital in Sheffield. They wanted Alex to come in as soon as possible and preferably immediately after the weekend on the Monday. They had looked at his X-ray and they knew now what was wrong. They had a diagnosis! Maruška asked for details and initially could not get any from the caller who explained that they weren't involved in that Department and they had just been tasked to make the call. Maruška insisted that they tell her what the name of the illness was and feared they would say Cancer. They said Alex had Perthes Disease.

Perthes Disease. This was the first time I had ever heard that word. An appointment was made for us on the Monday at Sheffield Children's Hospital. I immediately checked the condition out courtesy of Google and the NHS website. Perthes Disease is a condition that affects the hip joint in children. It involves the loss of blood supply to the femoral head (the top of the femur that is like a ball and fits into the hip socket). This lack of blood supply causes the bone tissue to die and collapse.

When Maruška shared the news with me the relief on her voice was palpable. I had checked and Perthes matched the symptoms Alex had: pain and hip irritation, pain in the knee, walking with a limp. I shared that relief, Perthes wasn't life threatening, a worst-case scenario may result in permanent disability or even the loss of the limb, but only in the rarest cases. Never-the-less it was life-altering but not life-threatening. At last we felt we had something resembling progress if the hospital knew what it was and therefore they could treat it.

The news I learned a little later was a pressure valve for Maruška who had begun to fear that it was cancer and now she had been told it wasn't. I would cling to that same hope a few weeks later. For now, we had a label and something that justified his absence from school, his poor sleeping, his limp. Something that gave us an explanation for his behaviour. It appeared to give us the direction we had yearned for, a path of treatment back to normality. At the time, I didn't question any further his weight loss and chronic fatigue: I just considered them a consequence of pain and discomfort from a lack of sleep and a lack of appetite.

We did our homework on the disease before our visit to the hospital at the start of the new week. Alex's illness had begun to affect me at work, I was tired more often and had spent more time away from work using time off owed and annual leave to get him to appointments or provide child care when Maruška needed to work. I had taken time off again at short notice to go to this appointment and Maruška had cancelled more work.

Monday morning arrived and Alex braved yet another journey in the car over a long distance. We dropped Sophia and our dog off at Maruška's mothers in Sheffield and attended at the Children's Hospital again. The hospital was busy and we attended the fracture clinic because it was the only way we had been able to get the appointment at such short notice. It was odd to me because several doctors and nurses as well as administrative staff exchanged friendly conversation with Maruška and it was clear that this was an area she had worked in regularly. Maybe that would stand us in good stead. I braced myself for another wait of many hours.

We were called into an examination room and the doctor confirmed to us that Alex had Perthes Disease. The head of that department was present also. He sat in the background and multi tasked with a myriad of jobs which occasionally involved us being interrupted or him leaving the room. A group of junior doctors ran the clinic for him. Maruška, my woman on the inside, explained to me that this was normal. It is a strange situation when you are told your son has a life changing and very painful illness and you are appreciative of that. We knew what we were dealing with and it wasn't as bad as it could have been. We were intoxicated on relief, he would get better and everything would go back to normal, to the structure that we craved.

In a moment of lucidity Maruška, recollecting the advice given to her by her mother's oncological colleague in Slovakia asked how did they know it was Perthes? Despite having taken no blood tests or having conducted no MRI scans. It was a good question, one that I waited desperately for an answer to. I had read the previous day on the NHS website that sometime bone scans or MRI scans were used to help with analysis. Their answer was decisive and reassuringly confident. They showed us the X-ray image and exclaimed it was "textbook Perthes". This was an exact example of Perthes Disease, this is how it looked. We were told that further tests, as well as being unnecessary would place further stress on Alex and as a child they wanted to minimise that.

We were advised to take Alex swimming and make sure he exercised as well as attend physiotherapy sessions. We were given information on what exercises we could do with him at home. Our first physio appointment would be arranged and we would return in six weeks' time for a check up on his situation. At that time, I was satisfied. Armed with a folder full of leaflets to read, I was settled now. We knew what we were dealing with and what we could do to help. As well as his physio, our lives were concerned with pain relief, exercise and swimming. I was determined to do everything to get him better.

Three

The relief of knowing what was happening and the feeling of some satisfaction was sadly fleeting. We passed on the diagnosis to the school right away, thankful we could now pin his absence to something credible. Upon receiving this information, the school were very supportive and that made life easier. He tried to stay at school and took pillows to make the seating more comfortable. This helped but he still suffered greatly with pain and discomfort. He almost seemed to be getting worse and was deteriorating further.

The exercises he was required to do were performed by Maruška or myself, and involved rotations, extensions and forms of what I would describe as massage, stretching and joint manipulation. The exercises were clearly distressing for us all. They were designed to grind the bone down, breaking off the affected areas so it could build up again and fit better into the socket.

He had physiotherapy at both Sheffield Children's Hospital and much closer to home at the Leicester Royal Infirmary. He was still not given crutches until some three weeks after diagnosis. This was explained to us as necessary to avoid him becoming lazy, as the objective was to exercise the bones to cause the breakdown, which would allow it to grow back. He needed to be using the leg to maximise the effectiveness of the treatment.

I remember in early April 2016 I walked home from school with Alex and observed his limp. For some reason, still unknown to me today, I videoed him on my mobile phone. That short video, just six seconds long of him hobbling home in his school uniform still crushes me to this day. This period was a difficult one. He seemed to be getting worse. He had lost a lot of weight and was exhausted. He was coming home from school and was going to sleep early, while he had lost his appetite and was not eating properly. As a parent, I was filled with self-doubt. Was he getting worse? He had lost more weight but he was exercising often so was he just getting fitter? The exercise and manipulation of his leg and hip must have been taxing on him, was that why he felt tired all the time? He was exercising regularly and that included frequent swimming.

In order to make sure he could swim regularly we joined the local sports centre at Lutterworth. We had to pay for family membership so that either Maruška or I and usually both of us could go with him. We would take Sophia as well. It wasn't cheap and came to over £70 per month. We attempted to get this need to swim prescribed by a hospital referral but were unsuccessful. I was reliably informed that people who are fighting obesity were often prescribed and received subsidised gym membership. It didn't seem fair that we couldn't get it for Alex.

It was at this time, around the middle of April, that I remember contacting our local doctor's practice by telephone to complain about the fact that we had heard nothing from them or indeed our local regional healthcare trust. I made an official complaint with regards to the treatment that Maruška told me she had faced when taking Alex to our local doctor and that it had been compounded by the fact that we had been informed that after peer review we would be updated. I spoke directly to the doctor that Maruška had met almost three weeks previously and she apologised for failing to inform us of what was happening. The doctor's office seemed unaware of the diagnosis Alex had been given from the Sheffield Children's Hospital and I informed them of the situation. In truth, I wrongly dwelled on our success during that conversation. We, it seemed, had found out what was wrong with Alex with no assistance from our own doctor or our local Accident & Emergency Department and gloated on it. In fairness, the local doctor had apologised and I appreciated her candour. This was however, only part of the situation with regards to our dealings with our local doctor. The rest would not come to my attention until conversation and meetings with the head doctor at our local family practice some 15 months later.

Back in April 2016 we had, what we thought was a diagnosis and stuck to the plan as directed by the hospital. As I mentioned earlier when Alex was at the Accident and Emergency Department at

Leicester Royal Infirmary, we place our faith and confidence in the health care professionals because we assume they know best and we don't know any better. I carry this guilt of putting Alex through a gruelling regime and the physiotherapy undertaken by us at home. I pushed him and we tried our best to keep him at school as much as we could. He would cry as we performed the leg and hip movements and sometimes when we made him walk or met him from school after sitting for hours in class, it was too much for him. His tears were met with my motivational rhetoric: "come on be strong" "it's going to be alright" and similar responses. I wasn't being cruel, I was just attempting to reassure him and help him to push past it as it was what he needed in the long run. I remember, when we knew the truth, reflecting on my response to his misery during many sleepless nights as I watched over him in the coming months.

The check-up date, back at the Children's Hospital, was approaching and we had a physiotherapy appointment just before it. We had decided to push our concerns about his continuing decline and increase in pain and decrease in mobility. We were gripped with worry; it couldn't go on any longer, he was waking up more often now despite the increased frequency of pain relief. At this time, he was using a cushion to sit comfortably all the time either at home or elsewhere. Furthermore, he was now using hot water bottles on a regular basis on his leg particularly around the shin and knee area.

On 4th May 2016 we attended at Sheffield Children's Hospital with a heavy heart. Alex was in tremendous pain and was barely able to manage sitting in the car, even with cushions, for the 80-mile trip from home to Sheffield. Prior to his check-up meeting with doctors he had a physio appointment and we explained to the physiotherapist our concerns about his weight loss, pain and fatigue. He genuinely seemed to listen and said we needed to "voice that strongly to the doctors".

The examination room was busy: two doctors and a nurse as well the consultant and head of the department in the background. As rationally and calmly as possible we expressed our worries and concerns, detailing all that seemed relevant: the hot water bottles, the pain relief, the weight loss, tiredness. The answer seemed to be another X-ray. The X-ray was done and then we waited. After some considerable time, The X-ray came back and we were called back into the room. The Head of the Department was positioned in the centre of the group and was no longer at the periphery. Even before he started speaking with us I knew that something significant was going on in that moment. We had managed to get an audience with the boss. I felt anxiety as this obviously meant something serious was wrong.

At that point, we were told that they thought there was something else wrong with Alex. The bone had continued to deteriorate and the affected area had increased. We were then informed that he may have a severe bone infection and he would require an urgent MRI scan. Interestingly and much to my chagrin I had obtained in July 2017, over a year later a copy of a letter sent by the Sheffield Children's Hospital on this matter to our local doctor in Lutterworth. The word used to describe the change in position following the new X-ray was "sinister". Had I known that now I would have pressed home Maruška's original request for the myriad of blood tests and scans instead of being satisfied with the MRI scan alone.

I sought clarification that they had discounted Perthes Disease for sure and the likelihood of a "severe bone infection" instead. They regarded it as unlikely that it was Perthes and reiterated that Alex needed an MRI scan. We would receive a telephone call from the hospital with an appointment. The Head of Department escorted us out of the examination room personally and then seemed to divert to another task. Surprisingly Maruška received the call before we had even left the hospital building. "the Head of Department has personally requested," said Maruška, having quoted the administrative assistant on the phone. We had been allocated the earliest available appointment and that was less than two days away. On reflection and considering my experience and exposure to another health system, this was a ridiculously long time to wait. However, at the time, it seemed a very brief period, almost no time at all to wait. At that time, it remained the case that no one even mentioned cancer to us either to confirm or discount it. We left and Alex endured another uncomfortable and painful journey home and Maruška and I were then placed in a position of uncertainty. That uncertainty was a breeding ground for anxiety and worry and was a common theme throughout the time prior to December 2016.

Alex's MRI scan took place that same week of May and this was when the now distinctive social media profile photo of Alex was taken by his Aunt Lenka. It has sat on his profile ever since we set it up: broad smile, laid on the bed in his batman t-shirt with his headphones on. The photo also shows a heavily bandaged arm. When attending for the MRI scan the hospital needed to take some blood for analysis. They couldn't seem to find a vein and made several attempts to draw blood which was very traumatic for Alex and resulted in several skin punctures. This is why he has a bandage on his arm in the photo and he developed, from this incident, a serious phobia for needles. This phobia would influence how his treatment was delivered; his response to some aspects of the treatment regimen and ultimately, during his few moments of sleep, due to nightmares on the issue.

He had managed his MRI scan without sedation, however what followed was a complete shock to us. We were fully expecting to travel back home after the scan and await the results. Unfortunately, that didn't happen. We were told by the staff in the radiology department to sit and wait. This was most unusual. I looked at Maruška and she knew that something wasn't right. She had experienced, with her job, many cases of patients coming for scans and leaving once they were finished. We didn't have to wait for more than ten minutes when an emergency on call doctor came to us and escorted us to an office to discuss the situation. We were told that Alex would have to be admitted onto the ward as a matter of urgency and future investigation into his condition would be conducted. The doctor didn't specify the exact condition or diagnosis but it remained at that time, even then, as a suspected serious bone infection. Several departments were contacted including infectious diseases and oncology.

Maruška stayed with him but I remained there as long as possible before leaving them alone. The doctors were lined up from different departments to discuss the different possibilities of his diagnosis: infectious diseases, haematology to name but a few. The one department that we were told to expect to speak to was Oncology.

I recall Maruška recounting the unfolding events to me in one of the many telephone conversations that we had. As the office hours drew to an end, and no one had been, she had asked the same Head of Department whom we had been dealing with, when someone from the oncology team were coming. She was told, "they will not be getting involved, at this moment in time as they don't feel it is necessary".

What we were blissfully unaware of at that time was that the national bone cancer centre in Birmingham had been contacted and made aware of Alex's condition. Again, no one mentioned cancer that evening as Alex and his mum remained at Sheffield Children's Hospital.

They were, however, told that a biopsy would be performed on Alex. This meant he had to stay 'Nil by Mouth' that night for the procedure the following morning. It is important to note that he had already fasted prior to this decision for the MRI scan in case he required sedation: but he did not. Ravenous, he ate late at night and remained in the hospital to be monitored. The next day being Friday 20th May he was again 'Nil By Mouth'. During that day, after yet more long waits and uncertainty, we were told that the national bone tumour centre in the Royal Orthopaedic Hospital in Birmingham would carry out their own biopsy and he would not be having a biopsy at the Sheffield Children's Hospital. This was a heavy blow. Not only had Alex spent all day waiting, unable to eat or drink anticipating a procedure he was so fearful of because of his recent experience with the needles It was also then and only then that any reference to cancer had emerged. Maruška told me weeks later that she laid in bed just days before this date weeping silently as she knew that Alex had cancer.

We went home and Alex deteriorated further. His pain was unmanageable now, it was incessant. We were constantly using hot water bottles to ease his pain and give him some relief. The biopsy that we had anticipated having on that Friday hadn't happened and we were sent home. It had been rescheduled for the 2nd June some weeks later. More delays. More uncertainty.

When you are dealing with a serious illness affecting someone so close you can drown in it. Changes, physical and psychological are gradual but because you are with them all the time you don't see them. Alex had always been a gentle boy who was kind and sensitive. That sensitivity and kindness was often construed by more belligerent or pugnacious boys as weakness. His circle of friends was small and he yearned desperately to be accepted and included throughout his formative years and beyond. I recalled, in all the places where we had lived, seeing him trying to mix with large groups of boys or be popular and it resulted in him being abused or manipulated. I constantly urged him to ignore those boys and seek out those who cared and would reciprocate his kindness. For some reason, he was persistent and tried to befriend the children of neighbours. One of the many things that I admired about him, despite the pitfalls he encountered, was that he didn't change his character to be accepted or relinquish his values. He had always been friendly and kind and had a smile and a kind word for all. Sadly because of his predicament, I could see this was starting to change.

When you step back from a situation and attempt to look back in to gain perspective you are usually shocked by the changes that have slipped by unnoticed. Alex rarely smiled now and was constantly wrestling with pain and sadness. Our structure and routine had changed to one of continuous pain relief and comfort for a boy who could hardly move now without help. Sitting down without cushions or padding was painful and he often laid in bed or on the sofa with a hot water bottle. The hot water bottle didn't seem to remove the pain just reduce it to a tolerant level.

We waited for contact, for results, for a way forward from the hospital. At this point where we were still seeking a correct diagnosis we had dealt with three separate hospitals, two of which were both over forty miles away from our home. This may not seem like a long distance to travel in the United States in such a vast expanse of country but here it entailed a one to perhaps two-hour journey at least.

This vacuum of information and a constant waiting would plague our time in the United Kingdom as we waited for news and action from the NHS. We could offer very little words of comfort to Alex and he was astute enough to sense the despondency in us too. When you know what something is you can meet it, rationalise it and come to terms with it if that is all you have left. But if there is some chance, some window of opportunity, there is hope.

Alex had become a shadow of his former self and he had become absent from school permanently. By this stage he spent a lot of time sleeping the pain off and we had started noticing his reluctance to get carried out of bed.

Maruška had thought it was cancer for some time and had spoken several times to the Paediatric Haematologist as well as an oncological consultant in Slovakia who said we needed a PET scan and his oncology markers needed checking. We had asked previously if it was going to be done and told it wasn't necessary. She was desperate to have these checks done because she didn't want to be right about her suspicions, she wanted to be proven wrong.

We hoped and prayed for confirmation that it was a bone infection. Throughout this time I had tried my best to maintain normality with regards to work. I had been allowed to take annual leave at short notice to facilitate childcare etc when possible, as my immediate crewmates were aware that Alex was unwell and Maruška who was self-employed, was picking up work when she could take it. She had cancelled so many jobs at short notice to look after Alex who, in reality, was quickly reaching a point where he was no longer attending school. Whilst I had been at home on my rest days she had been able to take a few jobs and could leave Sophia who was still too young for nursery at my mothers or her mother's, both of whom lived in Sheffield.

The biopsy results came back from the Royal Orthopaedic Hospital in Birmingham on the 7th June, some five months after Alex's first visit to the hospital, around ten weeks after both the visit to our local doctor's surgery and the first X-ray at Sheffield Children's Hospital.

Alex had Ewing Sarcoma Cancer.

Four

I remember very clearly the moment when Maruška woke me from my sleep. It was during the day and I had been on nights. She was almost absent from her own body. She maintains to this day that she can't recollect anything that the nurse said to her on the telephone except for the words Ewing Sarcoma cancer. She was numb and visibly in shock. Trembling. Oddly, I cannot recall where Alex was at the time of her telling me or where he was when I made the call back to the hospital.

As a police officer I had dealt with trauma and the suffering and distress of others many times. My reaction to Maruška's pain was to become that police officer and I tried to process and manage that news in a sterile way. We had been told that Alex had this devastating rare disease by telephone by one of the Macmillan nurses which didn't seem right. As we held each other and Maruška sobbed I couldn't let go of my emotions because then I would crumble. My first priority would be to re-contact this nurse and obtain information and process it. Eventually after some time I managed to speak with her. She was very kind but didn't pull any punches regarding the reality of the predicament we were in. She passed information to me and I scribbled it down frantically on a jotter pad. I asked questions where I needed to obtain clarity. I clung desperately to any words of hope or any positives that we could draw upon. I had never heard of it before.

Ewing Sarcoma is a highly malignant very rare form of cancer that develops in the long bones, pelvis or ribs, usually in children. It is so rare that it only accounts for around one percent of childhood cancers globally.

There seemed to be so many variables with regards to survivability and that survivability was linked to whether it had spread or not. Many of my questions were unanswerable at that time because all we had was a biopsy result. Treatment involved chemotherapy, surgery and radiotherapy.

As I ended the conversation I remained seated at our dining table where I had made the call. My jotter pad in front of me I read my notes again; as things settled I began to feel empty as the realisation crept in. I was worried because of the nurse's comments about whether it had spread or not and how that affected survivability. Alex had been ill since before Christmas which was six months previously. I wanted action and things to happen. Instead, I just sat. The nurse had explained how the treatment would work and how he would be a patient with both the Leicester Royal Infirmary (L.R.I.) and The Royal Orthopaedic Hospital (R.O.H) in Birmingham. Our Paediatric Oncological Consultant and the day to day treatment and care would be based in Leicester and he would likely have surgery in Birmingham. Other hospitals would be involved as other elements of the treatment became relevant like Nottingham Hospital for example with the radiotherapy.

It suddenly occurred to me that had we have stayed in St. Bees in Cumbria treatment at Leicester Royal Infirmary would have involved a five-hour car journey of over 215 miles. I would later learn that another alternative for us would have been Newcastle which would have still been two and half hours travelling away.

The Macmillan nurse had also given the contact details for the children's cancer ward in Leicester and I intended to reach out to them immediately and speak to the doctor that would be managing Alex's care.

After a few unsuccessful attempts to contact the doctor in the ward I finally had a conversation which was similar to the one with the McMillian nurse. I had mistakenly and extremely naively assumed that we would be taken into the ward immediately and Alex would begin the treatment within the next few days. That was not the case, he would require minor surgery to have a Hickman Line inserted and he would also need a number of tests and scans to make sure he was able to deal with the demanding physical effects of chemotherapy. Our first appointment at the ward would be on the 16th June as well as attending at another hospital for some of the checks on the same day. That wait of almost two weeks would be a long wait but one we had no choice but to endure.

Despite all of this happening around me I was still at work and was operational. I had the support of my crewmates. Being on a firearms team, like any specialist unit meant that you worked closely with a small group of people. You trained together and worked together and because of what we could potentially have to deal with you formed tight bonds of friendship. Even though I was relatively new to the team I felt part of it. I was sharing regular updates with the guys on Alex's situation and it was becoming apparent that it was all beginning to get on top of me. My emotional state was clearly frayed but in addition to that I was exhausted from the permanent and total care that Alex required. I probably couldn't see it at the time but the other team members and my Sergeant were looking out for me. They had seen my physical, mental and emotional deterioration.

Just before I took time off from work I remember discussing Alex's situation with Craig 'Creamy' Marshall who was on the team. Creamy was ex-military and had many years in the job having been on the Armed Response Vehicles for a good period of his service. I tended to work with him and he was a solid guy whom I would build a strong bond of personal friendship with over Alex's journey. I liked his unassuming demeanour and how it seemed to belie his eccentricity and streak of dry humour. I had no real idea why his nickname was Creamy. I had heard many explanations but frankly none stood out as being more credible than the other. Some of the stories around the nickname were off the wall and it seemed that as one of the older serving firearms officers on the team no one was actually left who could have confirmed his back story. Craig never let on to anyone the exact origins of the nickname and he would confirm or perpetuate one reason over another with different people at different times.

Creamy would become a regular visitor to our home to visit Alex and check up on how I was doing. Our friendship grew and he was a powerful force in getting Alex the funds and more importantly the support he would need.

When Alex was finally correctly diagnosed, one of the discussions I had with the MacMillan Nurse was about a diary. In days gone by, children fighting life threatening illness would create a diary which recorded their trials and tribulations and allowed them to document and vocalise their fears and anxieties. In the age of social media this had taken the form of a Twitter or Facebook diary page. Creamy ran the teams official Warwickshire Police Operational Patrol Unit account and was to all extent a bit of an expert with it. We talked about an account for Alex and the benefits that could bring. Social media is a double-edged sword. It can be a potent force for good but can also bring problems to your door in the form of trolls and unwanted attention. We had always been quite private people and I had stopped using any social media account personally many years previously. Maruška had an account but did not put a great amount on it, particularly nothing of an overly personal nature.

We needed a name for the Twitter and Facebook accounts and I remember one night shift, as we patrolled the county's crime hot spots and after considering several names including Alex the Brave, Creamy proffered Alexander's Journey. I liked it and thus Alexander's Journey Twitter and Facebook accounts were born.

Ironically, the crushing news of Alex's cancer diagnosis didn't really impact on Alex. He was in a very dark place already; wrestling with constant pain and fatigue. The revelation of cancer merely gave to his enemy a name but that foe had been there and weighed heavy on him for so long that it had changed him. He lived in a constant cycle of pain relief, medication, cushions and hot water bottles to reduce the impact on his frail body. He had drawn into himself and I feared we would lose him. He needed constant care and would often be carried from one room to another. He slept often and never smiled.

Alex was passionate about nature and had an interest in animals especially birds of prey, dinosaurs and sharks. He was extremely wise beyond his years and despite the pain and suffering he endured throughout his journey, often astounded visitors and nursing staff with his knowledge and appetite for learning on these topics. When we did discuss the cancer with him he likened it to a parasite. A minute animal that had got into his body and attached itself to him draining his energy and making him feel pain. He wasn't wrong.

We shared the news with family and friends. As I look back now it was an odd situation but also a very poignant and revealing one. Personally, other than an actual loss of life, I cannot think of any other news that would be as devastating as the news that a small child connected to you in some way had cancer. This was made worse by his physical frailty and the fact that he had been fighting illness for so long without proper diagnosis. I assumed that family and lifelong friends would be devastated by the news and make every effort to visit Alex and us to offer support and actually see him and spend time with him just in case things worsened and Alex was no longer with us. Sadly, I was wrong. Some people came and did all they could to help, others did not. People who I had grown up with, shared good times and tragedy with didn't seem to care. We received messages of consolation and a few kind words but that was all.

Fortunately, we were blessed with some friends and family members that did care and some people came down to visit and spend time with us. On the 11th June, we were visited by old friends Claire and Natalia from Sheffield who had stayed in touch with Maruška over the years. Their children had formed friendships with Alex and Sophia and this was the tonic that he needed. These types of visits were vital for Alex and were essential for his wellbeing. As his journey continued we would have numerous visitors over the following months that all helped keep his spirits up.

When I informed my colleagues and the organisation of Alex's illness at the beginning of June the support mechanisms kicked in almost immediately. My Sergeant and our team's Operational Firearms Commander, Dominic or Dom as he preferred, was a prime example of one of many people who on the face of things seemed to be distant and not overly engaging while I tried to address Alex's illness over the previous months. Dom was a very tall and imposing man, a former firefighter and boxer he cut the stereotypical image of a firearms officer without the often-misguided assumption that he was arrogant and ostentatious. I had misjudged him and his level of support and interest due to his reserved manner. He was an 'over watch' type of friend and supervisor who had taken a position on the apparent periphery of a situation, when, in reality he was simply able to view the terrain ahead much easier from the wider angle and identify obstacles and challenges ahead more readily. Dom and I discussed my situation and in consultation with the firearms training school deemed it best that I voluntarily relinquish my firearms authority until my mindset and personal situation was better. He handled it perfectly and I shall always respect him for that.

Policing in the United Kingdom is almost unique in the modern world and the British institution prides itself on the fact that the significant majority of police officers here do not carry a firearm. In fact, I believe only around 15% of police officers carry a Taser and just 5% are armed with a conventional firearm. This is a statistic that surprised cops in the United States during my many conversations with them on the subject. Authorised Firearms Officers receive a specific authority to carry firearms and Officers are subject to rigorous and continuous reclassification and requalification assessments on handling, accuracy and use of related tactics.

With everything that we were facing at this time I felt I was not in a place to manage the enormous responsibility of potentially having to make a decision on using a firearm. It was appropriate for me to relinquish that role for a time. That decision was well received by my superiors and was the right decision at that time. Within a short time I found myself unable to work anyway due to the fatigue I was dealing with having to constantly care for Alex and his needs. With that physical exhaustion came the mental aspects too.

I was also obligated to share the news with my unit commander and supervisor Inspector Lucy Sewell. It was something I was apprehensive to do as I did not know how she would react and what level of support I would obtain or could expect. My apprehension was completely misplaced. Lucy would become one of Alex's greatest supporters and her input and assistance could never be overstated. She acted as the link to Senior Command and along with Sergeant Carl Beaumont helped to make sure all the fundraising that was to come and the monumental support from the police alliance of Warwickshire and West Mercia achieved as much as it did for Alex.

Lucy had a very rare ability to manage, on the face of things, her personal feelings and balance them with the Rank and position she had on our team. She remained professional but compassionate when required but I was present on a few occasions when she, the real human Lucy and her love and desire to help Alex and us as a family was brilliantly demonstrated to me. Lucy's mother also became one of Alex's most ardent supporters and regularly reached out to him on social media.

Sergeant Carl Beaumont was the team leader and Operational Firearms Commander on one of the other duty groups on our unit and when I first met him I, in truth, found that he came across at times as intimidating. He is a tough looking man, another former military man who didn't suffer fools or work-shy constables lightly. It was interesting to see this hard man soften so readily when in the presence of Alex. Sergeant Carl became a regular visitor to our house over future months to see us and bring the myriad of gifts and cards that would be delivered for Alex from well-wishers to my police station over Summer and Autumn while we remained in the United Kingdom. As time went on I admired him more and more for his absolute commitment to supporting us. He and his wife Jan visited Alex many times in hospital and played their part in keeping his spirits up.

It is often quoted and regularly espoused that the police *are* a family. In my darkest time since attesting my loyalty to the Queen and becoming part of that family, I witnessed the care, commitment and genuine love and desire to help "one of our own" who, this time, was me.

The numbers of colleagues that stepped up and became part of that supporting mechanism was unbelievable. In such a short time, friendships were solidified and made more profound. To name and thank a hundred of Warwickshire and West Mercia's finest would leave out a hundred more equally worthy of such thanks. That thanks would need to extend beyond the alliance where I work to officers in my old Police Forces of South Yorkshire and the Civil Nuclear Constabulary and further afield even within a mere handful of weeks of his being diagnosed correctly at this early part of Alexander's Journey.

I am unsure how people when dealing with such a malevolent disease as cancer can cope if they do not have the support of their employer and the people that work with them.

Dealing with a life-threatening disease is a test of one's self, particularly when it is a loved one who relies on you as a protective element in their life. You constantly battle that fear of loss and have to exude a sense of ability, support and love as well as positivity. You cannot help but feel a sense of desperation and impotency that would be made exponentially more difficult if you were worrying about your livelihood. That feeling of helplessness and potential loss is something that you would do anything to be rid of and equally do anything to take that sense of loss and physical and mental pain from your child.

After that one week whuch seemed like a lifetime, we finally made it to Leicester Royal Infirmary's Children's Cancer Ward on the 16th June. Maruška's brother Paul had come with us. He worked in the private security industry and whilst he lived and technically worked in London he travelled abroad with clients a lot of the time. We had talked and we shared the same anger and frustration at the situation we faced. The truth was that Alex has spent such a huge amount of time being misdiagnosed and receiving the wrong treatment for a very aggressive and very rare form of cancer. I had attempted to do research which would provide me with reliable and independent information on Ewing Sarcoma. That was a minefield as Google searches would bring all kinds of horror stories and conflicting information up. I was under no illusion that the situation was a difficult one and Paul, Maruška and I feared that the delay of many months without any treatment for the cancer may have meant we were too late. I cannot impart to you with any degree of accuracy the sheer feeling of fear and foreboding when we approached the hospital. Alex was in pain and endured yet again another journey in the car being supported by pillows. He had been given pain relief so was able to use his crutches.

One thing was for certain Alex had all the symptoms of Ewing Sarcoma and we had imparted these signs and our concerns in detail to several doctors. The symptoms listed in numerous places on the internet were described as pain at the site of the tumour, swelling, fever, fatigue and weight loss. He had ticked every box.

We ventured onto the children's cancer ward at Leicester for the first time. It is a place that is difficult to describe. A place of both hope and despair that over time becomes the norm. The ward was full of children going through the same battles that Alex was: only a few had Ewing Sarcoma but all of them fought the life-threatening disease called cancer in one guise or another. Alex attended on crutches but he left with a wheelchair. This was four full weeks after we were taken onto the ward in Sheffield for a biopsy to clarify a condition that was "more sinister" than the incorrect diagnosis of Perthes Disease. Alex would spend such a major part of his life in this ward over the next six months. He would endure terrible sickness and upset and we would endure a roller coaster of emotions and soul searching.

Alex forged some lasting friendships with children in the ward: Mia, Ben, Evan, Eve, Marcus, Harrison and Abdul. Maruška and I spent time with their parents and also made friendships and connections over the many nights we were there at Alex's bedside. Mia and her

Mum and Dad became dear to us but for me, I became close friends with her dad Chris. He was also a police officer with Leicestershire Police. Mia had relapsed having originally being diagnosed as a mere infant and fought brave battles every day. She hardly spoke when we were there but would always go and sit with Alex. Often they would sit on the edge of the bed and she would watch him or they would watch his iPad. They spoke little but a connection was made and both seemed comfortable in each other's company. As time passed over weeks of them spending time together they began to share toys and Mia began to talk to Alex. He had become a first port of call whenever she was strong enough to leave her bed.

I recall also how Eve, a wonderful young girl had been so kind to Alex when he was going to have his Hickman Line fitted. It was surgery and Alex was genuinely terrified of the prospect. He was always nervous before every procedure but this one was the first and he feared the unknown. Eve had been ill several months before Alex with Ewing Sarcoma. I remember seeing her being so kind to him and doing her best to allay his fears and comfort him. That was a wonderful thing to do when she was facing her own fears and trials every day. It saddens me to say that Eve lost her battle with cancer in July 2017 just before this book was published. She was a shining star in life and is now the brightest star in the sky.

On his first day in the ward Alex underwent scans, blood tests and echo cardiograms to prepare him for the treatment we were so desperate to get him started on. Unbeknown to me at the time Paul, Maruškas's brother, who met the doctor with us, had recorded the meeting so that we could make sure we hadn't missed any vital piece of information or, because of our emotions, fail to recall some important aspect of the meeting.

The meeting took place with our ward doctor, the paediatric oncologist and we tried desperately to get information to allay our fears and concerns. The treatment regimen was described to us in principle but there didn't seem to be any urgency or sense of pace to commence Alex's treatment. We had experienced months of delay through incorrect diagnosis and then waited further for the occasion to attend the cancer ward where the task of saving him could actually take place through required treatment. There were delays in having his Hickman Line done and delays in finding a slot for Alex to undergo other tests prior to starting the chemotherapy. They all seemed necessary and vital to ascertain his current situation. I expressed my concerns at how any further delays would make the huge delays in diagnosis even more of an issue. I recall the paediatric oncologist's answer which still surprises me to this day: "he has had it for so long now that another couple of weeks won't make any difference".

This quote would come to haunt me over the following months as we heard from numerous sources on the rest of our journey in both the United Kingdom and the United States as well as in Europe that treatment was always time critical.

The 16th June was an important day for another reason. We started Alex's social media account and he made his first video then. His first Follower was Michaela, an old friend of Maruška's who had stepped up and was one of the many fundraisers for Alex. She visited us at home with her daughter early on in his diagnosis and I know that both Alex and Maruška really appreciated it.

As a reward for his day at the hospital we went to Toys R Us as he had received a gift voucher from my work. This was the first of many gifts and donations that he would receive over the months and not the last one from Warwickshire police officers and staff.

On 16th June, we also managed to get a wheelchair which Alex so desperately needed. The wheelchair was, frankly, an old heavy metal monstrosity with a turning circle of a submarine. We were however grateful for anything we could get. It would be several weeks later before we were gifted an amazing wheelchair from a local group of trustees, independent to, but connected through history, to the ward. That wheelchair, complete with bespoke add-on's and dinosaur wheel covers has been both a close friend and a constant reminder to him of his frailty and dependency. I was surprised how expensive it was and at that time we simply would have not been able to afford to get one that was designed to meet his specific needs due to the financial problems we were facing.

The financial problems we were experiencing due to our geographical move and my change in role had been compounded by Maruška's inability to undertake work due to Alex's dependency on one or both of us. Maruška was self-employed, if she didn't work she didn't get paid. Alex was now so ill he wasn't attending school and required full time care. We were effectively reduced to one wage in a matter of weeks and were using our small amount of savings to plug the gap between income and expenditure!

As the support mechanisms were set up in Warwickshire Police I also reached out to my staff association and professional organisation the Police Federation of England and Wales and the Police Firearms Officer Association. The Police Firearms Officer Association (P.F.O.A) is my professional body and I pay a small membership per month for which I receive a professional magazine and the best support and assistance if I was to discharge my firearm at work. I never anticipated contacting them for anything more than legal and professional guidance and it was Creamy who suggested that I contact them with regards to my current position.

I made the call and I was pleasantly surprised. They exceeded all my expectations. I spoke with Debbie Williams who managed the administrative functions and then to her husband Mark Williams, a retired Metropolitan Police A.F.O and now Chief Executive Officer of the P.F.O.A. Our telephone conversation was very candid and he was obviously well versed in dealing with this kind of situation. He asked what I needed. I was honest, I wanted advice on how to manage such a situation in a firearms role with the obvious pressure and anxiety that this situation could cause. I also disclosed to him how fatigued I was and how a lack of sleep due to caring for Alex was my biggest problem at that time. I wanted him to assure me that my role as an A.F.O was not over, only suspended temporarily. The next biggest problem was financial. They immediately sent Alex and

Maruška gifts and after a quick discussion on where the financial shortfalls were they made up that shortfall with a monthly payment to my bank account. Throughout this whole situation I was completely humbled by their generosity and support which extended throughout. They sent Alex a gift of an iPad and some other accessories which he would use to occupy himself at times and to relax with whilst in hospital. Mark and Debbie visited us at home and became friends, that part of the family you choose.

Simon Payne, the Chairperson of Warwickshire Police Federation became a champion of Alex from early on and was involved in the huge fundraising machine that burst into operation as Alex was diagnosed. Simon and another Federation Officer called Steve helped me to get support from the benevolent fund to manage our personal finances making it easier to cope. I was also able to access some health care assistance through the Warwickshire Police life insurance, which included a private healthcare company called Red Arc. Red Arc provided us with practical advice and emotional support. That support came in the form of an experienced nurse and former NHS employee called Joy. Joy was a force for good when we were struggling to make progress. She was my nurse advisor; Red Arc provided another for Maruška also. Joy was much more than a sympathetic ear, she gave me practical help and advice. Her expertise and ability to be totally honest and impartial would be invaluable later on when we were trying to break out from of the lack of progress and seek much needed medical expertise and opinions elsewhere. Interestingly I would meet another, very similar and equally exceptional woman on a flight to Atlanta in August 2017 a whole year later.

Alex's cancer was not just a physical issue but spiritual and mental too. As the pain and discomfort and isolation took its toll he was clearly depressed and the psychological impact of his treatment and related events left him saddened and withdrawn. He was also haunted by night terrors associated with bad experiences during the course of his diagnosis. A recurring dream was of him left abandoned in an old derelict hospital: dusty and web covered. He was desperately seeking us out and trying to avoid the faceless nurses that were trying to hurt him with needles. He would wake in the night screaming and very quickly he would or indeed could not sleep alone. Nights at home from just a few months into the illness involved Maruška or I having to sleep with him. He lacked mobility and needed medication during the night for pain relief. He needed help using the toilet, cleaning and moving his position in bed. He had lost any sense of independence which was coupled with a nine-year old's sense of acceptance of a new way of living linked to pain and discomfort. He began to fade away.

The P.F.O.A also supported us with counselling support and Stuart, a counselor and all-round trouble shooter at the P.F.O.A visited Alex and gave me support to primarily manage his fears and recurring nightmares about hospital. Stuart did a great job in helping Alex. The anxieties remain and he occasionally suffers troubled dreams but nothing on the same scale he endured previously.

So far, I have retold Alexander's journey from the beginning of his problems to the time when we realized the enormity of the battle we now face. We had received the terrible news following months of uncertainty, frustration and a sense of foreboding. Even with the final correct diagnosis those negative emotions would remain, but in different sets of circumstances and for different reasons. Such a deeply penetrating and traumatic event affects you spiritually as well. I have handled significant trauma and stress during my life and due to my police training and martial arts training, I have managed to navigate it well enough to continue with life and remain centered and optimistic about the future. This had shaken my faith and belief to its core.

Five

The social media accounts had been set up and within a matter of weeks Alex had generated a huge following that just seemed to continue to increase. Initially the following had come from the police family as my works official social media accounts had supported and exposed his pages and posts to their audience.

The Twitter and Facebook accounts had the same profile and background pictures. His profile photo, as mentioned before, was my boy at the Sheffield Children's Hospital in May 2016, with a smile, sporting a Batman t-shirt and a bandaged arm. His background photo, now immortalised as the front cover to this book and accompanying DVD was taken in 2014 and is of Alex and Sophia walking from the beach at Seamill Lane to our home in St. Bees, Cumbria. I remember that sunny day. Maruška and I walked behind them with a weary, sea soaked dog talking of the future but completely unknowing about the battles that lay ahead.

Alex made video posts revealing the events of the day. We never filmed or photographed him when he was ill or was upset but he genuinely enjoyed the ability to share his experiences and the battles he was facing. The cancer had confined him to a wheelchair by now and he was constantly exhausted from a lack of sleep. The continuous use of hot water bottles to alleviate the pain had marked his skin and it took some considerable time before those marks would disappear.

Despite this, Alex had drawn strength and encouragement from this new world around him where he could speak about his day and what he was doing. His initial uncertainties when being videoed for his posts quickly dissolved away. He was a natural and seemed to find an energy and enthusiasm for his accounts. He relished the time we spent together looking at the many messages of encouragement. He rekindled his passion for nature and shared this with his new audience. The gentle kind boy had returned and so had his love of life and care for the natural world. His supporters and followers quickly picked up on the fact that he had a love for owls and birds of prey and was very knowledgeable about sharks and dinosaurs. He had loved reading before he fell ill and the social media had motivated him to once again read his books and watch his documentaries on the natural world. He did this to impart his knowledge in his messages and posts and engaged other people who he shared a common interest.

Alex would wake with an excitement to see what messages he had received from his fans. We would sit together and look through them and it created an intimate time for us to be close and escape the reality of his hospital appointments, the checks and scans for that day or his confinement to his wheelchair and hospital bed. He wanted to share his experiences with them and cared for the people that were messaging him, many of whom were going through challenging times of their own and perhaps found solace in Alex's posts. My son, regardless of his problems at that time, had found his smile and his positivity. The little boy who I admired so much for his kind and gentle outlook even when it had been used against him in the past had turned these attributes into a strength that motivated and inspired others to do the same. Here was this small boy fighting cancer who cared about the welfare of others and wanted people to have a nice day and be happy in whatever their endeavours were at that time.

Alex was in a better place now and we tried desperately to maintain that predicament for him. Maruška and I were dealing with other issues. The biggest problem for me was that we seemed to be beset by delays that resulted in nothing being done for sometimes weeks at a time. The delay in diagnosis created serious frustrations and we lived with the anxiety every day that the cancer was running amok in his body. We would learn much later once we had received analysis of the situation whilst in America, that in fact the delay in diagnosis and the further crippling delays in starting effective treatment in the form of chemotherapy had more than likely allowed the cancer to spread from the femur head into the cup area of the acetabulum. Furthermore, the cancer had metastasised and there were small pockets of disease on the opposite side of his body on the pelvis. None of this had come to light as Alex commenced his chemotherapy treatment. We had been assured that the cancer had remained localised and that was a good sign. This wasn't however correct.

I remember the specific meeting with our paediatric oncological consultant at the Leicester Royal Infirmary about the results of his first scan and further biopsy. She informed us that the cancer was localised and that was great news as its increased significantly his chances of survival. I wept a lot that day with tears of relief. The reality would come to light months later and I would weep again.

I had heard time and time again in the following months that treatment was time critical. It is overpoweringly frustrating having the feeling of anxiety over the passage of time and having no ability to influence it.

Obtaining hard facts about Ewing Sarcoma was difficult as was hard evidence on the efficacy of treatment. The condition was so rare and so few people were diagnosed with it. The treatment plan was presented to us at Leicester Royal Infirmary and we were offered the opportunity to take part in a clinical trial. The Euro Ewing Trial which ironically was comparing the standard treatment in the United Kingdom with the treatment given in the United States. This makes me smile now after that other continent had become a second home and who knows, maybe in the future my first.

At the time, we didn't really know which way to go with the clinical trial, as the information we had received was rather sterile and the hospital had indicated that they couldn't be seen to influence our decision and therefore they did not provide us with any opinions on the matter.

I turned to the Bone Cancer Research Trust for some help and advice as well as Joy at Red Arc. I also sought out credible websites where I could get information and this included Sarcoma UK, the only charity in the United Kingdom that focusses on all types of Sarcoma.

I was fortunate enough to obtain a great deal of information from Hannah at the Bone Cancer Research Trust, a U.K. charity who explained because it was so rare a condition that early diagnosis of the symptoms was difficult and they believed there was a need to raise awareness within the medical profession. The prognosis wasn't good. For Ewing Sarcoma, the five-year survival rate for a child under 15 years old was around 70 to 80% if the cancer had remained local and had not spread. If there had been a spread the chances of survival were drastically reduced and were as low as 20 to 30%. This news hit me hard and I was further troubled when they confirmed my fears that early diagnosis was important to maximise the ability to defeat the cancer.

But, at the time, we had been told that it was localised so I took comfort from a 70% survival rate over the next five years. It's amazing what, when you are in such a comprising position how a three in ten fatality statistic seems comforting and digestible.

What are statistics? My trusty Oxford English Dictionary tells me it is "the practice of collecting and analysing numerical data, especially for the purpose of inferring proportions in a whole from those in a representative sample". The Bone Cancer Research Trust as well as doctor's in the United States months later would explain that the statistics, were just that and the actual number of the sample was so low due to the rarity of this type of cancer and the limited amount of records that there would be fluctuations due to the unique set of circumstances in every case. I hoped, as I still do, that this was a good thing.

The Bone Cancer Research Trust also explained that in the NHS significant funding went into the main cancers particularly in children but the rare ones, including Ewing Sarcoma, were woefully neglected. I did understand this when I thought rationally. There is a saying: that the needs of the many outweigh the needs of the few. But when you put all the children suffering from rare cancers together, they become many. Far too many souls to ignore or neglect.

With regards to the clinical trial one thing was certain that if he was accepted on the trial then the hospital would have to ensure that treatments and checks were delivered on time and comprehensively to ensure parity with other participants nationally and internationally. This key piece of information from both the Trust and Red Arc was the key decider for me. Would it stop the delays and the often absence of communication? I truly hoped.

Armed with this information I requested we be considered for the trial. We submitted our request and were later informed that we had been accepted on the trial and he would receive the United States model of treatment. This model was obviously was very significant albeit completely coincidental some six months later.

Prior to commencing chemotherapy Alex needed a central line surgically implanted so as to allow the delivery of the chemotherapy or other medication and to allow the withdrawal of blood. Two kinds of central line were offered and Alex wanted a Hickman Line which was the older type that involved using an external tube. He wanted this because the other type used needles to extract and inject into a pad and he now had a significant phobia of needles that remains with him to this day.

Alex was admitted having his Hickman Line put in on the 20th June but the procedure was cancelled due to the surgery slot being required for an emergency. The Hickman Line was put in the following day. One more delayed day.

On 22nd June Alex went to his school to speak to everyone about the cancer and the Hickman Line. He gave a presentation to his school friends. Maruška, Sophia and I went with him. He had gone to great efforts to explain that he would lose his hair and that they shouldn't be scared of him or worry. My heart swelled with pride on that day and I watched him at the front of the class talking about his life-threatening illness and seeking to reassure all these children about the changes that would occur in his body as he fought the cancer and how he was the same person.

He had changed in so many ways. He was so much thinner and his body always contorted through the constant need to take as much weight off his diseased leg and pelvis as possible whenever he walked or indeed whenever he moved. It is difficult for me to write a description now of how he was because it is so wretched and upsetting. This physical frailty and pain was constantly masked by medication. It had affected him physically but his spirit and mind remained so strong, but they too were affected. He had awful nightmares by night and with a fear and uncertainty of what was happening to him by day.

We had spoken before we went to the school and he confided in me how nervous he was and how he hoped that when his hair fell out and he became more ill that people wouldn't be scared of him or make fun of him. But while he was there, there wasn't a shred of that anxious self-conscious little boy only Alex the Brave, Alex the Kind and Alex the little boy who cared more for others than for himself.

The school and the Parent Teacher Association had organised numerous fundraising events for Alex over the course of the following months. Like me, he had only been in his new surroundings for a handful of months, but he was one of their own and the support was phenomenal.

The village in its entirety is around 900 residents, a School, Pub, Post Office and Church and they had taken Alex into their hearts. Whenever we walked in the village, from then right up to today as I write this book, people would stop and ask about him, ask about us. They cared and it was, in perhaps a tiny way, their fight too. Several of the villagers helped in so many ways: our neighbours Esther and Craig, Eleanor and Andy, Hannah and Emily visited often. Dog walking duties were taken on, afternoon tea with Sophia and her dolls and at times, over a glass of wine, a shoulder to cry on for Maruška.

74

Many months later in December, Emily and Genie brought their horses over for Alex and Sophia to see and ride.

Craig and Esther own a printing company called Blink Print, who are based in Lutterworth and with the help of their son, an aspiring and very promising graphic designer, made and produced hundreds of prints of a variety of fundraising events and promotional posters. All for Alex and all at no cost to us.

From June to November 2016 it was a constant relentless diary of hospital visits, checks and treatments. He would spend 50% of his life in hospital during this period primarily at the Leicester Royal Infirmary but also at the Glenfield Hospital in Leicestershire and Royal the Orthopaedic Hospital in Birmingham.

It was towards the end of June as we waited for Alex to begin his actual treatment to fight the cancer that we discussed, from time to time, the disease with him. It was evident that, with the exception of a few books, there was very little about cancer in children for children. What there was appeared to be written by adults. My first plan was to help Alex write a book about his cancer for children of his age. We have started it and perhaps he will finish it when he is home and healthy. He continued to liken his cancer to a parasite inside him, it suited him because of his passion for nature and constant reference to it. Besides it was rather accurate.

Alex remained in a positive mindset for most of the time and talked about defeating the cancer on his video messages. We had begun our martial rhetoric. Never-the-less I remained astounded by how positive he was at times. He seemed genuinely to care about other people and what was happening around him. This would be more evident as we continued the journey. The times where he wallowed in self-pity were so few. That didn't mean he wasn't in pain and he cried and was sad but he didn't languish in a state of despondency. The number of times I saw him suffering mentally and physically was just too many to count but there were certain occasions which are prominent in my thoughts.

I remember one night at home, he slept during the day more often as the crippling fatigue associated with chemotherapy set in, but before then he went to bed at a normal time and I had a ritual of going to bed with him. We lay together and I held him tightly in the usual position that allowed him to be hugged without feeling the pain or pressure on his hip or leg. We settled for the night and then from out of nowhere he asked me … "Am I going to die". Those words from his mouth choked me. I couldn't stop my tears no matter how hard I tried: they just flowed, relentlessly. We held each other tighter and I swore to him that he would live because I wasn't going to let God take him from me. God and I had some serious issues at that time but my writing on that can wait for another page.

I promised Alex that he would live, the medicine would make him better but he would need to help it: by being strong and brave. The treatment plan, the clinical trial, that I had waited desperately for him to commence was about to begin.

Alex had his first chemotherapy on the 27th June. That was three weeks after we had been told he had cancer and was the first actual treatment to deal with it specifically. It hit him hard, very hard and he vomited constantly for almost 48 hours snatching precious little sleep. We didn't know how he was going to react and his body, whilst it had dealt with pain, have never dealt with the chemotherapy process. That process pumped poison through his veins with the intention of attacking the cancer regardless of the collateral damage. He was begging us to help him and there was nothing we could do about it. Maruška was with him that day and she told me he kept saying, "I'm so sorry mummy, I don't know what's happening, I don't know why this is happening. Please help me". What can you say to that. The feeling of impotency that I have spoken of previously gripped me yet again.

Chemotherapy treatment are chemicals that are designed to attack fast growing cells like cancer. Unfortunately, they don't just attack cancer, they attack any fast-growing cell structure in the body because they have no way differentiating. Blood cells are damaged and the life and health-giving benefits they contain are destroyed and other cells like hair and nails and skin are affected too. The side effects are brutal and in many ways as bad as the cancer itself. Over the course of this treatment he would suffer the loss of nails, ulceration of his mouth, chronic fatigue and sickness and the one usually associated with the treatment- hair loss. Chemotherapy also made sure that the healing process took longer and this was a significant issue when he had the major surgeries on the journey ahead.

When Alex was diagnosed Maruška, who had always leaned towards the use of natural remedies, and her mother Anna, searched and studied natural products that could help in the fight against cancer. They had some experience previously as they had used them in the fight against cancer when her father, Frank, fell ill with cancer when Alex was just a few years old. He had won the fight initially but relapsed shortly after. I believe the natural remedies had helped Frank but it was his lifestyle and mindset that made him succumb to the disease.

Alex took a plethora of natural compounds and supplements that had been well researched by Maruška and tried and tested on the field of battle. Vitamins, herbal and plant derivatives and other metabolic supplements combined with enzymes that would ensure they were absorbed by the body and not simply urinated away. I am convinced that they reduced the impact of the chemotherapy on him and improved the recovery rate of the white and red blood cells within him. This was evident in his tests and results because, right up to the last few weeks of chemotherapy after his first surgery, he never failed to recover the blood counts required to commence the next period of chemotherapy whereas almost all the other children in both the U.K and the U.S. failed at some point.

This fact also left the doctor's in the United States slightly bemused and interested in why it was happening and the only material physical difference between him and other children were these supplements to his treatment regimen. They considered it and even now as I write laboratory tests are taking place in the hospital to see what and why this was happening. I look forward to the results.

When Maruška shared this additional treatment with the U.K. doctors it was met with indifference. They asked for a list of the products and the dosage and amounts which we readily provided but then, like so many other things, we heard nothing else from them. Amusingly we needed a letter from the hospital in Kansas City to allow us to travel with this supplements across the Atlantic and when we arrived they also requested specific details like they had in the U.K. We received a response from the team which requested that we stopped using some of them and gave us the green light to continue with others. To her credit and thanks to her conviction, Maruška continued with them all.

We had several messages and posts from people during the journey advising us of miracle cures and natural substances around the cure of cancer. Most of these were cannabis related or derivatives thereof. As a police officer I made a decision not to go down this route and maintained the "conventional" treatment and the natural supplements. Had it been me with the cancer I may have sought other alternatives but I wasn't prepared to take the chance with my son's life. Despite this huge assault on his body we managed to maintain the social media posts and throughout June his followers continued to increase at a rapid rate.

Alex returned home on the 30th June after a weeklong regimen of daily chemotherapy treatment. It was then we found that the first batches of presents started arriving from his followers and well-wishers. This raised his spirits but he was so weak and feeling sick all the time. I decided, using the power of social media to try and contact his idol Steve Backshall to lift his spirits. I did the same a few months later with a time travelling zoologist called Nigel Marven. Both Steve Backshall and Nigel Marven are both very popular and successful naturalists, writers and television presenters of nature and wildlife programmes in the U.K. I reached out to them and hoped for a reply: they did not disappoint.

Whenever he was well enough between chemotherapy treatments he would turn to nature or draw pictures. This was a common theme throughout his treatment, whether it was chemotherapy, recovering from surgery or radiation therapy. He would escape to his favourite places and paint and draw the dreams he had for the future or escape into his world of monsters, dinosaurs and sharks. He spent time with his geckos, Riptor and Serena, whenever he was well enough. It was strange to see that he had such a natural affinity with animals. The geckos, like the birds of prey he would handle so comfortably and confidently in the near future, would happily sit on his hand or shoulder as he pet them and regardless of what he was doing: watching television, reading or giving all his attention to them they clearly had a bond. I hope that, when he returns to the U.K and to his geckos, they remember him.

Immediately following the first chemotherapy treatment we saw an improvement. The intense pain had reduced and subsequent scans indicated that the tumour had shrunk. He was still on regular pain relief but I remember getting him out of the bath one evening at the beginning of July. Alex still needed lifting and carrying around. I can see him very clearly in mind's eye standing at the edge of the bath, held by me to steady him. He looked very frail and tired, wrapped in a towel that almost covered him completely. It was then that he told Maruška and I that he couldn't feel any pain. The look on his face was priceless. He looked so emotional and so relieved as well as surprised. He wept then, silently and for some time, as we held him.

Six

The chemotherapy would continue for months and Alex began to dread the cycle of treatment often sobbing the night before we would go to the hospital. Maruška or myself would keep a constant vigil at his bedside over those arduous weeks. We tried to comfort him and always give him love, encouragement and our presence so he knew he was never alone.

The nurses at the hospital always tried to keep him happy and engaged. They were always busy, flitting from one job to another, one patient to another.   Some of them were closer to Alex than others and we built a rapport with some of them due to the length of time we were there. We connected with some of the more experienced and longer-in-service nurses who, I guessed, like police officers, had begun to take the continuous demands and pressure in their stride a little more.   They also seemed to talk more personally and directly with you about the illness and I have fond memories of sitting with one of the nurses overnight sipping tea and processing the obstacles we faced with her guiding words that gave me truths and direct answers.

The wards in the U.K are communal with individual rooms only for patients that have an infection risk or who are teenagers. This was hard to endure for Alex and both Maruška and I. can you imagine going through terrible treatment for an awful disease along with everyone else in the same room, separated at night by just a curtain of cloth? Children as young as two years old shared those communal areas with us. I remember, one-night laying in a fold out bed alongside Alex's hospital bed, listening through the curtain to every child crying and screaming outside in that communal room all night. The psychological and physical impact of this on an anxious and distraught child seeking to rest and snatch a few hours' sleep between vital signs being checked and regular pain and sickness relief cannot truly be appreciated unless you are there.

The only positive aside from spending time with my son and never being far from his side was that I succeeded, fuelled with emotive and profound deliberations, in finishing writing my own book - a crime thriller horror.

Spending so much time at hospital also brought support from the charities connected to them: particularly Macmillan Cancer Support and CLIC Sargent. Ann, an advisor at CLIC Sargent would often stick pieces of paper and forms under our noses for us to sign that helped speed along the processes of obtaining a Disabled parking badge, small financial disbursements, discounted parking and many other things. They were very helpful and a harbour in the rough seas of the Leicester Royal Infirmary.

The fact remained that the current treatment of chemotherapy despite its heavy price was working for Alex. The incident in our bathroom as he got out of the bath confirmed that for me as readily as any scan or comment from a doctor. Things seemed to be under a degree of control and the hospital believed that the tumour was still localised. I allowed myself some hope. Unfortunately, we learned much later when in the U.S. that scans already taken in the U.K. to this point had not covered a sufficient area that incorporated parts of his pelvis that would pick up the other pockets of disease. We wouldn't see the evidence of the spread for months to come and we wouldn't learn about the scan problem and what would have greatly helped until much later still.

Weeks passed and Alex spent considerable time in hospital. We had a treatment plan and we focused on getting through it. It was strange how, with the help of the right dosage of anti-sickness medication, Alex began to adapt to and endure the worst of the sickness associated with the chemotherapy.

As Alex developed some endurance to the treatment and he responded and recovered well (thanks primarily I believe to his natural supplements) he would count the days, hours, minutes down to when the treatment and subsequent hydration was completed and he would be going home. We began a ritual where we would go to our local public house in the village called The Dunton Bassett Arms and have a Chinese meal there. Alex would share his plans for the visit and what he would eat with his Twitter and Facebook followers. Eventually they would ask him what he planned to eat a day or two before his treatment finished when he was coming out of hospital. These things helped to motivate him and help him pass the time as did regular visitors.

We had lots of visitors at hospital when he was there and at home when he was not. The visits were from some of our family members and from both the Police family and close friends but particularly from those that were in both latter two.

My good friend Stuart and his wife Shari made the journey down from Yorkshire to see us. They came with us to fundraising events and spent hours playing board games with the children. Alex, having been unable to play outdoors for some considerable time now, had taken to board games. He seemed to enjoy the comfort of a communal game and relished the company and moments of fun that everyone, including himself was part of. Stuart and Shari were always ready to play Ludo, Snakes and Ladders or one of his dinosaur quiz games as soon as they arrived.

Stuart had been my Sergeant when I was in South Yorkshire Police and we had remained in contact. He was a constant in my life and despite the amount of time that had passed since we had seen each other last the next time we spoke it was like we had seen each other just a few days before. We had gone through some memorable and often pressurised incidents together in the police and had also fought together against some rather unfriendly and aggressive individuals whilst we served on the same duty patrol group and he was a custody sergeant. He had seen me at what I thought was my worst and my best and that was before my current predicament. Stuart was a larger than life man, he was short but broad and barrel chested and had a booming voice that I had seen shrivel the most aggressive and disrespectful criminals when they had been presented before him in custody. He was another example of a hard man who was so kind and gentle when spending time with my children.

My team visited regularly and Alex would get all excited when he saw one of the Armed Response Vehicles or traffic cars pull up at the house. Dom, "Creg" (as Craig was known to Alex and Sophia), Lucy, Rich and Carl were the mainstay but other crewmates came too. Every visit was valued and memorable and he particularly enjoyed visits made by Amy a dog handler and her dogs Duke and Rebel. He was very fond of Amy and her dogs and he got excited when they arrived because he knew he would interact with the dogs. I think back to watching him hobble around the courtyard hiding items for the dogs to search for. Despite the discomfort and fatigue he always wore a genuine smile when they were around.

It was interesting that as time passed other police officers and other members of the police family from my Force and further afield would contact me or visit us offering words of support, prayers and positive thoughts for Alex and me. People endured long journeys and brought wonderful gifts. One friend Colin from Essex Police visited with his wife and brought a beautiful owl photo he had, as a keen amateur photographer, taken himself. That photo now adorns Alex's bedroom wall. Lee from the equivalent of my team in Cleveland & Durham (made famous as 'The Interceptors' that was once a weekly documentary series on U.K. television) made the journey southwards bringing a bag of cash raised at one of his teams many public appearances and a large Garden Gnome (long story).

Some of my old friends from Cumbria were a constant support too. I had forged strong bonds through mutual interest and mutual appreciation that would not diminish because of geography. One of my aikido students and friend Jason visited often. He took Alex's illness very hard as they had built up a connection through a shared interest and passion for sharks and conservation. It was warming and confirmed my faith in humanity to see Jason, a huge tank of a man who worked in and owned nightclubs in a former coal mining and shipping working class coastal town, wipe the tears from his eyes when we discussed Alex's health at various times during the course of his journey. Jason went on to do a gruelling sponsored swim of just under 11 miles in Lake Windermere in challenging conditions for Alex.

Another friend and fellow aikido student of mine I had left behind in Cumbria for my post in Warwickshire Police was Shona. Shona, a short fiery red head with Scottish ancestry, visited often and always checked not only on Alex's welfare but mine and the rest of the family too. She had just joined Cumbria Constabulary and despite the pressures of being a new recruit going through initial Police training made time to check how Alex was and if I was okay. Having practiced martial arts with her she was the person I would happily have at my back on a Saturday night, preferable to 90% of the people I had ever worked with! She played her part, at times, in making sure I didn't give in or give up and for that I shall forever be in her debt.

I remember Shona sent down a pennant for Alex when his chemotherapy had just begun that had the embroidered words "Be Brave" on it. It had arrived on a day that I was at home with Sophia and Alex was in hospital with Maruška. Sophia was desperate to share news of the pennant with Alex and the words it contained. She insisted we send Alex a video message. There she was, in her pyjama's brandishing the pennant and the words it displayed like a talisman gazing into my mobile phone camera for one of the first times.

"I'm Sophia, I'm Alexander's sister and I love Alex and all my family. And my ponies".

I love that video, as do we all.

When Alex was really suffering, Sophia was, I feel, side-lined on many occasions. This was completely unintentional and I regret it. She is quite the opposite of Alex in character and is more outgoing and headstrong. It was interesting to see, as I look back, how she dealt with Alexander's illness and the impact it had on our now less than normal life. I remember her insistence on several occasions after donning a children's nurses fancy dress costume from the hospital playroom to care for Alex when she visited him during treatment. They would also curl up with one another on Alex's bed and watch movies. This brought them closer together. She would often talk about "Alex's cancer" like it was influenza. I remember on one occasion when she had to take a trip herself to our local hospital because of suspected croup (an upper airway infection). When she was being examined by the doctor she casually asked, "Will I have to have a Hickman Line?". Maruška quickly explained the situation to the puzzled doctor.

These months have been a journey for Sophia also and she seems to have adopted many of the roles that Alex as older brother performed when he was healthy and at home. It will be interesting to see how the dynamic works when Alex returns home and Sophia is once again a little sister.

Around the 11th July, after several periods of chemotherapy treatment the inevitable happened and Alex's hair began to fall out. At first it was just like he was moulting loose strands. Then it continued and worsened where he would lay down and initially leave deposits of hair behind which a few days later became big clumps. He found it distressing more so when it stuck to his clothing and irritated his neck and back. We had talked about it and rationalised it many weeks before it happened, but when it happened, still hit him hard. Alex and I decided to shave off his hair while he was in hospital and we did that on the 15th July.

In solidarity, I shaved my hair off as well. Alex was really happy about this and he obviously found it comforting. As the weeks passed and my hair began to grow back he would often ask me, perhaps as a gentle reminder, of my commitment to him to keep it shaven whilst he remained bald. Within a short space of time most all my colleagues did the same and hair shaving quickly spread along the thin Blue and Green line. Alex's Uncle Paul, God-father Stuart and my mum's partner Peter shaved their hair too, as did many others. Many did it to raise funds for us as it was now, from July onwards, we began to seek donations through fundraising.

The police service and our team in particular have a very close bond to the other strands of the emergency service family: fire, ambulance and search & rescue. Many serving police officers in the U.K. wear the union flag with a distinctive thin blue line running across its middle. I have noticed more and more now seem to wear the same flag with the four colours (blue, red, green and orange) in a band rather than just the traditional one (red for fire, green for ambulance and orange for search & rescue).

My unit has a very close working relationship and strong camaraderie with the West Midlands Ambulance Service (W.M.A.S.). We are Firearms Officers and because of this receive enhanced medic training as part of the portfolio of skills we possess. This often results in us delivering first on scene treatment to injured persons at incidents, particularly road traffic collisions until W.M.A.S paramedics and ambulance crew arrive. We will also force entry into locked properties where they believe a vulnerable or injured person is located within.

Two of the W.M.A.S crew based at the Warwick hub along with one of the police officers on my unit were the first of many to shave their hair off and raise funds for Alex. I remember Alex was too ill to travel to watch the ceremonial shaving of Rich, Ian and Paul at the ambulance station but we watched it live via a Facebook stream. These three guys became devoted supporters of Alex and would also step up on many occasions thereafter to help, support and lift his spirits.

July was a month of highs and lows for Alex and for us a family. Most months were like that but July has a special place in my mind with its many highs relating to special events and life experiences that took place for Alex in that summer month in 2016.

After a demanding period of chemotherapy in the hospital and shaving off his hair we were invited to a summer event that weekend at the local racetrack and airfield of Bruntingthorpe. This place, a former RAF base during the second world war was now the home of a working racetrack and a rather impressive collection of privately owned cold war era military and civilian aircraft.

Ann from the CLIC Sargent came to see us before Alex left the ward explaining that the children in the ward and their families were invited to a day of fun at Bruntingthorpe that very weekend. There would be helicopter rides, vintage and sports cars to drive on the racetrack, Go Karts to enjoy as well as the aircraft on display.

It was a hot and wonderfully sunny day and we made it to the event which was memorable for all the right reasons. We all managed a helicopter ride and Alex was taken around the race track in a Ferrari with Simon who was such a help that day. Just a few weeks earlier and Alex would not have been able to have endured that brief trip in the car due to the agony in his hip and leg. I recollect spectating as he went around a track in a Go Kart. I was, naturally, unsure as to whether it was a good idea. Any jolt or collision could have had serious consequences but he was so very excited to get into that Kart: I couldn't take it away from him. As I watched him raise his fist in achievement at crossing the finish line I knew it was the right decision. He was happy and felt a sense of victory. I swore at that very moment that we would have that same victory against his cancer.

That event had previously taken place annually for the children on Ward 27 at the L.R.I. because it had such significance to the people who were involved at Bruntingthorpe. We learned that one of the organisers had lost his son many years previously to Ewing Sarcoma and that made the day all the more poignant.

This was such a memorable day, and we forged strong friendships with several people that helped make that happen Simon, his wife Mandy and Judy. These people visited and supported Alex so very much which included arranging the procurement of Alex's amazing wheelchair from local company Modern Mobility.

On 22nd July, we enjoyed more flying fun as one of my aikido students Jamie took us to Leicester Airfield to meet a talented and very kind pilot called Angela. Alex and I flew with her in a small single propeller aeroplane and Alex actually took the controls for a brief period of time (which gained him a rather splendid certificate from the Leicester Aero Club). I recall flying over our village and home and seeing, with some certainty, Maruška, Sophia and Bojar waving to us from our courtyard.

The best day in that month however was Wednesday 20th July. That, in light of the truly amazing things he had got to do with truly amazing people, is not an insignificant statement to make.

The 20th July is a day that Alex will never forget. He often talks about it, even now when he has endured, experienced and enjoyed so very much over a year later. Not only was it the day that we reached 2,000 followers on Twitter but also the day that Steve Backshall, his naturalist and wildlife presenting idol, replied to my contact with a video message for Alex! The video was short but full of energy and sincerity. That video made him so happy and so very content at a time when both feelings were in significant short supply. Finally, and this was the icing on the cake, Alex met a woman who was to have such a profound impact on him and his life: a woman named Anita Morris and she brought with her a little burrowing owl called Murray.

Seven

Anita Morris is a psychologist, behavioural coach and therapist who uses animal assisted therapy and is, most importantly for my son, also a falconer.

A falconer; the title used to describe a person skilled in the art of falconry, has in modern society, a much broader connotation to its original, centuries old meaning of hunting wild animals in their natural habitat using a trained bird of prey.

Alex dreams of one day being a falconer. A lover of nature and conservation, he has always had a fondness for birds of prey above almost all other creatures: but his favourite is the owl. This dream has never left him and acted like a warm glow and beacon light in his darkest and most derelict days. He has drawn many pictures of himself; owl or falcon on arm sat in a beautiful garden of fresh vegetables and flowers.

Murray and Alex's paths first crossed with a Tweet (or should that be a tweet-twoo). I can still remember the incandescent excitement from Alex when he received that message and then the subsequent ones that followed. It must be said that even to this day, that overwhelming joy still manifests itself whenever he speaks or receives a message from Anita. Alex and I owe a debt of gratitude to another lady as well called Denise. Denise is part of the original 'old guard' of Alex's followers on Twitter and also like Anita and Murray is from Cheshire. It was Denise who contacted Anita initially and that is where the falconry, where Anita learned her profession is based.

After a few messages and a phone call, we arranged for Anita and Murray to pay a visit. Anita runs a Community Interest Company called "Hack Back". I had never come across that phrase before but after checking their website I now know that it is the word for a gradual release technique to allow a bird of prey to successfully return to the wild. Hack Back is, in essence, a charity and it relies on donations and the small amount of funds it can raise from the handful of patrons it has and from sales of Murray memorabilia that Anita has had produced.

Anita and I spoke on the telephone and after feeling reassured that she wasn't a lunatic we agreed on a date for her to visit. I was so pleased that she was able to make the journey to us as Alex would definitely benefit from meeting them. At that time I wasn't aware of the huge positive impact that Anita and Hack Back would have on Alex's life and how it would shape and bolster him so entirely in his fight.

Alex was full of excitement and that exhilaration was also evident in Sophia. They both waited eagerly and impatiently for Anita to arrive. When she pulled into our courtyard in her small van emblazoned with photos of birds of prey they were fit to burst. It was so warming to see Alex acting like a little boy again and he hobbled outside to Anita and he embraced her as if they had known each other for years.

A mutual passion for birds of prey and nature as well as Anita's natural ability to transmit enthusiasm and a genuine joy for her craft would guarantee that their first meeting was a major success. Alex exuded confidence and shared his knowledge effortlessly in his conversations with Anita. Behind this frail boy and his tired drawn face was someone so very alive. The vivacity in his eyes and his broad beaming smile never left his face throughout the entire time Anita was with us. Murray was such a delightfully cute and curious little owl and he perched comfortably on Alex from the outset. I was proud and remain so to this day of Alex's natural affinity with animals and his ability to reassure them and handle them confidently whilst remaining awestruck by them. The energy and joy was infectious and we all would look back on that as such a memorable day.

This was one of many visits that Anita would make, not just with Murray but with her other owls Idris and Mango. Murray was a burrowing owl which is a very small owl, weighing just less than 200 grams and standing fewer than 10 inches tall and is indigenous, ironically, to the American mid-west. Idris lay on the other end of the spectrum as the African Spotted Eagle Owl is twice that height and four times the weight. Mango, a rather handsome Barn Owl was somewhere in-between them both. Those first few visits laid the foundations for the intention for Alex to undergo his professional falconry training under the tutelage of Anita and the other trainers at Cheshire Falconry.

I was surprised, as was Maruška, just how well trained and disciplined Murray was for such an apparently playful little bird. When Alex is better we will commence the United Kingdom's national falconry training required to have a bird. Due to Alex's age I would undertake the course with him but he would have, handle and care for his own bird. This aim and dream for the future has helped Alex steer a course through the most challenging times of his journey. We would spend hours over the next 12 months discussing which owl he would like. At first, he wanted a burrowing owl just like Murray but as he spent more time with other owls at another special place across the pond he would have to choose between three different species of owl. It was these kinds of things that we could use as a diversionary tactic when he was upset and in pain or feeling despondent.

Despite being focussed on the present in our actions and mindset, we always tried to discuss the future. The falconry training and owning his own bird was a key component to that hope and planning. When Alex got better...... we said that often. He had started his chemotherapy treatment but the reality was that he may not survive. This remained a constant in the back of my mind but I didn't dwell upon it. I hoped and prayed and we always spoke like that in front of Alex. He knew in his own way the reality of his illness and he would say, on the topic of Ewing Sarcoma, that "It can kill you" as if speaking as a bystander and that whilst Ewing Sarcoma could do that: it simply wouldn't do that to him. We daren't think otherwise. We had put our trust in the hospitals and Alex was doing what they had said. He endured the treatment and we counted the sessions and the weeks passed by.

The treatment regimen given to us by the hospital involved a course of chemotherapy followed by surgery to remove the diseased area and then depending on the analysis of the tumour once it had been removed they would then consider to what extent he would require consolidation chemotherapy or radiation therapy. The chemotherapy cycle lasted for four weeks: one week of six days of treatment and then rest and then one week of three days of treatment followed by rest and then it would begin again. The chemotherapy left his body in a fatigued and weakened state vulnerable to infection and illness. This was because the treatment damaged not only his red cells (that would at times need a blood transfusion) but also his white cells. Interestingly you cannot have a white cell transfusion as they can't survive the transfer. Your body needs to stimulate the creation of new ones as quickly as possible and you are given injections of "white cell boosters" as we would call them to help with that process.

The chemotherapy treatment was scheduled to continue until the end of October which gave us and Alex weeks of routine. One week of treatment and hospital stays and then one week of "rest" to recover. The reality was that those rest days were far from restful as he had endless blood tests and checks. He also required the white cell booster (called Filgrastim in the U.K and Neulasta in the U.S) for several consecutive days. If the blood tests indicated that he hadn't recovered sufficiently then the next chemotherapy could be delayed until Alex was strong enough. The white cell booster was delivered at home by community nurses. This group of nurses were from part of the NHS called Diana's Community Children's Services. Named after Princess Diana they were established through specific funds and donations made by Diana and her estate. They wear a distinctive purple uniform and when I asked about the unusual colour I am reliably informed that it was Diana's favourite colour and she signed all important documents in purple ink including those relating to the nursing Service that would bear her name. This was a small team of nurses that covered Leicestershire and we usually had the same five or six nurses. This meant we would get to know most of them with some degree of intimacy. Over the passing of a few months some of them became close to us and we would discuss Alex's situation and our frustrations with them. The ones we became close to would give us good advice and we felt some degree of comfort from them as time passed on and our situation and Alex's prognosis deteriorated. Just a few months later the only lines of communication we seemed to have was with these nurses.

The Neulasta white cell booster injection was delivered to Alex via his Hickman Line over a period of around half an hour. It was usually administered instantly by needle injection directly under the skin but because of Alex's phobia of needles that didn't happen. This medication, designed to aid recovery and prevent him lacking the means to fight illness and infection was, like almost all cancer related treatment as impactive on the body as the affects it was trying to counter. It had numerous side effects including nausea, fever and bone pain as well as coughing and shortness of breath.

Alex would often have photographs taken with the nurses when they visited and I have lost count of the number of tweets and posts put on his account over those months from June to November explaining that Alex had white cell booster treatment.

Despite this cycle of chemotherapy in hospital and medication at home he always bounced back and was ready for the next cycle of treatment. This, as stated previously, was due to the natural remedies and supplements that Maruška was giving him. The other factor of visits from friends and family, the enrichment of his free time and the plans made for the future as well our daily interaction with social media were the essential psychological elements. Their positive impact cannot be ignored. We were doing all we could physically and mentally to fight the cancer and to maximise his chances of survival based on the treatment plans of the experts.

July passed into August and the chemotherapy continued. It dominated our lives. Despite his resilience and the natural remedies to counter the worst of the toxicity of the relentless treatment Alex still suffered. It was taking its toll and I knew it would have decimated his body if not for the natural remedies that he was taking. He had a few blood transfusions and the ulceration affected him for brief periods before we managed to clear it up. I watched other children in the ward gripped by these adverse effects and I felt so much pity: the ulceration of their mouths and anuses and absolute fatigue must have been torture. The weakened state brought a high susceptibility to illness: coughs and colds could be life threatening and infection was an everyday risk. When your child is so vulnerable you have this tremendous fear when out in public. Next time you go out into a crowd, a shopping centre or a bus or coach perhaps see how many people cough, clear their throat or sneeze without using a tissue or handkerchief directly around you.

Twitter and Facebook gave him some solace from his constant treatment and we shared some light-hearted moments with his followers. I remember he would count down the hours until the last chemotherapy treatment of that cycle. He would draw flamboyant pictures of the time remaining before he could go home which we would capture with a beaming smile or a thumbs up and post to social media.

It was at this time that I remember browsing the internet with Alex one morning at hospital. As we navigated the growing number of messages, tweets and posts that he was now receiving daily, I came across one from a Dr. Max. This man, Dr. Massimiliano, would become another close friend who would have a direct impact on Alex's wellbeing. An archaeologist, Egyptologist and lover of natural history, Dr. Max would play his part in sustaining Alex through his darkest times. They would share a love of nature and history that would also impact on me personally. The post Alex and I found was one of Max attending radiotherapy treatment. The photo showed a sign on a hospital wall indicating the direction one should go to the Radiotherapy department. Max had positioned himself directly under the arrow as he announced his upcoming treatment. Max and I have also become good friends and I admire him greatly because of the love and care he has shown my son when he was fighting his own battles. Max has a condition that is an adult version of the sarcoma that Alex has. I explained the post and photo to an inquisitive Alex who immediately insisted that we sent him a message urging him to be brave and that Alex was thinking of him as they fought cancer together. Max replied and thus began a friendship that spanned generations through a common love of learning much like Anita and Alex had done just a few weeks earlier.

He was highly motivated by his regular communications with Anita and she visited again in August but this time she brought Idris and Mango with her too. I remember taking a photo of Alex holding Idris in our courtyard in the bright sunshine of a rare sunny day. He stood so tall and upright for those brief moments as he smiled and held such a heavy and majestic bird on his weary arm. Here he was again: Alex the Brave, Alex the Kind, Alex the Amazing, Alex the little boy who cared more for animals than himself. He was lost in the moment again and dismissed the cancer that had impacted so much on his life as he stood there with that owl. That photo is one of my favourites and it adorns the back cover of this book.

Alex had received such emotional and psychological sustenance over that period. He had also continued to receive messages via social media and by letter and telephone as well as parcels and presents. He had been gifted with so many presents of toys, clothes, memorabilia, vouchers and money it was astonishing. Despite this, Alex had saved his pocket money because he had wanted, even prior to him falling ill, some Godzilla and other giant robot figures. They were expensive, but I told him that we would travel to our local Forbidden Planet comic and toy store in Leicester to get them. I would pay half if he managed to save money for the other half of the total cost. The time came when he achieved that result so I remained true to my word. He assured me that all the figures he wanted were at the store as he has researched the fact that they stocked them there. One of Alex's strong supporters from the very start Sara, a friend of my crewmate Creamy, had contacted Forbidden Planet prior to our arrival and through her skills in coercion, had arranged for Alex to be given the VIP treatment. All this was totally unbeknownst to us.

Alex and I made our way in his wheelchair to the shop. As we approached Silver Street via a pedestrianised area in the centre there was a man up ahead sitting down at the side of a building wrapped in blankets. He was begging. Alex stared at the man and smiled at him as I pushed him past. The man, unshaven and bedraggled, smiled back.

As we went past Alex fell silent, which was in sharp contrast to his excited chatterings moments earlier. I knew something was wrong. He was preoccupied. He asked me if we could give some money to the beggar. I wasn't of a mind to do so: I noted that he had an opened can of extra strong lager at the side of him. I replied that he could if he wanted but that would mean he would have to buy one less toy today because I couldn't afford to make up the difference.

"Okay Dad," came his reply and he continued a few more yards before he spoke again. This time he told me he wanted to give him some money and he would have one toy less. He sounded so sure and definite that I obliged and turned the wheelchair round. "There you go," said Alex, with a warm and loving smile as he handed over the three shiny one-pound coins he had to this man. He accepted them somewhat ruefully but he took them never-the-less. We then made our way to the shop. After a few seconds of reflection on my part my heart swelled with pride. This was my boy, who despite being in a battle for his own life, wanted to help others. Alex the kind, Alex the giving, Alex the benevolent.

The shop incidentally gave him the royal treatment and gifted him several of the figures he wanted. Thank you Forbidden Planet and thank you Sara.

Eight

On 16th August, they sent us for an MRI scan. This was a pivotal moment that would, when we received the results, give us an official indication of how successful the chemotherapy had been so far. I had already placed my confidence in what I had witnessed and believed that the reduction in pain had justified the suffering that Alex had endured with the treatment itself. We would wait such a long time for the results.

But before we had received any results we had to accept the realistic possibility that the chemotherapy had not been successful. We decided that we wanted to try to raise funds to take Alex and Sophia to Disney: to give him the holiday of a lifetime in case the worst happened or indeed he became so ill or the treatment so life changing that he would not be able to go in the future. Thus, our first fundraising account was born. We decided to use something that was easily accessible and was also complimentary to our social media accounts. After some consideration of the myriad of fundraising platforms available on the internet I decided to go with Just Giving. All the accounts I had considered top sliced the amount of money raised in one way or another but I thought it better to lose a small percentage and have something that all Alex's supporters could readily access, have confidence in and transfer money to easily and without fuss. Our target was £10,000: it seemed such a lot. I remember discussing it with Jonny one night and how it seemed an unrealistic amount to hope people would raise. Maruška and her friend Claire who had visited Disney recently went through realistic costings so we simply weren't plucking a figure from the air.

The response was phenomenal and immediate: people began fundraising and donating at a tremendous rate. We had already been blessed with a hard core of followers on both Twitter and Facebook that messaged Alex daily. The number of followers continued to increase rapidly and we had pretty much doubled that amount by the end of August. These people helped get Alex's message out there and provide him with the motivation to face the day. Maruška and I would, a year on, refer to these people as the 'old guard'. This group, aside from a small handful, were people we had never met: they were strangers who would, ironically, exchange more words with me than some of my family members and old friends over the course of this journey. They were the daily bearers of motivational and uplifting messages that stimulated his interest or simply made him smile. It was always a profound moment to finally meet someone who you have exchanged messages and received tremendous support and encouragement from over many months.

As his message spread, his supporters increased across the Atlantic, into Europe, Gibraltar, Australia and South Africa. Dozens of my old school friends and old work colleagues were supporting him and sending messages of support. I hadn't spoken to some of them for decades, yet they were here, helping, encouraging, motivating.

I recall Sue, the wife of an old friend I knew through aikido was one of the first people to organise an actual event as a fundraiser for Alex. On the 28th August Sophia and I made the journey northwards to Chesterfield to take part in the Summer fete she had organised. Alex wasn't well enough to attend but as would happen on several occasions during the journey Sophia took on the role of Goodwin family ambassador perfectly. Family members also attended and I was surprised to see some old friends make an appearance. At this fundraiser one of Alex's followers on Twitter made a long journey to be with us. It was a thought provoking and memorable moment meeting someone for the first time, despite interacting with them almost daily for the past few months. It was an experience I would enjoy several times across two continents over the course of the journey.

As August drew to a close we still awaited any results or information on Alex's MRI scan. We carried on and Alex did the chemotherapy and endured the side effects as well as the long stays in hospital. It was sad how this had become our normality. Alex just kept going, sometimes he cried, sometimes he complained but he just kept going.

We tried to comfort him, motivate him and keep him engaged whilst ensuring he rested. I would sometimes catch him gazing through our large French windows into the courtyard beyond. It consisted of flagstone and a shallow surrounding of earth with some plants and shrubs. There was a tree that would sometimes house song birds in the morning but beyond it was the communal car park. It was no garden but it's all we had at that time. This saddened me as Alex would have benefitted from somewhere private to enjoy some fresh air and sunshine in those hot summer months.

I remember one weekend when his Uncle Paul had come to visit we had been working on some things in the garage. Paul and I noticed a small flower had broken through the paved parking area. Not only had it grown but bloomed a beautiful wash of lilac and purple colours. It was strange to me now, on reflection, how two grown men both doing the jobs that we did were standing and gazing reverently at this flower. We were thinking the same: this flower had managed not only to push through the gravel ground from the earth below and through stone pavement but had survived the numerous cars of our neighbours driving dangerously near it threatening any time to crush it. But, it wasn't crushed, it had endured and thrived against all the odds.

I would check up on that flower every day that I was home.

There was another memorable moment left before August drew to a close. On the 25th August Alex received a response from the zoologist Nigel Marven who had produced a short film for Alex of him in his garden with his own animals consisting of several exotic reptiles and a huge Great Grey Owl. It was a wonderful video message of hope and support and Alex watched it repeatedly. I remember watching him crying with tears of joy as he watched and we replied to Nigel Marven immediately via video message. Nigel has kept in touch and has promised to meet Alex later this year. This was a phenomenon that was completely alien to me: people coming together with words of support, encouragement and a commitment to help either financially or through other efforts. Some were famous, many were police and ambulance personnel across the world, many were members of the public. One thing was constant: all were strangers at first but so many of them touched our hearts that they became much more.

A lot of money was raised especially within the alliance of Warwickshire and West Mercia Police and other local emergency services. Fundraising also took place outside of the police family from family, friends, local people and other people who had become aware of Alex's plight. So many people gave their time freely and came up with ingenious and sometimes radical ideas to raise funds.

The recurring theme, even in these early days of fundraising was that people who I had never met and would probably never know, were coming together to help my son. This says something about humanity and despite all the ills of our society and indeed the world is facing, people still come rally in times of trouble to help. I was astounded when Maruška's sister's partner began fundraising at work and his company and its employees raised money for Alex. These people had never even heard about Alex yet had handed over their hard-earned money for someone else's cause.

The situation was the same when my brother and his partner had organised, with the help of his national company, a football tournament and Sophia and I attended. I spoke to these guys that had paid to spend a warm summers day competing against other employees from different offices and shops and thanked them in person. One of them bought me a pint of lager and shook my hand and he thanked me!

The support continued and work remained steadfast in their commitment to me and my family. Colleagues at work continued to visit and spread the word. Fundraising had begun in earnest at work too and several officers at Rugby police station were instrumental in invigorating a culture of support for Alex as the whole station took him under their collective wing. This support permeated across the alliance and he was firmly fixed in everyone's mind. The P.F.O.A also remained in constant contact and had arranged a surprise for us to attend London the following month and they would sort out the train and hotel accommodation down there!

We had regular conversations and occasional visits with Mark, Debbie and Stuart of the P.F.O.A and I shared with Mark my frustrations at our problems around transporting Alex for his hospital visits and trips out. My old and previously faithful car, now over ten years old, had started to show its age and had become somewhat unreliable. This culminated in it failing its annual Ministry of Transport roadworthy test and it required several repairs as well as the likelihood of several other repairs being required soon. In addition to this our other car, whilst very economical for city driving and well suited to Maruška's commuting was so small we couldn't fit Alex's wheelchair and bags in its boot (trunk). I was absolutely overwhelmed with the P.F.O.A's generosity when a few days later Mark told me that they would give us a car to use for the time being. We were told we could collect the car from London whilst we visited. Mark and I became close and he is and remains a remarkable and selfless man. The P.F.O.A is an organisation that Firearms Officer's in the U.K. join on a voluntary basis. They have been such an assistance to me and my family in so many ways and I would recommend any such officers not in this organisation join immediately!

Our visit to London was arranged for the 1st September and Alex's Uncle Paul would meet us down there. Furthermore, much to Alex's excitement and mine as well, if the truth be told, we had arranged to meet Dr. Max who had eagerly agreed with just as much enthusiasm to meet us at the Natural History Museum in London during our visit!

Nine

The first of September arrived and not only was it Sophia's 4th birthday but also the day we set off to Rugby train station to travel to London! We were all excited. Alex was struggling with discomfort that day and was weak but he was genuinely thrilled at what was waiting for him just a short train ride south. We arrived at Rugby train station to a police escort from some of my colleagues in Warwickshire Police's community policing team and The British Transport Police (B.T.P). I look back now at how this was the first of many times when we would arrive at a transport hub and be greeted by my brothers and sisters in blue. There were a few, who I would owe so much more to, but I valued every effort by all of them.

Mark, an officer with B.T.P and I had spoken a few days earlier and I was pleased to put a face to a name. I was proud that some of my fellow officers had made the effort to join us and Alex felt very special. I had contacted the train station ahead of our arrival to make them aware that Alex was wheelchair bound and we met by a member of staff called Seema from Virgin Trains. This was our first experience of Virgin as a company and they were great. It is interesting that this was also the first of many times we have relied of Virgin and its employees and been so grateful for their help and assistance. The photo taken as we were about to board the train speaks a thousand words as Alex, regardless of his ailments that morning, was happy and beamed with excitement.

Alex's passion for life and the way he conducted himself everyday despite his pain and sickness was infectious. He left a positive impression on everyone he met and would continue to do so throughout his journey. People seemed genuinely moved by the experience of spending any length of time with him. We gained followers on his social media site from every encounter: this was no exception. Seema began to follow Alex's endeavours on Twitter and sent us a kind and moving message. It would seem that this meeting also affected Mark as he became another champion for Alex. Both he and his wife Sarah, also a police officer, would walk with us for the rest of the journey and were responsible for raising thousands of pounds for Alex.

This is when I began to see that not only was Alex gaining followers and supporters but he was a force for good in other people's lives. We began to receive messages and letters from people from all walks of life that were inspired by Alex. People fighting their own battles and facing their own demons were reaching out to Alex to wish him well and to thank him for crossing their path. I remember getting into a lift with Alex one time and we were joined by a woman who worked at the hospital and was also a part time Search & Rescue officer. She began to talk to Alex with a strange excitement that I would liken to a fan meeting a favourite celebrity. She asked for a selfie with Alex as a follower of his journey on Twitter to which Alex and agreed. Within ten minutes that selfie was posted on social media and we gleefully retweeted it.

It was true that Alex drew attention to himself by the very fact he had no hair and was confined to a wheelchair. The fact remained that after just a few minutes of engaging with him he left a lasting impression that was far more than just sympathy for a child with cancer. He did the same thing on that train journey to London: we arrived with several more followers on social media than we had when we had set off.

Paul was waiting for us when we arrived and for that I was grateful. Working in the private security industry in a role which included chauffeuring his client in one of the world's busiest capital cities was a tremendous asset to relatives who had no idea how to get around. He was happy to see us too and had quickly taken us to our hotel and outlined the itinerary he had prepared. Alex was anxious to meet Dr. Max and we did just that the following morning.

Meeting Dr. Max was another of those key moments in Alex's journey. He met us promptly and immediately embraced us like family. I had scrutinised his photos on his Twitter account and had been surprised how young he looked for an Egyptologist. Meeting him in the flesh was slightly different. I could see he was weary and his illness had aged him. He was clearly in discomfort as he hobbled on crutches to greet us. This however was insignificant to his character: his energy and passion shone through just like it did with Alex. They were kindred spirits and no pathetic life-threatening illness was going to stifle their thirst for learning and discovery. Alex looked up to Max in awe and they viewed each specimen and exhibit with ardour. They moved around that museum with such zeal and we rushed to keep up. He insisted on pushing himself in his wheelchair so that no one could control where we went and what speed he arrived. That exhausted him, but he was happy. He was so very happy and his love for that museum and the person he was sharing it with shone radiantly. I posted the photos on Twitter that evening with so much pride for my boy: Alex the Radiant, Alex the Passionate, Alex the Conversant.

I remember that evening in the hotel whilst Maruška was having a shower, I was watching Alex and Sophia chatting excitedly on the bed together. They were singing and holding each other tightly. I can picture it in my mind's eye so clearly and it still brings tears to my eyes even now as I hit the keys on my computer.

"I love you, so much, you are my little baby."
"I love you," Alex would sing, to which Sophia would reply, "I love you.".

I kept out of their view using the slightly ajar door as cover and videoed that moment on my mobile phone. The children never knew.

We awoke the following morning and met Mark and Debbie of the P.F.O.A at Park Lane BMW. I was shocked when they handed the keys over to a brand-new BMW MPV (multipurpose vehicle) with seven seats and huge storage space at the rear. I drove that car home feeling so very grateful.

The eventful week continued and when we arrived back home and Maruška & Sophia joined our neighbour Hannah along with almost the whole female population of our village at a fundraiser arranged by Hannah on our village cricket field. This wasn't the only time that Maruška and some of the ladies from the village got involved in fitness fundraising for Alex. Michaela, Maruška's friend from Sheffield, organised a huge Les Mills fundraiser. Maruška travelled up with a friend from the village and some of her work colleagues. It was yet another occasion where people who had never met Alex had come together to support him.

Amidst these events and life changing meetings we began to grow increasingly frustrated with the lack of information and updates from the hospitals. September and October were months of significant concern for us. One of the biggest problems came from the lack of information. We had been made privy to the proposed treatment plan at the beginning but aside from that other than being told that his bloods were okay for his next series of chemotherapy that was all. It was also this crippling sense of delay, always delay and waiting.

Alex's case was managed by doctors at different hospitals and a national multi-disciplinary team (M.D.T) made the decisions or were at least consulted on with regards to his case. All information and results went through this M.D.T and as time passed, whenever I asked about the remit and constitution of this group the answers I received changed. Sometimes this group were consultative and offered comment and advice to the doctors responsible for Alex and other times they were the decision makers and issues could not be addressed or progressed until they had gone through the M.D.T. I understood and appreciated the benefits of such a group as it ensured that the best experience and knowledge could be drawn upon for the benefit of Alex. I recall discussing this with the doctors in the United States many months later who explained that peer review was normal and professional best practice. The problem we faced though was that the peer review was taking place across many different hospitals with people who never actually physically met. The M.D.T that was dealing with Alex's case (and that of many other children) met one every two weeks by conference telephone call.

I understand the practicalities of getting professionals across the country physically together but I was still surprised that the meeting, albeit by telephone only took place once every 14 days. Unfortunately add the fact that these people were radically overworked and as we discovered later, were often absent from the telephone meeting and you have a situation that clearly can't be conducive to providing timely and well-informed actions when dealing with a life-threatening illness.

Throughout this time, I was constantly aware of the importance of timely treatment for a disease like cancer. The delays and absence of updates were causing me some anxiety and combined with the crippling lack of sleep because I was either in the hospital overnight or at home waking up every two hours to care for Alex it was making me ill. Maruška and I were almost wearing two faces: the first with Alex was always upbeat and motivational so he could see we were with him and it was all going to work out in the end. The second was one of pressure, weariness and exasperation combined with a sense of helplessness. We tried to pick each other up and leaned on friends and family. I felt exhausted and drawn all the time like, to quote one of my favourite authors "I feel thin, sort of stretched, like butter scraped over too much bread".

We tried to get answers and clarity on issues around Alex's progress and treatment. He was continuing with his chemotherapy and we wanted to know the next steps… surgery? Radiotherapy? It was being discussed at the M.D.T and they were deliberating over the results of his scans. I remember receiving a promise that we would be updated on his plan following the M.D.T meeting. That call never came. It was a regular occurrence and I was constantly making calls to doctors and nurses and leaving messages. I remember making over half a dozen phone calls and leaving messages with other members of staff begging for an update from the last M.D.T meeting. Eventually another day later I received a telephone call from a nurse who informed me that the meeting hadn't happened because there had been an I.T issue and the conference call couldn't take place. Alex's case would be discussed at the next M.D.T the following week. Another week would pass by without any update or clarity. More delays. More waiting. Always waiting.

I had reached a breaking point and decided (considering these real issues of delay and a feeling that no one was really listening to our concerns) to start recording conversations with doctors like we had done at that very first meeting. We were, at this time, considering our options and I made complaints. I realise that is was probably not the most honest or polite thing to do but we were desperate. I remember speaking with the doctor in Leicester and the senior nurse in Birmingham about this lack of communication. The doctor told me that they too encountered problems in getting in touch with doctors at other hospitals and she was the oncology consultant! The nurse, less bluntly and more resigned to the fact, agreed that it was a problem and she had grown weary of apologising to parents because she too found it impossible to obtain information and replies from beleaguered doctors also. The nurse's honesty threw me that day. I really felt for her, she was an experienced nurse and had been kind to us.

In addition to these anxieties around his prognosis and treatment we still encountered everyday problems. On the 5th September, we had taken Alex into hospital for his scheduled chemotherapy treatment to find that no actual beds were available in the ward. He received that treatment all day in the play room. It was night time before he finally was allocated a bed.

Regardless of all this taking place around him Alex remained his kind, motivated and remarkable self. His support on social media continued to grow and he was always well received by the staff in the ward. His education had obviously suffered and he had not attended school for months. The hospital education service sent teachers to work with Alex whilst he was there and this helped to some degree. I was impressed by these teachers who managed to inspire Alex into studying despite his physical limitations and constant fatigue and nausea. Mathematics, English and Science were, on the face of the lesson, fun exercises involving the things that kept his attention: dinosaurs, sharks and nature.

When he wasn't in hospital we continued to try and get out to places to enrich his time away from the harsh and relentless treatments he had. It wasn't just for Alex but also for us to escape the house as well as the hospital. We visited Chatsworth House in September which isn't too far from us. We would go there often before Alex was ill. Chatsworth House, originally built in 1552 is the stately home of the Duke and Duchess of Devonshire and almost all the property and its wonderful gardens are open to the public. We would go and feed the ducks and enjoy a spot of tea in the café there. We loved the day and Alex was touched by the visit. He talked about going many times when he was better.

On the 14th September on one of Alex's "rest days" from chemotherapy treatment we went to The Royal Orthopaedic Hospital in Birmingham for another scan and to discuss the case with the doctors there. We were desperate for progress and information. It was important to understand that we had received no clear action plan or prognosis from Alex's previous scan on the 16th August by this time. That was a whole month of stress. I had complained and pestered but it hadn't really yielded anything. I felt so impotent that I couldn't get the information to support Alex in what was to come or know the plan of treatment to save my son. It was a common feeling amongst the parents that we spent time within the ward as our children fought for their lives. It was an awful time for us that was only going to get worse…

We arrived for our morning appointment and presented ourselves to the reception point before taking a seat in the waiting room. It was an unusually busy room that day and the fact that it was also an unusually hot sunny day didn't help. There was no air conditioning in that cramped room full of ill and weak children. The heat was so unbearable that one of the members of staff came in and distributed ice lollies to try and curb the stifling heat and our frayed tempers.

We waited all day. I enquired as to the reason for the endless delays and how much longer we would be waiting. We had been sitting there an hour by which time I was told there was a busy clinic that day. Finally, following a further two hours, I lost my temper and complained. We were told that our appointment was in the afternoon and we were only just behind schedule. I pointed out that we had arrived that morning and checked in yet no one had thought to mention our seemingly incorrect arrival time - some three hours before our apparent appointment. This error would mean that we wouldn't be at home for the arrival of Diana's Children's Services to administer Alex's white cell booster treatment. The nurses at Birmingham couldn't administer it there so we would have to drive to Leicester Hospital that evening to receive the medication he required.

It was with this background that we finally were seen by a doctor at the hospital. Not Alex's actual orthopaedic surgeon who was responsible for Alex and would, under the proposed treatment plan, perform the surgery. It was one of his colleagues. We have never met that actual orthopaedic surgeon… even to this day.

Devastatingly, it was at this meeting that we were told Alex's cancer had spread.

Ten

It was during this meeting in Birmingham that we were shown a scan for the first time. It was the scan from the 16th August which had been taken one month earlier. Not only did we see the scan but to the doctor's credit he spent time explaining the detail of it to us. This viewing was such a significant event that I took a photo of the scan on my mobile phone. I did ask his permission but in truth I would have, in my dishevelled, emotional, heat exhausted state, taken it anyway.

It didn't look good. Maruška and I looked at each other again as we flashbacked to the meeting at Sheffield Children's Hospital and the X-ray that had also been the harbinger of terrible news. The information the doctor was telling us just didn't seem to correlate. It wasn't localised and the chemotherapy had obviously failed to stop the spread. That word - *spread* - pierced me like a spear and I felt sick to my very core. The disease has gone down the femur into the acetabulum (the socket cup of the pelvis that connects to the ball joint of the leg bone). I was so shocked by this news that I asked the doctor to say it all again to me. He did. And it was the same news he had shared seconds earlier. I hadn't been mistaken. It confirmed and compounded that Alex was in a dark place.

Things were unravelling at a terrifying speed. I was desperate for someone to step in and tell me it was all under control and that it was okay. No one did. I wanted answers and reassurance of action but we were told we had to wait until they had had a chance to discuss it: presumably at the next M.D.T meeting.

This was one of those moments where now if I could go back in time I would have challenged every aspect of what had been said. Why hadn't we been told this earlier? The scan was a month old? Why hadn't the results been discussed by now so that even at this point we would have had a solution. How did this affect Alex's chances of survival?

110

I left that meeting broken.

Trying desperately and pathetically to keep a painted smile on my face, we drove home with Alex and Sophia in the car. Maruška was equally torn apart. Alex and I eventually arrived home late that night after visiting the Leicester Royal Infirmary. He was exhausted and crawled into bed. I crawled in with him and as I held him to me and felt his chest expand and contract in his deep sleep - I wept silently, I didn't want to wake him.

Later that night when all was still in the house and both Sophia and Alex slept, Maruška and I sat together and talked softly about the terrible predicament we were in. Alex's statistical survivability had reduced significantly because of the spread of the cancer. It seemed that now the chances of him surviving beyond five years were at around 20 to 30%. We were just a few sessions from finishing the proposed chemotherapy treatment before the next step and then we had received this news. Now, the implications of it spreading and it being either a progressive cancer or a metastatic cancer was never mentioned to me at this stage. All I knew was that it was taking over his body and growing and there was seemingly nothing I could do about it. I couldn't even get people who could do something about it to take action and help - or so it seemed. As a father, you take the mantle of protector and carer and I seemed to be failing. I experienced this overwhelming feeling of futility.

At the end of that week, Alex became ill and had developed a fever. He had picked up a cold and was rushed into hospital and placed in isolation. His weakened state had been made even more fragile by the travelling and waiting we had endured earlier that week and I feel that it could have contributed.

The next few days he spent in isolation and he was ill. He was also extremely depressed as he was spending even more time in hospital and away from the comfort and company of the other children in the ward.

Alex had to go for a chest X-ray while he was in isolation. His face mask on, a nurse and I took him to another part of the hospital. We then sat in a waiting room for our X-ray surrounded by dozens of people and their families that had just come in from the street as outpatients. Every cough and sniffle was like torture to me and I was in despair. I remember the nurse that was with us went to the reception area to insist we jumped the queue. She met with opposition at first from the member of staff in that department and they argued. We won through and Alex was seen next and we were back on the ward in no time. I thanked that nurse and she smiled but said nothing. Just in case she is reading this, I shall say it again. Thank you.

Alex recovered and was well enough for the next cycle of chemotherapy. Still we waited for news and for an update. I was vocal and constantly seeking news. I was told to wait. Around this time treatment options had been discussed and we had visited the radiotherapy department in Nottingham. This was another hospital in another county in England. The doctor and nurse we spoke to at the hospital discussed how and when radiation therapy may be used on Alex but nothing was concrete. It was around this time that I first heard about proton beam therapy and how it may be useful to Alex.

Proton beam therapy is a form of radiotherapy, but it differs from conventional treatment in that the beam has a narrow focus and can target specifically the area it needs to treat. What is also important and distinctive with proton beam therapy is that it stops at its target and doesn't carry on through the body like normal radiotherapy. This significantly reduces collateral damage especially less damage to surrounding tissue and has fewer side effects. It is used mainly against tumours that are close to other major organs.

At that time, the NHS in England sent its child cancer patients to hospitals in America under a financial arrangement between the two countries. One of the boys in the ward who had cancer behind his eye went to Oklahoma in the United States and received treatment. He is here today and seems to be winning the fight following his treatment there. We were given the details of the person in the NHS would arrange the trip for us if Alex went and we were put in touch with other people who had also been for that treatment. It seemed very promising and in a dark place gave us a glimmer of hope.

September became October and we continued to wait for a definitive plan. The chemotherapy continued and I remained anxious and exhausted most of the time.

Murray came to visit again on the 11th October and that filled Alex with joy. I found it very difficult wrestling with matters of his life to share his joy. Anita had been sponsored to visit once a month and received donations to cover her fuel expenses. I was aware that she ran her company for the benefit of others with very little financial support. She had made the effort, yet again, to come and spend some time with Alex and he was happy for it.

On the 12th October, we went to Birdland in Gloucestershire and Alex loved every minute of it. The name says it all really and Alex was treated like royalty during the trip. He could get close and interact with the penguins, bird of prey and of course specifically an owl. The trip was thanks to one of my colleagues, Matt, who basically harassed anybody and everybody to get us free tickets for local attractions. We had spoken about Alex and how he, who had also fought a battle with cancer, understood how important it was for Alex to get out whenever he could. It is true to say that these trips out were such an important positive element for Alex. He spent so much time at hospital and when he was at home he was constantly taking medication and resting. This was like a tonic for him and despite us having to stop several times so Alex could vomit from the nausea he was experiencing because of the journey he loved and cherished that day.

The middle of October marked what should have been the final chemotherapy treatment for Alex prior to his surgery. We were informed that his chemotherapy would continue and that they were currently deliberating on whether the surgery would go ahead. This period of time is difficult in places for me to recall the specifics as I was existing with very little sleep and tremendous anxiety with regards to Alex's very survival.

On the 16th October I recall Alex, Sophia and I making chocolate coins for the nurses as a thank you for looking after him. He should have completed the chemotherapy treatment by then and he, as astute as ever, felt like he wouldn't see them as often because of his understanding that this part of his battle with cancer was coming to a close. I didn't have the heart at that time to tell him exactly what was happening just that he may need to do a few more sessions "just to make sure". In my already emotional state I was so moved by the fact that my son, regardless of his sickness and depression, wanted to not only take a gift but make it himself for the nurses that had become such an integral part of his life. I was proud of him, my son: Alex the Kind, Alex the Giving, Alex the Thoughtful.

It was under this terribly dark shadow that we received a tweet from a man in Kansas in the United States who thanked us for the follow and for being so inspiring. He had started following us just a few days before and we had followed him back. That man was Chief of Police Terry Zeigler of Kansas City, Kansas Police Department (K.C.K.P.D.). He had reached out to us on the 14th October saying he wanted to send Alex a care package so I furnished him with the address details and we received the parcel on the 31st October. It was a myriad of police memorabilia including patches, police challenge coins, a K.C.K.P.D. bag and other items. The thing that stood out for Alex was a Kansas City, Kansas PD badge and an Identification card with Alex as Deputy Chief!

Both Chief Zeigler and Trooper Ben Gardner of Kansas Highway Patrol were the start of a number of United States Law Enforcement Officers (LEO's) to send Alex personal messages of support. Trooper Gardner was also the first to send him a video message. At the time, we had no idea or expectation that we would ever meet either of them but I can say, now, that I have the honour of knowing them both very well and I am proud to call them both friend. They were now part of an army of police officers and LEO's of all ranks and nationalities that were following Alex.

We were receiving parcels and packages every day from well-wishers but Alex was in hospital most of the time. The packages were received and stacked up for Alex to open when he was home and felt well enough to go through them. We tried to take photographs of every gift and card and letter and post them or send messages privately. Alex insisted we do that and I was so proud of how much he appreciated the support he was getting and the effort that people were making. He is wise beyond his years!

A new week began and Alex was back in hospital receiving chemotherapy. That week beginning on the 17th October was going to be one the worst since receiving that awful news some five months earlier. I was staying with Alex at the Leicester Royal Infirmary whilst he had his chemotherapy and ironically had been trying to speak to the Orthopaedic surgeon at the Royal Orthopaedic Hospital in Birmingham for a few days. I was told that I would receive a call updating me on Alex's situation. I had sat waiting all day desperate for an update. I received a call that evening whilst I sat at Alex's bedside.

The news from the Orthopaedic surgeon was shattering. Not only had the cancer spread but it had also metastasised across his body to the other side of his pelvis and to the top of the femur in his other leg. This news was delivered based on the scan taken on the 14th September, one month earlier and two months since the first scan in August that indicated it had spread. This meant that it was likely that the chemotherapy hadn't been successful and the cancer had continued to grow. I can appreciate more now how Maruška felt when she was told that our son had cancer: that surprise, numbness and her complete lack of retention of information.

I clambered for answers to key questions but had to be so careful what I said: Alex was laid mere inches from me in his hospital bed. He was looking at me as I had that conversation. I forced a smile on my face and bit back at the pain and anguish that flowed over me like a torrent. He smiled back.

I struggle now to recall the exact words that were used. Alex would need a full body MRI scan immediately to ascertain if the cancer has spread elsewhere. His prognosis was beyond bad. The surgery may now not even go ahead because it would damage the quality of life he had left. It could be weeks or months and even if the surgery went ahead it would be so impactive that he would suffer significant loss of functionality and likely be confined to a wheelchair for the rest of his life.

These words… *"quality of life"*, *"weeks or months"*, *"Significant loss of functionality"* hammered around my head. The conversation ended with them saying that he would ensure that our Paediatric oncologist at Leicester would arrange the full body MRI scan immediately. Then he was gone and I was left wearing my painted smile again.

Eleven

I had no sleep that night. I had called Maruška and shared that information with her as it had been shared with me. I didn't want to, I had struggled handling the news and I knew she would too, but I felt like I had no choice. She couldn't come to me at the hospital because she had Sophia and I couldn't leave Alex. Even if I could, I would not have left his side under any circumstances. I decided to make the call to her quite simply because if the situation was the other way around I would want to know. We cried together and when we had finished she held Sophia at home and I held Alex's hand. I held it almost all night as I thought about what I could possibly do.

I analysed, probably unfairly and unjustly, all my shortcomings in how Alex's illness had come to pass. I had focussed on my career and assumed all would be well. That assumption was borne out of complacency and in truth, if I was completely honest, laziness. I had to do something, do my best or I feared that I would lose this most precious thing to me. I had, despite my misgivings at the time, prayed in the night. I wasn't sure why, but I did. I wasn't knelt at the edge of the bed, hands clasped in prayer, but I was in deep profound thought and dwelled on the events that had come to pass with such a stark honesty like I had never done before.

It was time to relax my grip on other things and to try and save my son and become Jeff the Father.

The morning arrived like a car crash and I faced the day with such a heavy heart. Just the evening before I had received such a forceful message via telephone from another hospital as I sat with my son in another one. No one at the hospital had come to see me personally, yet I was sure the doctors knew. As a police officer I had delivered life changing messages to members of the public several times. The look on people faces when they open their front door and see you standing there. Bad news was always delivered face to face, or so I thought. I was determined to speak with the Paediatric Oncologist and get the scan sorted. I needed to do something but I felt totally reliant on the hospitals. But maybe, I didn't just need to place my faith in them alone.

Whilst I waited that morning I managed to contact Joy at Red Arc to inform her of the terrible news and seek her advice. I needed to know exactly what was happening and in truth had lost confidence in the hospitals we were dealing with. I needed to have other perspectives on Alex's situation. I wanted her help to obtain second opinions: but I had no idea how to go about it.

Joy was her usual calm and supportive self and she explained how we could tackle it and navigate the pitfalls of getting the NHS to share the information they held about Alex with a wider medical audience. She would consider it and draw upon the advice of some of the sarcoma charities as well as speak to former colleagues in the NHS. She also advised me to inform our doctors that we wanted a second opinion as soon as possible.

That morning I tried to find our doctor and asked the nurses to pass on my request to meet with her. I am sure they did but that meeting did not take place until the late afternoon. The doctor invited me into a meeting room along with a nurse. I knew what was coming and the doctor repeated almost word for word what the orthopaedic surgeon had said to me the night before. I had no words and felt the anguish again. This time though it was coupled with frustration and anger that swelled inside of me. I asked for the scan to be done urgently and I was assured it would be sorted and I would be contacted tomorrow with a date and time. I also informed the doctor that we would be seeking second opinions. The doctor seemed surprised but said they would produce the necessary reports.

Alex completed his chemotherapy and we returned home that same day. Maruška and I held him and his sister all that evening and exhausted I fell asleep laid alongside him that night. But before I did I checked on the flower in the courtyard. It was still there.

That following morning, the 20th October, I set about moving forward on Alex's treatment wherever I could. Joy and I spoke and I relayed the progress to Maruška. She had spoken to contacts at Great Ormond Street and University College Hospital in London and was arranging meetings for us. She had also drawn information from Sarcoma UK and their American equivalent the Sarcoma Alliance.

I felt that things were moving. I knew this was simply because we were moving them and no one else but this gave me a sense of purpose and direction. I had also, through a work colleague, managed to contact someone who worked in the NHS and had some involvement in commissioning treatment in other countries particularly in America. I had received confirmation that the Proton beam Therapy in the United States funded by the NHS was no longer an option because Alex didn't meet the criteria anymore because the sarcoma had metastasised. This made me extremely angry about the delays that had come to plague our journey. That anger didn't turn into rage, it just stiffened my resolve to save my son with the help of those that could and were in my eyes more motivated to do so.

Furthermore, I was given the name of a children's charity based just north of where we lived in another county called Derbyshire. This charity specialised in taking children from the UK who were not eligible for NHS support. They raised the funds and appeared to have connections with hospitals in the U.S.

I was still waiting for news of the promised scan... The 20th October became the 21st.

The first few hours of that next day went by and I waited. It totally consumed me and I felt the tension and anxiety as the minutes ticked by. Minutes became more hours. I contacted the Leicester Royal Infirmary and spoke to the doctor's secretary who assured me that she would pass the message on. I stressed the importance of the call and the situation and I was assured by the secretary that, whilst she hadn't actually seen the doctor yet that day she would make sure they got the message.

119

That morning I also sent an email to the hospitals that were dealing with Alex's care. I needed to record the events of the last few days and the promises made to us. I hoped it would assist in making sure things were done better if it seemed like there was something like an audit trail. I had nothing to lose by sending it. Perhaps it also helped arrange my thoughts.

More time passed. I needed the scan doing and the next day was the weekend. It would then be a new week before anything could happen. I had spent so much time waiting I couldn't endure it anymore. I decided to go to my local family doctor's office and try to get the scan sorted privately or something. One way or another it needed to happen. It was a race against time. It had to be done now.

Once Alex was diagnosed with Ewing Sarcoma I made sure I visited our family doctor to pass on this news especially in light of the problem we had faced there many months earlier. I also visited for my own health at the time because of the sheer exhaustion I was battling since December 2015. The head of the practice dealt with our family matters now and we have had many open and candid conversations. I bare him no ill will. The actions of one of his colleagues was the issue and not him personally. I respected his openness and willingness to engage with me and he was clearly well educated and experienced in his field. He had said to me previously that if I needed anything I should go to him.

So I did.

I waited at the reception of his practice and firmly pressed my need to see him as a matter of urgency. I made sure I maintained a sense of calm but was clear to myself and him what my objectives needed to be that day.

Eventually I made it into his examination room. I explained our situation and outlined the help I needed. My son's life was at stake and I wasn't going to leave until I had achieved the scan booking which he so desperately needed… that I so desperately needed… so we knew exactly where we were and what his realistic chances of survival were.

I sat on a chair at the side of his desk while he made calls to the hospitals to check up on whether a scan had been arranged "as a matter of urgency". The responses were not very favourable. It appeared nothing had been booked. He contacted the Leicester Royal Infirmary to speak to the doctor I had spoken to in the company of a nurse as they delivered the news to me. He had placed the phone on loud speaker so he could make notes as he made the telephone calls. Eventually he managed to speak to the doctor's secretary who, not knowing I was listening, informed me that the doctor was away in Ireland on a course all day and wouldn't be returning until next week.

My despondency had been replaced with anger, but it wasn't a rage. It was more like a focus and a determined drive. That doctor who was in Ireland and I spoke later that day as they called me at home from the conference. I was clear about how I felt and I was equally clear to them about my view on the situation.

A scan was arranged just two working days later.

Within this constant labour of effort to progress things, life went on in its routine for Alex. He had become a social media sensation and his story had been covered on regional television, radio and in the local press. He continued to share his goodwill messages inviting his followers to "have a great day" and hoped that they would "enjoy spending time with your pets".

I am a great admirer of Alex's desire to care for nature and animals and how he puts the welfare of them above his own. I remember an incident where a fellow police officer dog handler, PC Dave Wardell in Hertfordshire Police and his police dog PD Finn were seriously injured. On the 4th October 2016 they responded to a report of a robbery and PD Finn apprehended the suspect but he was stabbed in the head and chest during the struggle. PC Wardell was also injured in the hand. The police dog had, despite his injuries, kept hold of the offender. He needed extensive surgery and was recovering at home. Alex and I had been following the incident and we followed Dave on Twitter and he followed us. In the U.K., unlike the U.S. when a police dog or horse is injured it isn't classed as an assault of an officer but only criminal damage. As a result of this incident, PC Wardell and some of his supporters had started a petition to the British Government to have the law changed. It had gained tremendous support and momentum. I shared the news with Alex.

Alex was immediately concerned about the situation and, wise and mature beyond his years, wanted to do a short video to his followers about the situation and encouraged his followers to sign the petition. The video went viral and helped to cement a connection of friendship with Dave and Finn that remains to this day. That connection brought more followers and supporters to Alex and vice versa. One of the people who set up the whole drive to seek a change in the law had become a strong supporter of Alex and helped us with fundraising. We also, via PD Finn, received the support of the Countess Bathurst who was a strong supporter of great causes and the police.

Both Dave and PD Finn and Lady Bathurst attended the video event of a certain song for Alex that would bring the police, fire, ambulance and search & rescue services from all across the land to Warwickshire in support of his cause.

Alex has always had a fondness for nature especially owls. Here he is at Muncaster Castle, Cumbria age 5.

Before he fell ill, Alex was a keen swimmer.

Alex's knowledge of pre-historic creatures astounds both adult and child alike. This is a megalodon at the Blue Planet Aquarium in Chester.

Alex with one of his pet geckos, Riptor.

First photo after Alex was finally given crutches in April; four months after his pain began.

Alex at Toys R Us spending his first of many gift vouchers at the start of his illness. Note the skin damage to his right leg due to continuous use of hot water bottles to lessen the pain.

Alex in Sheffield Children's Hospital in May 2016 for a MRI scan. Note the bandage on his left arm following the problems taking blood. This is the famous Batman profile photo courtesy of his Aunt Lenka.

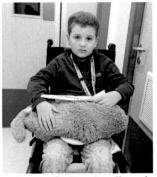

Alex was feeling the effect of numerous delays including two canceled operations for his Hickman line.

Alex's first day at the LRI Children's Cancer Ward. Due to his phobia of needles, he was given gas to calm him down in June 2016.

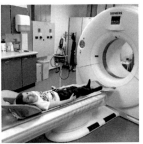

Before Alex even began his cancer treatment, he had blood tests, echocardiogram, MRI and CT scans. Here at LRI getting a CT scan.

Due to Alex needing full time care, Maruska had to quit her job to tend to him 24 hours a day.

On the 22nd of June, Alex went to his primary school to explain to his class about his cancer and his Hickman line.

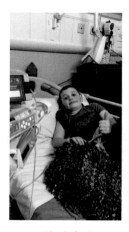

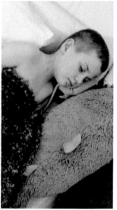

Alex's first chemotherapy took place on the 27th of June 2016 at LRI. This is one month after his biopsy.

Drained and exhausted from vomiting continuously for 48 hours as his body fought the effects from the chemotherapy.

Maruska and I maintained between us a constant vigil at Alex's bedside during long periods of treatment.

Alexander's battle with cancer brought him and his little sister Sophia closer together.

Alex's illness had a profound affect on Sophia who, for a three year old, grasped the need for Alex to fight and defeat the cancer.

As Alex's hair began to fall out he was very distressed, so he decided to shave all it off on the 15th of July 2016.

Thanks to CLIC Sargent and some very special people connected with Bruntingthorpe Alex attended an annual fun day at the racetrack.

Alex was practically a permanent resident at the LRI Children's Cancer Ward from July onwards. He forged profound friendships with many children including pictured Mia (pictured twice), Abdul, Evan, Marcus and Ben. Also pictured is Noah whom he met at Children's Mercy in Kansas City, Missouri.

The 20th of July 2016, was a great day! He met Anita and her owls for the first time, reached 2,000 followers on Twitter and he received a video message from his hero Steve Backshall. He finally met Steve in November.

A day at the museum

Alex also met Dr. Massimiliano "Max" Pinarello and visited the Natural History Museum with him twice. Sarcoma U.K. wrote an article about his second visit.

Anita visited several times during his chemotherapy treatment in the U.K. These visits were uplifting and continued to encourage him to look to the future.

We were lucky enough to fly in both airplane and helicopter at Leicester and Bruntingthorpe airports.

David Jones gifted the song Horizon On My Mind to raise funds for Alex. The video for this song was filmed at Warwickshire Police HQ Leek Wootton where hundreds of police, fire, and ambulance personnel came together for Alex.

After numerous medical checks, Alex was allowed to fly to America. Virgin Atlantic have been tremendous supporters of Alexander's Journey from then on.

The reception awaiting Alex in Kansas City was overwhelming. Hundreds of Kansas and Missouri officers braved subzero temperatures to welcome him to the United States. Alex and his family enjoyed a presidential-like escort to Dr. Wetzel's home.

The Doctors responsible for Alex's care in the U.S came from Kansas University Hospital, Kansas and Children's Mercy Hospital, Missouri. Left to Right: Dr. Katherine Chastain, MD, Dr. Howard G. Rosenthal, MD, Dr. Vickie L. Massey, MD, and Dr. Louis Wetzel, MD.

The connection made between Dr. Wetzel and Chief Zeigler came from the murder of two Kansas City, Kansas Police Officer's; Captain Robert David Melton and Detective Brad Lancaster. Their devastating and untimely deaths caused the Men and Women in White to reach out the Men and Women in Blue. That connection paved the way for Alexander to access the skills of specialists from two hospitals, thanks to the efforts of Chief Zeigler and Dr. Wetzel.

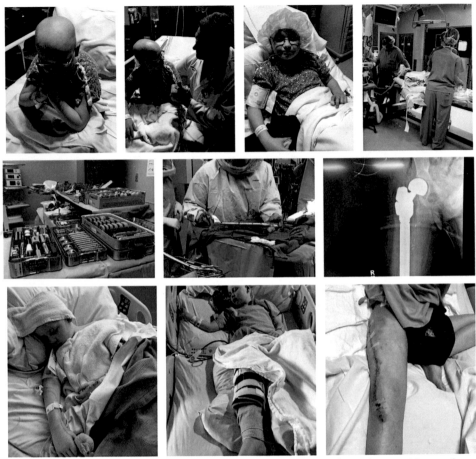

On 11th January 2017 following the finish of his chemotherapy Alex underwent 6 hours of surgery to remove the cancer in his leg and pelvis.

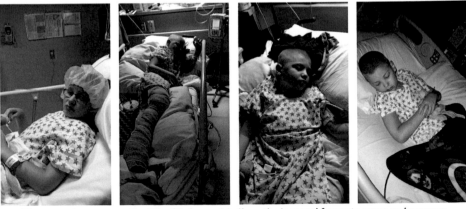

The second surgery on the 5th of July would allow Alex's metal femur to grow as he grows.

Alex's treatment involved intensive physiotherapy to ensure that the leg would work after such a major surgery. Alex's whole femur ravaged by the cancer was removed, as was his knee. His pelvic bone was reconstructed as well. Sophia showed some solidarity.

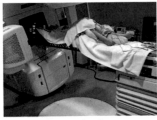

Following his first surgery and the finalization of chemotherapy, Alex underwent specialist stereotactic radiation therapy.

Our time in the United States created profound friendships with Lou, Jane and the Wetzel family. If it wasn't for Dr. Lou Wetzel, Alex would have never received his treatment.

Thanks to Make a Wish Missouri, Give Kids the Word, and the initial fundraising done for Alex, we managed to go to Disney twice during our stay in the United States.

Here are some of our supporters in Kansas City including KCTV5, KMBC9, Fox4KC, Black Sky Radio, Kansas City Chiefs, Kansas City Royals, Planet Comicon and Rainy Day Books. There were many more. Thank you to all!

Congressman Kevin Yoder was instrumental in helping Alex stay in Kansas for the remainder of his treatment.

Kerry donated £6,000 to Alex that had been raised for her mother Jill. Jill tragically lost her fight with cancer before the money could be used. Rachel visited Alex in hospital in November to try and help reassure him that the surgery could work and he could live a normal life. Rachel has a metal prosthesis too.

The Thin Blue Line extended all the way across the Atlantic from the U.K. to the U.S. but Police support came from all over the world too: primarily from Canada, Australia and the Netherlands.

At his darkest times, Alex would draw and paint pictures depicting dreams of his future and drawings that allowed him to escape his situation. He would often draw pictures of himself with lots of flowers and his own bird of prey.

Alex loves animals and nature but is especially passionate about birds of prey. He dreams of one day becoming a falconer.

Alexander's Journey strengthened and created profound bounds of friendship and showed that good people come together in bad situations. Thank you to everyone, not just those pictured above, that did their part and walked the path with Alex for the past 18 months of his life. Dum Spiro Spero

ALEX'S FUND RAISING EVENING

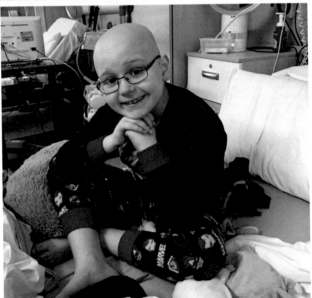
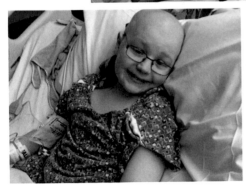

Despite living in so much pain and distress for so long, this little boy always has a smile and a kind word for other people and has won the hearts of thousands across the world.
Dum Spiro Spero

Twelve

Even though I was taking some time from work I would visit on occasion. An unofficial working group had been set up that were looking at fundraising for Alex and I shared with them my news and our recent terrible update. I had also received some positive news that some of the treatment options that Alex was no longer eligible for were possibly a viable treatment method for Alex. I remember the outpouring of support and how it spurred everyone to do even more. I felt uplifted - as if someone with an outstretched hand was pulling me up to the top of a cripplingly steep mountainside.

I smile now when I think of those meetings I attended. My Inspector, Lucy, presiding over a group of extremely motivated and loving individuals. They were all good people who had come together in horrendous circumstances to help. The fundraising that was taking place was across the spectrum of activities. One of this group - a patrol officer called Laura - was a strong supporter of Alex and had visited him often. She had managed to process an option where people could give money directly from their salary. This was amazing and so many people across the alliance did it, giving so generously. More brilliant work came from Simon, from the Warwickshire Police Federation, who had managed to ensure we could send information about Alex and his plight nationally and this had increased the number of police officers following and supporting significantly.

These was two of the many gestures that would create fundraising streams that were helping us. Up the road from my police station was the Halifax bank in Rugby and many police officers would attend there often to put money into a specific account that had been earmarked for his funds.

All these people, who had never even met me or didn't even know of my existence just 12 months earlier, were helping us fight this battle. Why? Because they were my brothers and sisters on the thin blue line but also because they cared and were inspired by Alex's energy and kindness. My son: Alex the Kind, Alex the Inspirational, Alex the Brave.

I returned home invigorated from this particular meeting and spoke with a rejuvenated energy with Maruška. We drew strength from each other and those close to us. I also drew strength from Alex who despite being this frail and so often ill and sometimes too weak to support his own weight, talked of gentle things and life. He spoke of nature and growing things and simple dreams for the future where he would grow flowers and vegetables in a garden and care for animals. I swore to myself that I would make sure he could fulfil these dreams and, with the help of others, he would.

I also mentioned to Maruška that there had been some talk of a song being written by one of the people at work. That's all I knew at the time. I didn't really pay it much attention if I am honest. I was genuinely grateful for all that everyone did for Alex: great or small, but I assumed that it was someone who was going to send a video for him of them singing something to cheer him. How wrong I would be!

On the 26th October, we all attended the Police Federation conference to make a speech about Alex and his fundraising with the P.F.O.A. Some old colleagues were there including Andy from the C.N.C. It was good to see him and he had clearly been following Alex's journey. Andy, another person who was touched by meeting Alex, would get involved in fundraising and give tremendous support. He cycled across the U.K. from Lands' End to John O'Groats in 2017 just before Alex returned back to the U.K.

Alex made a speech at that conference as Mark from the P.F.O.A and I stood at the side of the stage. He was amazing. There he was, my nine-year-old son speaking, to police officers of all ranks at a national conference about his journey. He talked about his cancer, about his dreams and about the kindness of others. Mark and I hugged him as he hobbled to his wheelchair to a symphony of applause. I wish I could have recorded or documented that speech but it had not been prepared in advance: he just spoke sincerely and honestly. Perhaps that was his strength? In that moment, Alex the Inspirational, Alex the Articulate and Alex the Courageous had won the hearts of everyone in that room.

While Alex was still buzzing about the conference, I was desperately trying to engage with other people and obtain second opinions. It wasn't as easy as you may think. The whole idea of obtaining a second opinion in the U.K. is quite an alien one. It is a common occurrence in mainland Europe and in the United States but for whatever reason it isn't here. My close friend Jonny and I discussed this and he encourage me to seek the knowledge and input of others. Perhaps it was just in our culture that because the NHS is a public institution we don't question it. I suspect it is something to do with our propensity to place total confidence in the doctors and not question or doubt what we are told. We were at the point. But no longer.

It was essential that we were able to reach out to other professionals but it was far more difficult than I had anticipated. Joy from Red Arc was sending emails to hospitals that had been identified from lists obtained from the Sarcoma Alliance but responses were slow and almost hesitant. Several hospitals across Europe and the United States simply didn't reply. I desperately wanted to progress things but again, it felt like we had hit a brick wall.

In a bid to remain optimistic, I also reached out to a few people on Twitter who Alex and I had built up somewhat of a rapport with. One of them was a doctor in the U.K. but had lived in the middle east. She had been a fervent supporter of Alex and we had exchanged several messages about Alex's condition over the previous months. When we reached this critical stage, she said she could no longer help because colleagues had warned her about getting personally involved with a patient. I was devastated, but I knew that other people would not share that philosophy. There was a solution out there.

I had also built up communications with Jill from the U.S. who had worked, I believe, in a consultancy role within the medical insurance sector. We spoke often in a short period of time about how to reach out to the right people in the U.S. Her advice, although non-specific, was invaluable in making sure I could navigate to credible sources and that would be invaluable later. It was at this point in one of our conversations that Kansas and the mid-west was mentioned. I paid it no further thought at the time, just put it to the back of my mind and noted to myself that perhaps I would reach out to Chief Zeigler in Kansas City, Kansas Police. Perhaps he would have some contacts in the medical professions?

The health insurance I had through the Police Federation had been of great assistance in connecting me to Red Arc and providing some immediate financial support. They also had a scheme called 'Best Doctors' where you could obtain second opinions. I jumped at the chance but was so deeply disappointed at the red tape that was involved. After spending a tremendous amount of energy in trying to progress this line I was informed that someone would be in touch in around six weeks. I didn't have six weeks. Alex didn't have six weeks. We needed help now.

I had made contact with a gentleman called Mike from the Derbyshire charity and we spoke on the phone at length. He seemed a very direct but passionate man and he was sure that he could assist us. I had sent him a very detailed email asking specifically for his assistance in making contact with organisations abroad. I also explained that we had fundraising in place. He needed access to the scans and documents we had in order for him to obtain a second opinion for us. I was impressed how enthusiastic he was about this and he wanted the information immediately. So much so that, on the 27th October, he arranged to meet us off the motorway to collect the information when we were travelling north to meet a very special role model for Alex.

Meeting Mike from the charity was, at the time, a tremendous relief. We had someone who clearly wanted to make it happen. I checked out their website and was touched by the passion they had for helping children to get the treatment they needed in the United States. I handed over the documents and the scans with an understanding that I would be connected with his doctors in The United States. We then drove to Nottingham to the Royal Concert Hall to meet, none other than, Steve Backshall!

The trip to meet Steve Backshall had been arranged several months ago by the Round Table Children's Wish charity. Cathy from that organisation contacted us months earlier and sent Alex some Steve Backshall related gifts before booking us tickets for the event in Nottingham where he was presenting his "Wild World Tour". Arrangements had also been made in advance for Alex to meet Steve backstage during the event!

We had gone together as a family and we were all very excited but it was nothing compared to the excitement Alex was feeling. He was luminous at the prospect of meeting his hero. He had been a fan of his before he fell ill but as he declined and he was confined to home or hospital Alex would look at nature through Steve's programmes. We arrived at a packed auditorium full of animated children clutching books, t-shirts and other memorabilia of the event.

I was so impressed by his presentation and after the tumultuous roar announcing his arrival the hall was silent in reverence to their hero. You could hear a pin drop. Alex was also completely engrossed. There was a section of the show where he interacted with the crowd displaying close ups of oddly angled photographs on a huge screen and inviting his audience to identify them. People from all over the hall would shout out the answers. One picture came on the screen and the whole room was silent. One boy shouted up in a weak but confident voice identifying the odd shape to be the tooth of a Sand-tiger shark. That boy was Alex and Steve Backshall nodded his approval.

At the interval, we were invited back stage and Steve Backshall came and spoke to Alex. It was such a pleasure watching them interact. I was mesmerised by their discussions on wild things and nature. Alex asked insightful questions and I was yet again swelling with pride. I was so happy that Alex had met him and for a second I was gripped by the fear that he may never do so again such was the situation we were facing with such a terrible prognosis. I quickly dismissed those thoughts from my mind and settled back in the moment enjoying my son's joy: Alex the Wise, Alex the Passionate, Alex the Nature Lover.

Just a few days after meeting Mike in a road layby whilst travelling to Nottingham I was meeting him again, but this time at his offices in Derbyshire. The office was plastered with photos of children that were fighting the deadly disease and various celebrities who were supporting the charity's cause. We spoke of his efforts and he explained that a conference call had been arranged with doctors in the United States who specialised in dealing with Alex's condition at a proton beam therapy centre in the southeast of the country. That call would take place very shortly. He was a very confident man and obviously well-travelled. He shared his experiences of working with some of the European proton beam therapy centres explaining how he found the ones in the United States better. He also boasted that they had only lost one child from the last twelve they had helped. I am sure that statistic is how he said it, it was also on the charity's website – but I can no longer find it on the internet.

His assistant made us tea and he began flitting about outlining his plans to get Alex over to the U.S. as quickly as possible. It all seemed a little bit premature to me but I was open to help, real help that, as he explained how we would save Alex. So, perhaps casting aside my natural inclination to be cautious I began to lose myself in the prospects of prompt treatment. But, I am a cop, and I have been for many years. As we spoke and as he moved around the office I was, probably subconsciously, scanning my surroundings. I noticed reports from the Charities Commission (the regulatory body for charities in England & Wales) on Governance in a shelf on the wall and demand for payment from what appeared to be utility companies. There were letters from the council amongst other things.

Despite all the issues we were facing and the whirlwind of events and commitments as well as the full-time job of managing Alex's social media, I had tried to do some research on the charity. Due to my lack of time, this 'due diligence' consisted of scrutinising the internet only. I had viewed the website and also noted an article about a Charities Commission investigation into the charity in 2014. There had been issues but, due to how busy I was I didn't give it the attention it probably deserved. I asked him almost absently about the Charities Commission investigation and he gave me an account of how they had changed trustees and it had created problems about accountability. We then discussed the meeting and I sat eager to engage with these doctors and find out what I could.

When I originally contacted the charity, I had asked specifically to obtain their assistance to make contact with hospitals abroad and obtain second opinions. This had progressed to this centre in the United States being able to treat Alex. He assured me that everything was in hand and he had spoken already with the doctor. The conference call was made and I found myself speaking to two doctors in the U.S. They introduced themselves and it was explained that both undertook work at various centres across the U.S. and they also did work commissioned by the NHS on British children. This was a thorny issue in regards to Alex's situation. I had previously explained that he was deemed no longer eligible for NHS funding for the proton beam therapy as the cancer had metastasised. As a result of this they didn't want to create a compromising situation where they had treat Alex despite the NHS saying that they couldn't.

They explained that they had reviewed his records and scans and were able to treat him using proton beam therapy. In fact, because of the area of the spread it would prevent collateral damage to his intestines that may occur with conventional radiotherapy. No surgery would take place, just the proton beam therapy.

This was amazing news and I left that office so relieved. I immediately called Maruška and informed her of the situation. She too, was happy and relieved. I explained to her that the meeting had ended with me asking for a treatment plan and report on their proposal as well as costings. Mike agreed to liaise with the doctors and get that to me the next day.

Everything seemed to be going in the right direction and we seemed, finally, to be making some progress through our own efforts. We had been given a solution which stood in stark contrast to the issues we faced with our own hospitals who had proposed radical surgery in the event it was deemed worthwhile due to Alex's deteriorating situation. We had sought other options too, including other proton beam therapy centres, but we had yet to receive any news from the hospitals we had made contact with in Germany and the Czech Republic. I had also attempted to contact several hospitals in the United States but they were simply not replying to us. Furthermore, we were encountering frustration at fixing an appointment with doctors at hospitals in London. The situation was dire and only one route seemed open to us.

I had really hoped to make a connection with hospitals in the United States directly and was both surprised and disappointed that I was unable. I sent messages to several people who we had engaged with and who were seemingly in positions of trust and responsibility in the U.S. in the hopes that someone may have a connection. One such message went to Chief Zeigler of K.C.K.P.D.

Thirteen

"Horizon on my Mind" said Lucy. "The song is called Horizon on my Mind". I had gone into work to have one my regular discussions with my Inspector and visit work colleagues. We had discussed Alex and how he was, how I was and we also discussed fundraising.

The proposed fundraising plan was so interesting and sounded so promising. One of the civilian road collision investigators, David, had approached Lucy offering a song he had written to raise money for Alex. I had heard about something from my crew mates but didn't know the details until now. David and his son David Jnr. had written and produced the song and it was ready for release. The song had originally been written by David for his son who was battling Cerebral Palsy but when David heard of Alex's plight he decided to gift the song to him. David Jnr produced the song in his own studio under the label Mix Asylum which was his own company.

I had heard of David at work but knew him by reputation only as we had never actually worked together. He was regarded as a decent man who was quite reserved but was known for his passion and skill for music. I was genuinely surprised yet honoured that he had given this song to Alex with the intention of generating income from song sales and the significant majority of profit would go to Alex. Lucy provided me with his contact details and we spoke the following day.

That following day I heard the song. I must say right from the outset I was both surprised and impressed. It was a well put together rock song, carrying not only a catchy tune but a good set of lyrics that reflected the journey that Alex was on. I liked it.

The plan was to make the song available for download via iTunes, Amazon and by texting a specific code from your mobile phone. It would be officially released at the beginning of December but would be available for pre-order at the beginning of November. The plan was to build up an advertising campaign and saturate social media for pre-orders and try to really make an impact. After few short weeks, we decided to do a music video and we were delighted to find out that our Chief Constable, Martin Jelley, had approved our use of Warwickshire Police's Headquarters at Leek Wootton in Warwick to film it. I couldn't believe what I was hearing at first. Not only was the village mentioned in the Domesday Book, with the main building built in 1861 but it would now be the location for our fundraising music video!

David began plans to direct the video and thanks to one of the staff in our Corporate Communications department we managed to enlist the help of a Manchester based production company called Into Productions to film on the day. We would maintain contact with its founder and co-owner Damian and Into Productions and Alexander's Journey would cross paths again a few weeks later and then again in 2017 in the U.S!

Alex continued to post regular updates on social media and had become quite the professional as he updated, inspired and entertained his supporters. Sophia had flourished as well under his tutelage and she was now regularly interrupting and gate crashing his posts, much to his irritation. People had come to adore them and we received hundreds of Tweets, posts and messages every day. A considerable proportion of those followers were police or emergency services related and we used this opportunity to both rally the emergency services in the U.K. to come and take part in the music video and to encourage everyone to buy the song. The messages promoting the event and the song came thick and fast and people got behind the it. We hoped for some financial success as it was around this time we had begun seeking funds to look at the possibility of Alex having treatment abroad.

Preparation was now taking place for the filming of the music video and it was apparent from the early stages that it would be a huge logistical undertaking. In addition to the working group planning meetings, David and I had regular contact with updates either in person or on the telephone and Alex and I met his wife and son a few times prior to the event itself. David junior was a bright but reserved boy but he seemed to blossom when he was working with his passion: music. I was very impressed by his skill and his outlook on life. He had suffered as a child with Cerebral Palsy but now as an adult he seemed to cope with it admirably. I drew parallels with Alex and hoped that Alex would flourish in his passion and grow into a man.

In addition to the filming on the day we would undertake some filming at our home and I had the idea of seeing if we could ask some of our police followers in other forces around the U.K. to get involved as well as asking U.S., Canada, Australia and Gibraltar law enforcement to be involved in some way.

We continued to have huge support from the United States as well as Canadian police forces including the Royal Canadian Mounted Police and several police departments in Ontario including Halton Regional Police Service and Ontario Provincial Police who had all sent gifts and police memorabilia. This support would continue to grow as months passed by and we obtained a significant number of supporters in the Toronto Police Service who sent regular messages of support. We had many Canadian followers not connected with the police service as well. A family friend of Maruška's called Judy had emigrated to Canada many years ago and she was one of the first of now many Facebook followers from that country.

I had communicated several times with a police Inspector in the Midland Police Service in Ontario so I decided to ask him if he would do some filming and lip sync a few lines of "Horizon on my Mind" so we could include it in the music video. I was so very pleased when he agreed. He and his officer did a great job and I will be forever grateful for his contribution. I also approached Chief Zeigler of Kansas City Police and a former U.K. police officer who emigrated and is serving in Western Australia and they agreed too. Officers in the Metropolitan Police Service in London were also on board – it was all very exciting! All delivered. When I think back it humbles me to think that all these people continued to help and give their time and energy for my son.

On the 6ᵗʰ November 2016 hundreds of officers, staff and friends from the uniformed emergency services descended onto Leek Wootton and the music video for Horizon on my Mind was filmed. It was a day I will never forget and it began with me driving Alex to the event with a motorcycle escort from officers in my unit at Rugby. When we arrived, we marvelled at the rows of police, fire, ambulance and search & rescue officers that braved dark cloudy skies to support us. Thankfully the weather held until the end of the day when the heavens opened but that didn't dampen anyone's spirits especially Alex's.

When I watch that video I am completely overwhelmed by the numbers of people that came together. The lines of police dogs and their handlers when we arrived, the police horses dancing outside Buckingham Palace, My Inspector rocking out with an inflatable guitar, The Police and Crime Commissioner and Chief Constable for Warwickshire 'getting down' with all their officers, a Canadian constable checking his watch in time with the lyric, Australian police officers singing on the beach and the Kansas City cops, albeit like startled rabbits in headlights, doing their part too (I would meet some of them just a few months later).

I love the way Alex sings in the footage recorded at our house and how my crewmate Simon did his best impression of animal in the muppets (you may also recognise the guy attempting to play the bass guitar).

I would like to ask you, the reader of this book, to download the song if you haven't already done so. Join in with the experience at the cost of around 99 pence or 99 cents. Just type in "Horizon on my Mind" on Amazon or iTunes. (You can also view the music video by typing in "Alexander's Journey Horizon on my Mind" on Vevo or You Tube). Thank you.

On 7ᵗʰ November 2016 Horizon on my Mind (or HOMM as it had come to be known) was number 6 on the charts for pre-orders for release on 5th December on iTunes and 4th in the charts on the Amazon best sellers list! We were encouraged by the number of people that said they had downloaded the song, which included my mother in a feat of technological excellence, but it quickly slid back down the charts, such was the competitive environment it was in. Never-the-less the coming together of so many people in one place was a fantastic achievement and one that would stay with us.

Ironically, we nearly didn't make the music video event and I had to negotiate Alex's attendance with the L.R.I. as he had succumbed to an infection just a few days before.

On Thursday the 3rd November, just a few days before the filming for the music video, we went to London for a special event at the Natural History museum. Invited by an enthusiastic Dr. Max he informed us that a writer and photographer from Sarcoma UK wanted to meet Alex and write an article for their magazine about Alex and his friendship with Dr. Max. Whilst I had never spoken to Sarcoma U.K. I had made full use of their comprehensive and informative reference material on Ewing Sarcoma. We received a guided tour and managed to spend time behind the scenes in the museum's Mineral & Planetary Sciences Department, which meant Alex had fun with volcano and meteor related stuff. It was extremely interesting and we got to hold pieces of rock from space that were dated as being older than the actual earth itself.

It was great to see Dr. Max again but I noticed he was struggling that day with his leg. It seemed worse than before. Alex didn't notice, but I did. The article was written and was published later in the year. It covered their mutual appreciation and love of natural history and their support and the inspiration they drew from each other. It identified the similarities in the battle they faced but also that the passions and enemies they had were both the same. It was an excellent piece with an amazing photo.

Alex fell ill while we were in London and was rushed into a London hospital with an apparent infection. It turned out to be a cold: plain common cold, but his body couldn't fight it. He was transferred to the L.R.I. and kept in isolation again but again there were no beds free so he was admitted to the infectious diseases ward. It was here we met two of the kindest, hardworking and all round pleasant nurses I have ever met.

Using every possible shred of charm and making so many promises to ensure Alex was cared for we were allowed out of hospital to attend the event at Leek Wootton.

We also received the gift of a song from an actor called Stephen Walters, who had been in many films and drama's including Band of Brothers and Outlander to name just two. He and several other Outlander actors followed Alex and we would see their endorsements and likes of his Tweets from time to time.

It came months later, when we were in the United States but I feel it is appropriate to mention it now. The song was very touching and gentle which was in contrast to the Rock music edge of Horizon on my Mind. It was beautiful and simple with deep lyrics that were carried by striking, yet soothing, acoustic guitar. That song, called "Hold On" makes Alex weep every time he listens to it. I was touched as well and when combined with a simple yet moving video they had put together from his Twitter footage it was a very emotive piece. Another ardent supporter of Alex was the multi-faceted actor, singer and DJ Ross Owen, who sang on the song along with Stephen. As soon as we watched it Alex was, in an outpouring of emotion, desperate to reach out to them and thank them. Alex sent a video reply to Ross and Stephen but we had to stop filming because he broke down half way through. We eventually succeeded in sending an emotional message of love and thanks for their kindness when he was more composed.

Ross was a DJ on a music station called Black Sky Radio who have been and remain champions of Alexander's cause. They supported Horizon on my Mind and gave it playtime as well as inviting both David and Alex on to their show to promote its release. Ironically and quite possibly in yet another twist of coincidence that seems to permeate this journey, their main studio was in Kansas City with DJ Nightmare (a.k.a. Mike) at the helm.

Ross and I have spoken many times and he is also going through his own battles. Such is our sense of commitment to Alex and to each other that despite never meeting him I regard him not only as a supporter of Alex but as a supporter of me and more importantly as my friend. I remember him being instrumental in increasing Alex's followers and going around his home town of Cumbernauld, Scotland and obtaining video messages of support for Alex including one from a friend of his in Lanarkshire Police. I look forward to meeting both Stephen and Ross one day very soon: I want to embrace them as brothers and thank them for the gift of such a profound song. Its lyrics touch me every time I hear them.

Hold on little boy,
Give us one of your smiles

Out of the darkness,
You shine a light

Sometimes the road seems long,
All you got to do, is hold on

All you got to do is hold on

Whenever you're down,
Just look to the stars

Every step that you take,
Every beat of your heart

Sometimes, when hopes on the run,
All you got to do, is hold on

Hold on, hold on, little boy

A world full of friends,
A journey to ride

Even the animals,
Are right by your side

Sometimes, when things out wrong,
All you got to do, is hold on

Hold on, hold on, hold on

Fourteen

The recent events had left Alex completely enthused but also totally exhausted.

Unfortunately, he was placed back on a chemotherapy programme on the 8th November which included another six days stay at the L.R.I.. We were told that he needed to remain on chemotherapy until they could decide what to do as the next step. We were, yet again, waiting. This meant he had gone way past the original finish date for his chemotherapy and whilst that was frustrating for me I wasn't fully aware of the potential implications for Alex with regards to this until we went to America.

Summer had become autumn. Despite this, my flower remained steadfast. I told myself that I must do the same.

I had also received a response from Chief Zeigler informing me that he had reached out to a doctor at Kansas University Hospital and he would get back to me. I didn't realise where this would go at the time. It was one of many lines of enquiry I was hoping to find some success with: London, Czech Republic, Germany, United States. This didn't include, ironically, what the hospitals were doing where we lived, where Alex was being treated.

At this point it was still difficult to get answers and clarity. I felt that we were considered an irritation because, frankly, I was. Only through doggedness did I ascertain that because Alex had continued beyond the treatment plan he was no longer able to remain on the clinical trial. This was a big blow. But life continued in the ward, the strange half-life of routine and frustration. I remember speaking with one of the parents of another child who was receiving chemotherapy at the same time as Alex. We vented our frustrations to each other and I was informed that they and another parent had the same oncology consultant Alex had as the primary doctor for their children and they had complained and had been moved to another doctor.

That was interesting for me and it planted the seed that would result, very shortly after, in me taking the decision to complain and Alex changed doctor too. I gleaned something else from that discussion that night: we were stood in the parent's kitchen making a drink and this mum expressed her concern about her child's predicament. Nothing seemed to be working and she was desperate for something to change. I explained to her that we were seeking second opinions because of the lack of confidence we had and the need to naturally obtain other perspectives. She looked blankly at me, never even considering doing the same. To my knowledge, I don't know if she ever did. It really hadn't occurred to her to challenge the NHS' authority on cancer care. It just wasn't done.

On the 12th November Alex received an interesting visitor to his hospital bed. This lady had contacted us some months previously and had been following his journey with interest. Her name was Rachael, and she was a Ewing Sarcoma survivor who also had a metal prosthetic. She had visited to give him some comfort that there was life after cancer and that, even with a metal limb, you can lead a relatively normal life. This meeting was timely. So many things were in the melting pot and we were desperately trying to reach out for more options and answers. The hospital had decided that they would do the surgery and it would involve a metal femur and extensive work on his pelvic bone. We were, however, waiting for a date and until a date was identified he would need to stay on chemotherapy.

Sadly, the situation with Mike and the charity was becoming uncomfortable. He had mentioned a few times during our numerous conversations that they would ensure sufficient funds were available to pay for the treatment and suggested we transfer funds raised by us to them to maximise sums received as a result of their charitable status. They would cover any shortfall. It was a kind offer but I had declined this because I had every confidence in my team at work and they had made supreme efforts to help Alex. Going elsewhere for money or to manage money seemed wrong.

Mike had informed me of the plans to fly Alex and I out to the U.S. and make sure Alex could benefit from the treatment immediately. The sums required, I had been informed, for proton beam therapy treatment would be around £80,000 in addition to possible expenses for additional flights and accommodation. I was constantly requesting the information I had asked for in our first telephone conference which had been weeks earlier. The documents never came, regardless of my requests, and all information was passed via Mike. We reached a point when I had to explain my need for official documentation on proposed treatment plans or I would not proceed any further.

My instincts had told me that if something seemed too good to be true, then it probably was. This combined with the apparent absence of support from other avenues with regards to the use of proton beam therapy alone without surgery further led me to doubt and question whether I should consider my relationship with Mike and his doctors in the U.S. any longer. After a few more days of waiting and, after an exchange of emails that were, unfortunately, not very pleasant, Mike and I parted company.

In the meantime, despite Joy's best efforts, the appointments at all but one of the hospitals in London did not come to fruition for a myriad of disappointing reasons. We managed to visit a doctor at the University College London who did both NHS and private work. I asked her about proton beam therapy and she was clear that if any treatment was going to help Alex it was surgery.

She showed me a number of sobering graphs and charts about survivability comparing methods of treatment which still to this day haunt me. That was the first and only time in the U.K where a medical professional had really discussed Alex's likelihood of survival. She had explained that the previous week she had been at a conference in Lisbon where one of the topics discussed was the need for early intervention surgery in the treatment of sarcomas to maximise the chances of success and survival.

I was hoping now for a miracle.

Fifteen

So much had happened in October and November to support Alex and enrich his time during his treatment. This seemed to be in stark contrast to the crippling feeling of waiting for news during the same period of time: firstly, on scan results, then on the feasibility of surgery and then as to when the surgery would actually take place.

We had begun to fundraise, trying to obtain money for proton beam therapy and from a target of £120,000 we had raised a phenomenal £54,000. Sometime later we had set up a fundraising account to reach £20,000 to help us with his rehabilitation and we achieved that target. Money continued to come in from dozens of fundraisers: 'squash-a-thons' (thanks Cheryl), sky-dives, dog walks, cake sales and numerous other events.

The money was growing and I had become concerned that we needed to make sure it was transparent and accounted for: this was particularly important because my employer and a considerable amount of the rest of the police service had been involved in one way or another. I wanted to be able to demonstrate when all this was done how the money had been spent. Sergeant Beaumont was the main controller and manager of funds that passed through the Alliance and Maruška's accountants, Mike and his staff Linda, Gaynor and Michael of M.P. Beahan & Co., who were already supporters of Alex had offered to help. They had very kindly agreed to present financial statements and give advice. In addition to this, David, a Lawyer and the husband of Maruška's friend Michaela, had offered to act as an overseer of the integrity of the money and when the time came for the accounts to be produced he would serve as an auditor of sorts. I'm not sure that David really appreciated the volume of work he would give himself through such a kind offer and for a period of weeks, when fundraising was at its most crucial, he was inundated with correspondence. His assistance was invaluable and would continue. Our need for his and Mike Beahan's expertise for the final analysis was yet to come.

Fundraising and donations continued to come in and we did all we could to raise revenue ourselves. We received amounts both large and small, and all mattered. Our local fish and chip shop, Neptune's in Lutterworth, kept a bucket on the counter. As did a fish and chip shop called Merchants near to my Firearms Training School in Worcestershire. I remember earlier this year, when I was back in the U.K. having just returned from Kansas, going to Neptune's Fish and Chip Shop and being surprised at seeing Alex face on a poster on their counter. His posters covered the Police stations I visited as well. It was amazing!

The 'Finn for Change' organisation, who were at the forefront of trying to change the law for police animals, helped greatly and helped us to raise Alex's profile and also helped us with the actual fundraising of merchandise. I had wristbands produced that had the "Alexander's Journey" logo and the phrase 'Dum Spiro Spero' moulded on to them. This is a Latin phrase and it means "I breathe, I hope". It fitted our mindset now. We would continue and never stop hoping. As long as we had breath in our lungs we would continue to find a way to defeat this cancer. I was not prepared to lose him.

We had lots of support from numerous celebrities and it felt strange, and still does even now, to receive messages of support from people that I consider to be famous! Receiving a Tweet from Mark Hamill, William Shatner or Eric Idle always brightens up your day. One Tweet of support from their official account asking their followers to support Alex created hundreds more followers for us. I remember Twitter suspending Alex's account a number of times during this journey because, based on the huge number increase in followers in a short space of time, they assumed we must be using some kind of software or other unscrupulous methods! We received financial support from celebrities which was heart-warming. Further support came from other directions and we were very fortunate to have regular messages from the talented author Diana Gabaldon of Outlander fame. Alex and I spoke with her via telephone and she gave him wonderful words of encouragement and me words of advice about my book!

Mark Hamill and William Shatner also kept in regular contact and Mark has very kindly contributed to this book. We have arranged to meet William Shatner later this year and both Alex and I are very excited about that.

On 19th November Alex did an original drawing of PD Finn by a Christmas tree which was used as part of a limited edition set of Christmas Cards and sold to raise money for Alexander's Journey. Two print runs were made of that set and both complete runs sold out immediately. The original drawing was auctioned off and after a fierce melee of bids my teammate Rosie won the drawing. It is now framed and hung on her wall at home.

One of my aikido students and local artist, Eddie, drew a remarkable picture of a Tawny owl for Alex and had many prints done that we were selling off to raise money. His wife and her ladies choir were committed to fundraising for Alex as well.

This was the support he had because of the profound impact he had on people's lives. So much so that they would make such an effort to help.

On 23rd November, Into Productions returned to our home to start filming the documentary of Alexander's Journey. Originally, we had considered a production showing a "making of" the Horizon on my Mind song and music video but in truth it was quite limiting. We wanted, one day, to write this memoir and at an early stage Damian from Into Productions sowed the seed of a dual project. A book and film. Those early interviews in the documentary, whilst a significant way through from the start of the journey, were very interesting to watch when subsequent filming began months later in Kansas.

One important thing happened on the 9th November 2016 that I totally missed. I received an email sent via the Alexander's Journey website from someone who wished to support us. I had missed that message due to the sheer volume of messages that were coming through. I thank God that they persisted. I received a second message from them on Alexander's Twitter account and I made contact.

That person and their family wish to remain completely anonymous but they had suffered at the hands of cancer and lost a loved one. They extended an offer to pay whatever was required for Alexander's treatment. I thought it was a hoax at first but by the time we met them as a family and they had fallen in love with Alex and he with them, I knew they were real and their commitment to Alex was too. Could our prayers have been answered? Either way, we accepted with many, many thanks.

We have had other emails from people professing help. Some were clearly malicious but others were more cunning. I recall someone contacting us professing to be the director of a major company and chairperson of a major English football club. He wanted to meet at an odd location to discuss the offer of financial help he had made. I checked and the address was in an old almost abandoned derelict industrial estate in northern England. I didn't go and he failed to reply on his "private" email to my questions and requests for clarity.

However, this was irrelevant, now we had a plan and it was thanks to the benefactor and their family that we could act upon it. This was one component of the miracle we were seeking.

Sixteen

The rest of the miracle would take place across the pond in the New World. Whilst it involved the skill and abilities of many professionals it was down to the efforts and compassion of just two people.

From an initial contact on Twitter that had developed into the sending of a gift for Alex, I had, in desperation to find a credible and independent source for a second opinion, reached out to Chief Zeigler of K.C.K.P.D. He had replied saying that he would do his best to find someone for me and from that day to this, that is exactly what he has done for me and my family. He kept his word and did his best. He introduced me to Dr. Lou Wetzel of Kansas University Hospital and he too, right from the outset, did the same.

As things progressed and I spoke with Chief Terry Zeigler more and more often, it occurred to me that I did not know what he looked like. His profile photo on his official police Twitter account was of the Kansas City, Kansas police insignia: the American eagle, its wings unfurled as it sat on top of a disc of the great seal of the state of Kansas. He spoke, right from the outset, casually and relaxed. He laughed often and it seemed from his voice that he always wore a smile: this made me assume he was younger than he was. He had asked his staff officer, Michael, to contact Dr. Wetzel on my behalf to try and arrange for me to ask, directly, the questions I had and obtain much needed answers. It seemed that our original plan to seek support for Proton Beam Therapy had evolved into simply obtaining second opinions. That would progress further.

I remember, in November 2016, to satisfy my curiosity after one of our telephone conversations, checking You Tube to try and find images of Chief Zeigler. I found footage from May that year of the ceremony honouring the untimely death of one of his officers Detective Brad Lancaster. It was peculiar that this is what I found and whilst seeming to be completely unrelated to Alexander's situation it was, however, intrinsically linked to it. Also on that footage was Detective Danon Vaughn who sang 'Amazing Grace' in honour of his fallen comrade. Danon was another brother of the thin blue line who would, after meeting Alex, take him to his heart and both he and his wife would support us throughout our time in Kansas.

The story of how Dr. Wetzel and Chief Zeigler met is relayed in the DVD and in the forewords for this book I asked them to do me the honour of providing as part of the rich mosaic of this journey. It is a profound tale with a tremendous sadness at the loss of two officers: Detective Brad Lancaster and Captain Dave Melton. Their loss meant that Chief Zeigler and Dr. Wetzel met and Chief Zeigler was so easily and readily able to reach out promptly and with some confidence on my behalf. Furthermore, Chief Zeigler had been moved and inspired by Alexander's Twitter account as he tried to come to terms with and rehabilitate himself from those awful months.

Drop a pebble into a pond the water ripples outward.

I can relate the development of this relationship from our perspective. Chief Zeigler became Terry as we spoke more over those weeks. He was, rather affectionately by Alex and Sophia, called Chief Terry later on. While my friendship with Terry would grow in the U.S., for now I would spend much more time on the telephone with Dr. Wetzel.

My initial contact with Dr. Wetzel was very comfortable. He was more formal of course than Chief Terry but I genuinely felt his kindness even over the telephone. I was direct and candid with him. Not only because I needed to be forthright but because time was against me. I asked Dr. Wetzel if it was normal to get second opinions to which he replied that in the U.S. it was an everyday occurrence.

Like I had done for Chief Zeigler, I had sought out video footage of Dr. Wetzel on You Tube. Viewing this footage had revealed an interview he had given when he had been promoted to Chief of Staff at the University. He had never mentioned his prominent position to me in any conversation or via any title accorded to him on an email. This was a measure of a man without ego and with complete humility. This was a man I would come to respect greatly and regard as a father figure not just in Alex's life but in mine too.

This may seem strange but this memoir isn't just about my writing: it is about the story of strangers who contributed and by contributing became friends. That is why the DVD story is equally as important as the words I am putting here.

From the 8th November to the 9th December a total of 69 emails passed between Lou and I. We were on the telephone to each other every day, occasionally more than once a day. When I was living with Lou in their house I observed how busy he was on a daily basis and it occurred to me on more than one occasion – how on earth did he make time to correspond and speak to me so often!

Over the period of these weeks we formed a bond.

Dr. Wetzel and I spent many weeks trying together to find a way to save Alex. His herculean efforts did just that. Opportunities regarding Alex's treatment began to close down even more rapidly at this stage and as they did I clung more and more to the possibility and hope that Dr. Wetzel, Lou, would be able to help us. We were still waiting for a date for the surgery to take place in the U.K. and there were some issues as I understood around the procurement of the femur. They had made scans of the femur so they could get the measurements but things remained slow and fraught with delay. I had also received correspondence from Germany and the Czech Republic that they were unable to help and they further confirmed that proton beam therapy would not help Alex. His illness was too far gone.

Interestingly, the final letter I received from the German Hospital, whilst not good news, had come after several communications from them wanting further information. This was in addition to that which had been provided by the NHS initially. It also contained comments relating to the absence of certain tests that they considered should have been performed earlier. But this door was now closed to us.

My daily conversations with Lou became more intense and it was beginning to become clear that our list of options was growing thin. What had started as a request for a second opinion on what was available had become a quest – to identify a treatment based on the expertise that was out there.

The whole process of providing information from the NHS to the external hospitals in Europe and particularly to the U.S had been a laborious and frustrating one. It had taken time and effort which finally culminated in me physically attending at the hospital in Leicester and taking in my own hand a disc containing scans from the hospital and me sending these by courier personally to the United States.

I remained desperate for news from the hospitals that were caring for Alex here in the U.K. but still no date for his surgery had been set.

I recall one evening, asking our doctor and Paediatric Oncology Consultant in Leicester for a direct email address as Dr. Wetzel had offered to liaise with them directly on second opinions and sought to streamline and enhance the process of sharing information. The doctor refused to give it to me. This was the final straw and I remember ending that telephone conversation and deciding that I would make a strong official complaint the following day. I needed to replace that doctor with another one in a final attempt to obtain some degree of accord with the NHS with regards to my son's situation. I thought back to the conversations I have had with other parents and how they had also made complaints and then had their care transferred to another doctor. We had to do the same.

Within 48 hours Maruška and I sat face to face with the head of the service at the hospital and he became our new doctor and Paediatric Oncology Consultant. It was a breath of fresh air and he genuinely supported the transfer of information. I often wonder if, had we made that decision earlier, would things be different. I think, in truth, not. The issues we face weren't primarily down to personalities but were procedural and due to processes and the fantastic demands on those related structures.

My talks with Dr. Wetzel were centred around a need for information and for myself, a sense of direction. I was desperately seeking hope and affirmation that something could be done. I needed to move past the waiting, the crippling waiting.

Dr. Wetzel had put me into contact with Dr. Rosenthal but he also remained as my staunch ally and advisor. I reflect now on how over time our relationship became less defined from Doctor and "patient" and more as friends. It was odd at the time because he continuously reminded me that this area wasn't his field and he referred to others such as Dr. Rosenthal as a lead practitioner. Notwithstanding this he, continued to contact experts in the field so that his knowledge was increased and he could assist me further. He was regularly consulting with colleagues in his own hospital's sarcoma programme and several other major pediatric cancer centres throughout the United States: St. Jude Children's Research Hospital in Memphis, the Mayo Clinic in Minnesota and Massachusetts General Hospital in Boston to name a few. I recall registering Alex as an international patient at the Boston Hospital so that Dr. Wetzel could have a serious dialogue with experts there and seek their input on Alex's treatment and prognosis. During this critical period of dialogue, I tried to maintain some degree of normality and so did Dr. Wetzel: we spoke about his home and his family. About him mowing the lawn and his wife being busy. We spoke of home and mundane things one moment and Alex's reality the next. But what was certain in my mind was that for Lou Wetzel it had become personal.

It is important to know that at this time, particularly when Lou Wetzel was seeking second opinions, that he was still fixed on Alex getting the treatment he needed in the U.K. Once we had reached the stage of discounting any treatment plan involving proton beam therapy and we were certain any treatment would involve surgery. Dr. Rosenthal had assured us both that there was an able surgeon in the U.K. who had performed this kind of surgery. Not only was he known to Dr. Rosenthal but he was actually at the Birmingham Royal Orthopaedic Hospital, the very same hospital that Alex was attending. With this information and good news, I approached the hospital only to be told that this surgeon had retired a year earlier. His successor was our current orthopaedic surgeon but he had never performed this kind of surgery before. Thwarted again. Frustrated again.

It was at this point, having relayed this piece of news back to Dr. Rosenthal and Lou Wetzel, that I was then convinced that Dr. Rosenthal was the man who needed to perform the surgery. Why? Because when I told him that the surgeon had retired he offered to come to England and assist in it being performed here in the U.K! What happened then is a little unclear to me. It happened at a time in November when I had very little idea about what was happening and would happen now to my son. The treatment plan here was unknown to me. We had received terrible news and had been informed that surgery wouldn't happen. Then we were told that it would happen… but would be very radical and may still not save him.

I informed the hospital of Dr. Rosenthal's offer and it was received with an almost indifference. The initial response was that it was unlikely to be possible but it would be passed on to the appropriate parties for a decision to be made.

I received no reply.

I remember one key conversation with Lou that took place late into the night towards the end of November. The six-hour time difference would always ensure that our conversations took place very late at night or very early in the morning for one of us! I was broken, despondent and desperate for some breakthrough, some revelation. I had no confidence in the treatment here and believed that if Alex remained in the U.K. he would die.

This was the harsh reality that I shared with a man I had never met and had only known for a brief few weeks. It was then that I lost my veneer of courtesy and formality with Lou and I cried. He was upset too. I could tell from his voice. It quavered, he was emotionally involved aswell and now caught up in the waves of raw emotion that I had conveyed to him. I pleaded for help, for some positive outcome, for him to tell me what to do, how to react against this tidal wave of apparent apathy. I tried to control myself and stabilise the situation. I was so fearful that my emotional outburst would force Lou to back away. I spoke seriously and earnestly to him telling him that I would understand if he could no longer sustain the intensity of the situation and the sheer weight I, a stranger, was putting on his shoulders. I was giving him an out. A window of opportunity to walk away. I steeled myself for his response. It felt like it was the right thing to do but I was suspended in fear waiting for his reply. Seconds felt like hours until I heard the words I will remember forever,

"I cannot look at this just professionally or medically in isolation anymore, I can only approach this as if Alex were my own son".

Lou and I were bound together now to save my son: and we would.

Seventeen

Lou was working with the staff in the Kansas University's sarcoma programme and they had analysed in detail the records and scans they had received from the NHS. It became apparent to me that Lou and Kansas University Hospital was where Alex should have the treatment.

I needed to maximise my son's chances of survival and minimise the impact of the treatment on his body. We needed not only to defeat the cancer but make sure he would live after the battle and not just exist. He needed to walk again and not be confined to a wheelchair. I could accept him needing a walking cane but I wouldn't resign him to having "significant loss of functionality" and being wheelchair bound for the rest of his days.

Lou and I had spoken about costs and the reality of securing medical treatment in the United States. I had also, through occasional updates, informed the benefactor of the financial situation and they remained steadfast in their support.

As the end of November loomed ever closer Lou, after I had persuaded him to see the predicament I face here in the U.K. had presented me with the realistic options that we could take. I shared with him my thoughts and my desire to come to him and Kansas University Hospital. They seemed to have the expertise and they also had my confidence. I would pin my hopes on them, on Lou and the professionals he spoke so highly of.

He agreed. He would do what he could to make it happen.

Dr. Rosenthal was the driving force in the team. It was his expertise in surgery that was, aside from the confidence and faith I had in Lou to do his best, the main influence for the decision to go to Kansas. What I was to learn whilst in the United States was that Dr. Rosenthal was extremely well regarded and was esteemed in this form of treatment. He would pick his team from two states: Kansas and neighboring Missouri. Kansas University Hospital and Children's Mercy Hospital would be involved in his treatment and Alex would spend time in both. I would be told months later that only Rosenthal could pick his team that he worked in his own clinic off site from the main hospital such was his prowess.

I remember one evening, earlier in November, as Maruška and I discussed the situation and updates that had come from Lou that day. I imparted information top her about surgery and about Dr. Rosenthal. It was then she leapt up and grabbed the iPad. She had, months before, stumbled across a feed on her Facebook page. This feed was about a dancer called Gabi from Missouri in the U.S. who had received treatment for cancer in her leg. This teenager, a successful ballerina, had been diagnosed with osteo sarcoma of her leg below her knee. She had successful surgery to remove the sarcoma but it involved her losing the leg below the knee. The surgeon, so skillful in the procedure, had saved the shin and foot and attached it to her knee using rotation-plasty (putting it on back to front). She was then able to insert the foot into a prosthetic. She is now a successful competition dancer. The surgeon? Dr. Rosenthal.

I reflect upon the kaleidoscope of events, circumstances, coincidences and twists that took us to Kansas. The numerous lines that lead us to Chief Terry Zeigler, Dr. Lou Wetzel and to Dr. Howard Rosenthal. I was yet to be aware of all the factors until I would meet Terry and Lou but still, even before we flew to America, it seemed as if fate had a hand in things to bring us all together.

Things moved very rapidly then. I spoke, the majority of the time, to Dr. Lou Wetzel but also with Dr. Rosenthal and a Dr. Chastain from Children's Mercy Hospital. Dr. Rosenthal, the orthopedic surgeon, had a booming voice which, I would see when I met him, reflected his physicality. We spoke of the procedure and how he would require measurements of Alex's femur so he could order a 'made-to-measure' prosthetic. We would seek to obtain the measurements from the NHS. Dr. Chastain would be Alex's pediatric oncology consultant and would ensure that all necessary scans and tests would take place so they, as a team, could see the exact situation prior to surgery. We spoke on the telephone on one occasion before we flew to America's Midwest. She sounded very young on the telephone but very knowledgeable. This knowledge was underscored with a friendliness and warmth that I had not encountered with her U.K. equivalent. That friendliness wasn't unprofessional but seemed to exude a comforting warmth that put me at ease and made even more confident and assured in the steps we were taking.

I had also spoken with Chief Terry and explained the decision to come to Kansas and how I hoped for his support. I shared my anxieties with him about travelling to a foreign place neither Maruška or I had ever been to. I was honest and direct. It's always the best policy and had served me well. I explained, "I don't know you Terry and you don't know me. But, I am asking for your help to make our coming to Kansas City - your patch - a reality".

As we spoke I hoped he would reach out and proclaim his support. He did. I remember his reply. It would stay with me and personify the journey in many respects in my eyes....

"We went through our own problems and people helped us. You're a police officer and I'm going to be there for you".

The original plan was for us to travel to the U.S. after Christmas in the first few days of January. We anticipated Alex would have finished his chemotherapy and would have had a few weeks to recover and then he could make the journey to Kansas and have the surgery he needed. But that was not to be. Alex's health began to decline. He grew weaker as the chemotherapy continued. He took longer to recover, he was becoming frailer every passing day. I had seen this with other children in the ward: they succumbed to the relentless cycle of treatments that over time affected the bone marrow more and more. Alex had, so far, managed to withstand this due to his natural supplements but it seemed he was struggling. As this decline worsened I had begun to make preparations to cross the Atlantic Ocean. I was worried that he may not be strong enough to travel, that he would fall ill and be confined yet again to an isolation ward in the hospital in Leicester. I spoke with Lou and we decided that we would travel immediately. We would fly on the 14th December.

The scans and measurements needed by Dr. Rosenthal to start the process of having the bespoke prosthetic made were a problem. The images obtained by the NHS were insufficient in detail for Dr. Rosenthal and lacked depth and other key elements that would help ensure accurate dimensions. This did make me wonder how the NHS would have organized a correct fitting prosthetic had the surgery gone ahead. But, this time, I kept my opinions to myself. We had to go to a private hospital about 40 miles from home and have the scans done. I was impressed by the hospital and the staff. The scans were done and I viewed them immediately afterwards. They were saved to disc for us there and then and handed to me before we left the hospital. I posted them that day and they arrived by courier the following morning in Kansas. Less than 24 hours!

Dr. Rosenthal explained that such a high specification prosthetic was made to measure and only a few companies made them in the world. Interestingly, his preferred supplier was from a company in the U.K. and they were, in his opinion, the best quality and because of their manufacturing processes had the lowest risk of infection.

I would need to sort the financial arrangements with the hospital as well as flights and visas for us all. Children's Mercy Hospital had more experience of international patients and they took the lead in many respects. I spoke with Pam, their International Services Director and she provided with me with information and estimates of costs for the treatment. It wasn't cheap but, in truth, I had nothing to compare or contrast it to. This was unfamiliar and somewhat strange for me. Over $400,000 USD was transferred via bank wire within a matter of days. There would be more to pay but for now we were able to make the trip and Alex could have the treatment.

The next obstacle was securing flights to get us there. I reached out to Virgin Atlantic initially via Alex's Twitter account and they responded almost immediately. I had checked the costs of flying for four of us (potentially six) and it would be well in excess in £10k. I had contacted them to ensure that Alex would be able to fly and we would get the enhanced support that we needed to make sure he had leg room, could use his wheel chair until we physically got to the entrance of the plane etc. The medical information they required was detailed and we spoke at length with their staff via telephone. Our new doctor at the L.R.I. provided us with a report to give to Virgin confirming that, at this time, Alex was fit to fly.

They exceeded my expectations completely. They gave us financial support with Alex and Sophia's tickets and were supportive and genuinely nice. I thanked them and asked if I could put something on social media about their generosity. Their response was to assure me that it wasn't necessary and they were doing it to help us – no publicity was required. I was impressed and remain so to this day. Thank you Virgin Atlantic.

As we prepared at short notice to make the journey to the U.S. it was interesting to note that I had never had any inclination to go to America. I was interested in Canada because of the still tangible links between our countries, our shared sovereign and a more recent shared policing history as well as the great open spaces and proximity to wild places and nature. Never-the-less we were on our way. Events were now taking over and our original plans for an arrival in January had changed and that meant that we had much less time to arrange entry into the country. The original proposed treatment plan covered just under nine weeks and we were all scheduled to return to the U.K. at the end of February 2017. This would allow Alex sufficient healing time from his surgery but then make sure that he could continue with suitable treatments back here as part of a combined approach.

This would mean we could travel as a group on an ESTA visa waiver programme within a three-month window which was convenient for us and meant not only did we not need to apply for an extended stay visa but we wouldn't need to travel to London to obtain one and cause Alex to endure a further long journey and the further hardship of travelling then waiting could bring. The visa waiver was applied for online and I received the appropriate email notification within 24 hours.

As the travel day came ever closer we said our goodbyes to family and friends. People we would miss dearly who had walked this path with us to this point. And it was such a pivotal point. I was apprehensive because I felt we had been surrounded with a ring of support and we would leave this behind for the unknown. The local media, TV, radio and newspapers had covered in detail the last few weeks and the push to get us to the United States. One of the newspaper headlines read: "Community unites to help seriously-ill nine-year-old Alex". They had and I was grateful.

Eighteen

On the 14th December 2016, we left Manchester airport on a flight across the Atlantic Ocean to the United States of America. We would land in Atlanta and then connect to Kansas City. Uncle Paul and his fiancée Ulrika had joined us to give us the support with managing the sheer volume of luggage we had brought along with us. This included one full suitcase of Alexander's medication both prescribed and supplemental. We had been given letters from our new doctor and paediatric oncologist at the L.R.I. and Dr. Wetzel in case we had problems at the U.S. border getting them into the country.

On the day that we left, Lenka, Maruška's sister, had posted an image of a lit candle on Facebook for Alex and invited others to do the same. Dozens of people responded to her request and she produced a collage on Alex's page which was a very touching presentation of hope.

Hope. We were imbued with it, and we left the United Kingdom with such high hopes of success. We couldn't fail, it had to work. We were met at departures by some firearms officers from Greater Manchester Police and they wished us well and this was a welcome boost. I would take all the good fortune that anyone was prepared to give at that time. As the plane left English soil I cast my mind back to the conversations I had had just one week previously with both Lou Wetzel and Terry Zeigler. It is very strange that you can have two very different conversations within minutes of each other. My chat with Terry Zeigler was upbeat and we discussed our arrival and what the State of Kansas and neighbouring Missouri had to offer aside from the hospitals where Alex would spend most, but not all, of his time. The contrast with my discussion with Dr. Wetzel was unbelievable as he spoke of his commitment to Alex and of his intention to do what he could and seek the best care for him. However, alas, the odds may be stacked against us. I remember in a fleeting moment of lost control, sobbing down the phone to him pleading for him to save my son's life. This was the second time I would weep down the telephone with him. The other time, I recalled, we had wept together. He would do all he could and I could ask for no more than that.

The crew on our Virgin Atlantic flight were amazing. It was surprising and yet very comforting that one of the cabin crew, Maria, had actually been supporting Alex on Facebook and she had made all her colleagues aware of him. They were eager to meet him and learn more about his story and were so very supportive and genuinely seemed to enjoy the time they spent with not only Alex, but all of us. Maruška and I recounted the journey so far to several of them as well as a few other passengers during the flight over a gin and tonic while both Alex and Sophia snatched a few hours' sleep. We had made a connection with the staff and they would continue to follow Alex's journey on social media.

As we left the plane I was so pleasantly surprised at how smooth and worry free our checks at border control were. We had ensured we had all the necessary documentation to hand and the officer assessing us for entry was both polite and efficient. As we passed into Atlanta airport with the stamp's ink still fresh on our passports, he wished us luck and Godspeed in our fight against cancer. I hung onto his words as well. After more checks, we made the much shorter flight from Atlanta to Kansas City. It was a 90-minute flight but both Alex and Sophia were beginning to suffer the effects of almost no sleep for nearly a day, as we landed, exhausted, into a very cold and dark Kansas City.

Then things began to get surreal and I recount the night of our arrival with some fuzziness because, not only was it completely overwhelming but also somewhat dreamlike. The Delta flight had come to a halt and as soon as the seat belt light sign had been turned off people began frantically getting luggage from overhead cabins and preparing to leave the plane. We remained seated as we were dependant on Alex's wheelchair being recovered from the hold and brought to us. It was then that an announcement came over the tannoy that all passengers needed to return to their seats as there were officials on board. Both Maruška and I looked at each other as we both cradled one of our offspring and we joined everyone else on board looking around the cabin for the politician or celebrity that they were obviously referring to. At that point a female police officer from the airport police came on board with a member of ground staff and came over to us. It seemed we were the officials that had been announced!

Terry Zeigler, in one of our many telephone conversations just before we flew out, informed me, quite casually, that there was some media interest in our arrival and that a few cops would meet us at the airport. That was a total understatement and what was to come completely overwhelmed us. In fact, in my weary state I would describe it, in interviews to come, as like being hit by a baseball bat.

Following our VIP escort from the plane we arrived into the airport and into a whirlwind of activity. I was pushing Alex in his wheelchair, Paul, in an impressive feat of strength after 12 hours of confinement, was carrying almost all of our collective hand luggage and between them Maruška and Ulrika were handling the incredibly tired Sophia. I wish I could remember the female officer's name who was the first U.S. cop in Kansas City to welcome us. I recall the name of the Delta crew member who walked with us, Sue. It was Sue who would help us some three months later when we needed to make surprise changes to our return flights following changes in Alex's treatment plan.

We entered the arrivals hall to the bustle of hundreds of people. There seemed to be cameras everywhere and people holding placards adorned with Alex's name and other decorations depicting his favourite things: Godzilla, King Kong and Sharks. I was completely derailed for a precious few moments. I looked for a familiar face in the sea of uniforms, winter clothing, camera lights and boom microphones and then I saw Chief Terry Zeigler. That was an extremely emotional moment for me and I was overcome by a sense of joy and wellbeing. I didn't experience emotions like that anymore and that made it all the more meaningful. I had thrown aside my restraint and embraced him like a long-lost relative. I felt I knew him anyway. I then shook hands with a few of his command staff that were with us. Every handshake was sincere and I wanted everyone who had come out to meet us to know that I appreciated it. I now sought Dr. Wetzel, my eyes scanning the crowd for him. Like the humble and unassuming man that I already knew him to be, he had held back, to let other people be introduced first. Now he came forward and we held each other too. I had never met this man in the flesh, but due to the common purpose we now had and the raw emotions we had shared he was close to me like family. I could have easily cried there as a strange sense of relief and sentiment washed over me. This was a bizarre moment in my life and when I reflect back on it I believe, that with the backdrop of so much adversity and a fear for so many months previously of what was ahead, I felt almost as if I had been rescued.

Alex seemed to be coping well but I could see that he, despite his now natural affinity for the camera, was shocked by the sheer magnitude of things. He was asked questions by the media that were there, but what occurred to me straight away was that no one was pushy or intrusive. There was an air of excitement and exhilaration but nothing frantic. We took questions in an orderly fashion. I didn't understand why so many TV and radio stations were here and how they had come to have such a thirst for his story in such a short space of time. It had been less than four weeks prior to this that I had discussed tentatively any possibility of coming to Kansas with either Chief Zeigler or Dr. Wetzel. It seemed that Chief Zeigler had sown the seed and our social media machine had done the rest.

It was worthy of note that when we arrived that day into the United States we had approximately 7,000 followers on Twitter. That doubled within three months and now in August 2017 it has almost doubled again - to just under 26,000 followers. I find that remarkable.

As I tried to reconcile what had just happened in my mind we went outside into the cold air of Kansas City. It was well below freezing.

Thinking that the surprise was over, I wasn't prepared for what happened next. The whole area beyond the main terminal of the airport was bathed in the blue and red of beacon lights. We were bundled into Dr. Wetzel's car and were confronted just around the corner with a spectacle. In front of me were some 30 police cars and at least 20 to 30 police motorcycles. I remember getting out of the car to take photos and video footage as I had never seen anything like it before. I recall exchanging excited glances to Maruška and Paul as we set off from the airport. Chief Zeigler had jumped into the car with us and sat as the front seat passenger as Dr. Wetzel drove. They both commented how they had never seen anything like it either and they likened it to a presidential escort.

The escort took us from the airport across the Missouri river into Kansas City, Kansas and then into the district known as Westwood and to Dr. Wetzel's house. I was impressed by the motorcycle cops who rode with such skill. I had seen motorcycle units on operational escorts back in the U.K. and they were mightily impressive. This was no exception. As we passed through Kansas City we waved to police and fire officers that had blocked the side roads off for our approach. The Mayor of Westwood John M. Ye and Chief of Police Chief O'Halloran at Westwood P.D. had arranged a second reception for us as we arrived there. On that bitterly cold night in December around a hundred Westwood residents met us on the main arterial road into that district outside the town hall. Placards and posters were brandished and people were shouting Alex's name. We got out of the car and I held Alex and he hobbled out too. The cold air and the sheer energy of that experience had woken him up and he was enjoying the moment.

The events had been captured by a local media company called KJO media who, at the request of the Chief of Police at Westwood P.D. had got on board. They produced a brilliant piece about the night of our arrival and I remember watching it on local TV at the Wetzel's house. It was a night I will never forget.

As we arrived on that amazing night at Dr. Wetzel's house his wife Jane had prepared a buffet and made hot chocolate for everyone (and that included over 80 police officers). I met many officers that were part of the escort that night and forged some profound friendships with some of them during my stay. Many of them, whom I would meet again in the weeks and months ahead were there that night and I didn't realise! Due to tiredness and excitement it was a bit of a blur to me at times. Sophia and Alex were exhausted! Maruška was too. I remember after the event when everyone had gone home sitting at the Wetzel's kitchen table and just looking outside into their huge garden. We were thousands of miles away from home, but it didn't feel like that. There was a feeling of hope and new beginnings in a new chapter. I turned my attention to the house. It was beautiful with a Christmas tree up and a wonderful huge log fire burning. It was so inviting and relaxing.

When Alex ventured into the house he was smitten with the tree. He was exhausted and frail but the energy and light in his eyes when he looked upon that tree: it was magical. I remember Alex and I standing with Lou in his kitchen the night we arrived. We were surrounded by the police officers and their family members and we thanked them all for being part of this journey. Lou then said....

"The will of God brought them here, and the will of God is going to take them home"

Alex would not return home for eight months, over five months longer than we anticipated. But that is what would be necessary to ensure we did our best to fight his cancer, and win.

Nineteen

Within just a day Alex was in hospital. The plan was to quickly ascertain where Alex was medically and recommence chemotherapy. On the 16th December, he was at Children's Mercy Hospital in Kansas City, Missouri. We spoke with Dr. Chastain and her senior nurse Lindsey. Dr. Chastain looked very young and time had been very kind to her. She spoke warmly but articulately as did Lindsey. They were clearly a team who worked well together and respected each other. We learned more in just a few days about Alex's condition and where we were and what we could expect than in the several months prior back in the U.K.

Alex's cancer and the primary tumour in the top of his right femur had spread down the bone towards the knee and had also spread into the acetabulum (cup of the pelvis where the ball of the leg bone goes). It had also metastasised across the pelvis onto the other side of his hip bone and there were marks on his iliac crest and on the top of the leg bone on the other side. He was tired and frail and he could not put any weight on the leg now for fear of it shattering such was the terrible destruction to the right femur now almost completely diseased.

The immediate commencement of chemotherapy was essential to ensure the cancer did not grow in the absence of any further treatment. It was a necessary evil and needed to be part of the treatment plan here in the United States until he was ready for surgery. Dr. Chastain had inherited a difficult situation where the treatment plan in the U.K. had continued to use chemotherapy beyond the original plan whilst they considered and pondered on Alex's situation.

The treatment, internationally, for this kind of cancer was carefully laid down to maximise the results: chemotherapy, then surgery, with some chemotherapy after that to consolidate the treatment and then radiation therapy. The problem was that the body can only take so much toxicity from the chemotherapy doses before it becomes

165

seriously damaged beyond repair. The U.K. doctors had used up more of the chemotherapy doses than they should have, leaving very little options after the surgery, particularly as more doses would have to be used beforehand until he was ready to go under the knife.

She would do her best, and we would hope.

A few days later we met Dr. Rosenthal at his sarcoma clinic. Lou was with us and I was happy about that. Dr. Rosenthal was the man I expected, a giant of a man with a firm grip as he shook my hand. He spoke formally with us and in very serious tones but he smiled often and that would do for me.

Alex got to look at the metal prosthesis that would be implanted. I did too. It was heavy, so very heavy and seemed to be too big for Alex's thin and feeble lower body. I could see Alex was worried and Dr. Rosenthal noticed too. I marvelled at how Dr. Rosenthal knelt down and spoke softly and warmly to Alex. He made the time to engage with him and that seemed in contrast to his almost business-like approach with Maruška and I. I was impressed and would remain so throughout our frequent interactions.

All the doctors leading Alex's care did the same. They made time for him. Dr. Chastain visited Alex every time he was in hospital. Every time. Regardless of the reason or duration of the visit. It was sometimes literally for a few seconds but it mattered. It mattered to me, to Maruška and to Alex.

It was made clear to us and we were under no illusion that this was still a challenging situation. He would get treatment in two separate hospitals who would work as a team together. Children's Mercy would manage his chemotherapy and perform the scans and checks. Kansas University (K.U.) Hospital would undertake the surgery and radiation therapy. The team, the tumour board, would meet together on a weekly or sometimes fortnightly basis, in the same room, at the same time, to discuss his situation. That would make a tremendous difference.

He reiterated the plan that had been discussed in brief with me by telephone back in the U.K. now it had the detail. Information, information, information! The surgery would be in three parts:

- The first surgery would remove the primary tumour, the femur and replace it with a metal non-expandable femur. They would be able to view the extent of the tumour and also see the surrounding areas and how they had been affected.

- The second planned surgery would be to reconstruct the acetabulum and remove any diseased areas where the cancer had spread from the tip of the femur into the pelvis.

- The third surgery, planned for the end of the year or the beginning of the following year, would involve replacing the metal prosthesis with a telescopic version that, when activated by a magnetic device would grow the required length to mimic the growth in the healthy femur. It would grow as he grows. Regular three-monthly scans would be required, not only to make sure there was no recurrence of the cancer but to measure growth.

Two prosthetics were required, because the leg was too diseased and fragile to tolerate any further delays than those that were necessary. The first prosthesis would act as a transitional femur until the scope of the spread had been seen in the surgery and the second final telescopic version was made and that would take time.

The scans to check for the cancer would take place for five years until statistically his chances of a relapse were significantly reduced but the scans and lengthening of his femur would last for another eight to ten years until he reached adulthood and was not going to grow anymore. This would cost money but, at that time, it wasn't something we would worry about. Now we had to focus on the treatment plan to secure a future. The proposed date of the first surgery was the 11th January 2017.

We left that meeting in a daze. We had a plan! A clear definitive plan. For the past six months, I had endured frustration and anxiety and suffered fear to the pit of my stomach as to what would happen to my son. What were we going to do? Where were we going? In the course of an hour we now had the facts, the plan, a road map and most importantly for me in that moment, a date for the surgery! My aspirations of hope over the past few weeks, could probably and realistically been described as faith. But now they were solidified into a tangible credible hope.

That first week was full of revelations. We were given details on what had occurred from what they, as a team of professionals, had pieced together from the scans and records they had received from the U.K. Questions were asked, why had certain things not taken place or why certain conclusions had been made. They believed that the cancer was not progressive, it was metastatic only. This was fundamental because it would mean that the treatment had been effective. The cancer hadn't progressed and got worse during the chemotherapy. The cancer had spread aggressively over the time Alex was misdiagnosed and, in the opinion of the doctors, the scans that were performed were inconsistent in their coverage, so they did not pick up the activity. However, as soon as the chemotherapy was commenced it had stopped the cancer in its tracks.

This was amazing news.

He would spend the next few weeks around Christmas at Children's Mercy Hospital and then move to K.U. Hospital. Both were in Kansas City.

Kansas City was positioned on the state border between the State of Kansas and the State of Missouri. It straddles both States and is where the great Missouri river and Kansas river meet. Whilst not a capital city, it is the largest city on the Missouri side with a population of just under half a million. Over the eight months Alex was in Kansas City, we lived a great portion of that with the Wetzel's. The rest of the time we lived at a Marriott Residence Inn in the heart of Kansas City, Kansas.

The original plan was that we would spend a few days with the Wetzel's and then move to a Ronald McDonald house near to the hospital. Time at the Wetzel's in those first few days was so comforting and felt like a refuge. I had not managed to spend any quality time over the first few days with Lou's wife Jane but we did so shortly after. Jane was and remains the busiest person I have ever met. She was committed to her local church and volunteered locally supporting so many needy causes. Her stamina and her kindness were equally incredible. She spoke softly and walked gently but inside she was a lioness. Just as Lou and I had formed a bond so did Jane and I. The whole Wetzel family accepted us into their home, and there were lots of them! Lou and Jane had six children and the majority of them had wives, husbands or partners of their own. We felt welcome whenever we spent time there: by everyone, every single time.

This feeling of acceptance and a genuine kindness extended beyond the Wetzel's house. We felt surrounded by support, as we had done in the U.K. My initial worries about being isolated were completely dispelled. The thin blue line and their families were always near but no more so than Chief Zeigler's Kansas City, Kansas PD.

Chief Terry had made a promise to help us and he did. He made arrangements for his traffic unit to help us in those first few weeks: making sure we could manage hospital appointments and simply get around without relying on the Wetzels. The traffic unit mainly conducted motorcycle traffic and road policing duties but also managed many ceremonial and special escort roles. The division Sergeant, Don and his Wheel Unit of motorcycle officers, would become as close to me as my crew mates back in the U.K. They would, along with their families, and both on and off duty become our personal protection team and dear friends. Sergeant Don and officers Chris, John and Troy formed the core of our new crewmates with other officers helping out from time to time.

Master Sergeant Don was retired U.S. Air Force and now a veteran of the PD approaching his retirement date (he would actually retire while we were in the U.S.). Whilst I was told by a few people he was somewhat fastidious, he was well respected by everyone and no one seemed to have a bad word to say about him. As I spent time with him, he seemed to me like the epitome of an experienced sergeant: firm but fair, capable and with rectitude. He was always smart; his uniform pristine. He was a man of integrity and he always managed to help us whilst maintaining the delicate balance of not abusing public resources. It was clear to see that within a few short weeks Alex had a profound effect on him too.

It was interesting to see that Chris, John and Troy seemed to have contrasting personalities but clearly were close and tight as a team. It was usually the case in specialist units. It's the same in my team as I am sure it is the world over.

Chris is the youngest, tallest and most plucky of the three of them. When he and I were both taking Alex to the hospital or making some other trip together we would always exchange banter. He was garrulous and made me laugh often. But he wasn't a joker and to personify him as such would be wrong, instead he had a dry sense of humour, with a layer of sarcasm, akin to my own. I would find out that he had personally requested to be involved with us as it was something close to his heart. His son, Austin, had battled cancer years earlier as a small child. He had won that battle and had grown into a strong and capable young man. Chris and I spoke from time to time on the problems we had both faced and emotions and experience we had shared, albeit at different times in our lives. He had managed Austin's illness alone as a single parent and that was worthy of both my admiration and respect. He now lived with a southern belle named Lisa who, like everyone else who had met Alex, was touched by him. Chris and Lisa spent time with us and they regularly brought their miniature Maltese terrier to visit.

Troy and I spent the most time together and the close relationship forged between Alex and Troy was duplicated between Troy and I too. He was an outdoors man and shared Alex's love of nature and wild places. I often spent long periods of time just listening to Alex and Troy talk about birds, fish and the wild untamed animals of the American continent. Troy shared his personal experiences in those wild places with Alex and he would listen transfixed, as would I. Troy spent quality time with Alex and took him to nature whenever he had a break from his hospital regimen and more so when I was back in the U.K.

John seemed to change the most during our time with him. When he first met him, he was very reserved and was a man of few words. At first, he shared very little with us with regards to everything about himself (including his personality) but as we spent time together he allowed us brief views into his life and into who he was. Towards the end of our stay we had become firm friends and forged a friendship that would last a lifetime. He is a simple man but with such depth. I only wished I had known the real John much earlier. John and his wife Leah became very close to us and we cherished the few short weeks that we finally knew them. Alex and John grew very fond of each other and Alex was extremely upset when he said his goodbyes at the airport when it was time to come home.

It was interesting, that after such a short period, these officers became so close to us that we would spend a lot of time with them off duty and they would help us then also: getting Alex to appointments and supporting him to visit interesting places during his time out of hospital.

Another thing that was interesting and amusing was their conversion, like so many Americans that became part of our lives, to English tea. When we first offered it the look of revulsion on their faces to tea with milk and brown sugar was priceless but once tasted they were fans. I recall when they visited they would become accustomed to an English tea so much so that if we had an appointment they would arrive early to allow them to enjoy a cup before we had to set off!

We also were amused and strangely enraptured with two U.K. shops in the Kansas area: 'Redcoats' and 'The Brit'. They were interesting places that sold everything from H.P. Sauce to Beatles records on vinyl. They also sold one of Alex's favourite snacks... Hula Hoops! We purchased a box of them. One of Alex's followers Janet from the Missouri area who was also an Air Stewardess visited us and brought Alex a top up of the salty potato snack from a recent trip to London!

We very quickly fell into a routine of hospital visits and attendance and either Maruška or I would be with Alex while the other remained most of the time with Sophia. We were both very conscious of Sophia's mindset in all this huge upheaval which was, in effect, a move to another country and a new, albeit temporary, home. She had spent a great amount of time in Alex's shadow already back in the U.K. and out of sheer necessity our focus had been on Alex. Her character had changed and she became, out of her own necessity, more outgoing and at times more persistent. We made an effort to engage with her more and make her feel wanted and loved, particularly as we were thousands of miles from anything she knew: nursery, Grandmas, her favourite toys etc. The first part of our stay in the U.S. was spent at the Wetzel's house where we felt welcome, loved, safe and truly at home and this comfort had soothed Sophia also. This was only a temporary arrangement however, as we were going to stay at a Ronald McDonald charity house near to the hospital.

Our move to the Ronald McDonald House was done with a heavy heart. The staff welcomed us with open arms and were very kind but it didn't feel like home, or more precisely a surrogate home. Our first night there was a difficult one. Alex wasn't in hospital and the apartment we had was only two rooms and a bathroom. The large bedroom had two double beds which meant that none of us managed any sleep. Alex was awake at least every hour or so needing support, medication and reassurance and this woke everyone up including Sophia.

Lou and Jane came to visit us while we were at the Ronald McDonald house and despite our attempts not to burden them with the issues we had there, they insisted we move back in with them: even if it was just until we arranged somewhere else to stay. Attempting to contain our relief and excitement we moved back in immediately.

Whilst this was happening and within a few days of our arrival, Alex had been receiving chemotherapy treatment in Children's Mercy Hospital and had stayed throughout the week. It still dominated our days and nights even thousands of miles away from home and that hadn't changed. The nursing staff were amazing and very friendly. They were busy and flitted between rooms and between patients but they were kind and attentive. Things seemed to get done quicker in the U.S. and this was, in my opinion, down to numbers of nurses on the ward. The major difference for us personally, putting aside of course the clearly superior facilities, was this sense of involvement and association with the treatment.

Meanwhile, Alex's popularity continued! The huge reception at the airport was not an isolated incident and the interest from local media and the public continued unabated. We held a "press conference" in the playroom of the ward where Alex was receiving his chemotherapy treatment. Several TV stations and the local newspaper, the Kansas City Star were there. Alex was his usual charming self and he answered questions whilst being filmed painting and decorating a porcelain Christmas tree. The reporter, Donna McGuire of the Kansas City Star was there and she would be one of the regular faces that would become familiar to us. It was still unusual to me that the plight of a young British boy would gain so much attention. The support and interest from the media was nothing new to us but it was amplified here tenfold. It would become clear to me over the following months that the media stations were simply reacting to the sheer outpouring of support that we had received from the people of Kansas and Missouri who had taken Alex into their hearts.

As soon as Alex had arrived he had recommenced his chemotherapy and as soon as he was able, he would have the first surgery. This meant he was in hospital and ill or tired often. The chemotherapy made him more vulnerable to virus and other airborne nasties so we had to keep visits and visitors, aside from Lou and Jane and Chief Terry, to a minimum and only when a window of opportunity presented itself. This meant we had dozens of disappointed people who had contacted us wanting to meet him. This was difficult, but we hoped people would understand.

We had a similar problem here that we had experienced in the U.K. with complete strangers reaching out and wishing to visit. You have to find a balance, we didn't want to push away good kind people that wanted to meet Alex and help us on our journey but we had to be careful. I took some comfort from the fact that most of them were part of the thin blue line and that made exposing Alex to the unknown a little easier.

We had visitors from K.C.K.P.D. and surrounding police departments and their families. They were kind and they seemed genuine. They came bearing gifts of toys and home-made and home-baked goods that ranged from blankets to cookies. All were friendly and I actually enjoyed the conversations and time we had. Alex was tired and suffering from the chemotherapy and we were ever mindful of how susceptible to illness he was, but he always managed a smile and enjoyed the company when he was strong enough.

Alex missed spending time with children. Sophia was lucky because Jane and Lou had a granddaughter around Sophia's age who would come and play on occasion while we were at the Wetzel's. We also managed to organise nursery school locally for Sophia and she enjoyed that too. Alex however spent most of his time with adults and I think that, as well as the life-threatening battle he was fighting, matured him ahead of time. Chris, a Westwood Cop and his son Cody came to visit Alex in hospital. Cody was much older than Alex but they shared an interest in Pokémon and other similar games. Alex enjoyed the company and they played sometimes for hours.

174

Chris and I talked about the job and about his English heritage (his family had come from Warwickshire nearly two centuries earlier). His wife, Mariette and her two daughters Bella and Alexandria, would become close friends of ours and Maruška and Mariette spent lots of time together. We wouldn't meet Mariette or the girls until after Alex's surgery.

But despite the company and attention Alex was here to keep up the fight and to win. His first six days of chemotherapy treatment began on the 16th December and was full of memorable experiences!

On the 17th December Alex had a visit that night, whilst Maruška was with him, from a number of Kansas Highway Patrol State Troopers and none other than Father Christmas/Santa Claus himself! They brought gifts for Alex and I was surprised to learn that Trooper Ben (the first U.S. cop to send Alex a video message whilst we were still back in the U.K.) was not among them. It would be a few days later when he would make the trip to Kansas City to meet Alex and me. The events of that evening were so significant and were a measure of who Alex was. I cannot describe the tremendous pride and love I had for my son as I watched the video Maruška had recorded and sent to me. I am watching it now as I write this piece and it catches me every single time. When asked by Santa what he wanted for Christmas Alex replied…

"I want everyone to keep cheering me on and be happy, that's what my first present would be, for everyone to be happy. Be well, and I want no one to have the same cancer as me so I want to help them. If anyone here has this type of cancer I would, if they set up a Twitter, I would give money to them. To help them, those in need".

Santa Claus's reply, as he tried to stifle his own emotional response to that heartfelt and innocently kind message reiterated my thoughts at that moment:

"You're a special young man, I hope that you have a great Christmas. I hope your recovery is fast".

This was a measure of my son: Alex the kind, Alex the loving, Alex the selfless.

Alex then offered to get him a mince pie and milk with some carrots for his reindeer to which, still emotionally unstable, Santa uttered that he would prefer a chocolate chip cookie to a mince pie (the cops thought we were referring to a meat filled pie but traditionally Christmas mince pies, dating back to a 300+ year old recipe, are full of sweet dried glazed fruits and spices).

To this day Alex still believes that was the real Father Christmas that had come to visit him. He would tell us that he felt very special and that the real Santa had made time to come himself rather than send one of his helpers.

On the 18th December, I was staying overnight with Alex at the hospital and whilst he slept, I came outside for a breath of fresh air. When you spend long hours in a room it is essential to get outside and find a change of scenery whenever the opportunity should arise. I walked outside into the freezing night. It was dark and it had been snowing. I was alone, all the traffic of patients and cars coming and going were gone and I stood in silence savouring the stillness and freshness of the air. The forecourt was bathed in the richness of Christmas lights and I looked at the elaborate signage for the hospital that contained a diorama of children's toys. I reflected on the journey to date and how far we had come. It was Christmas soon and in truth I had never even considered what that meant for us in another country away from family and friends. I felt we were in the right place and despite everything I knew being so far away, I recognised this was where we needed to be. I remember videoing that moment outside on my mobile phone and posting it onto my social media account.

The following day, the 19th December was another day of note. Alex had a visit from the K.C.K.P.D.'s mascot LEO the Lion (ingenious use of the acronym for Law Enforcement Officer). The cop behind the costume was Tommy and occasionally Cameron. I was surprised just how much Alex loved the visit. He was excited and hugged LEO constantly. This reminded me that he was still a little boy, trapped in a situation that had torn his childhood from him. I wanted, desperately, to find a way of giving it back to him. LEO would visit Alex again and attended his birthday party many months later.

More sentimental for me was our next visitor that day. Kansas Highway State Trooper Ben. Ben was the first U.S. cop to send Alex a video message: it was a powerful message of support for Alex and an affirmation that he was with him on the journey. Ben and I had exchanged messages whilst I was in the U.K. and I was keen to finally meet him face to face. Ben was a very impressive and bold looking man. His uniform, including his leather Sam Brown belt and broad rimmed hat, harked back to another age, but now it was equipped with covert vest, pistol and taser-instruments of a modern policing era.

Ben had explained prior to his arrival that he was being accompanied by a camera crew and a reporter called Shawn Wheat from a TV station called WIBW and they wanted to run a piece about Ben and Alex that evening. He asked if that was okay and if not they would wait outside. Alex and I agreed. Ignoring the camera Ben and I embraced as friends and spoke warmly with each other. Alex was pleased to see him too and they seemed to speak comfortably with each other. It was obvious Ben had kids of his own and was accustomed to the presence of TV cameras. We would see Ben again before our trip home and I am glad about that. I also managed to ensure he was converted to English tea drinking too!

Almost as soon as we had arrived the TV stations local to Kansas and Missouri had run pieces about Alex. Three TV stations: KCTV 5, KMBC 9 and Fox 4 would become major supporters of Alex whilst we were in the U.S. and we would form friendships with a few of their anchors on the journey. That evening Alex and I watched the news article from our hospital room TV. It was an event that would become more regular as we spent more time in the U.S. and I would never get used to it. Not only was he a star of social media, now he was on TV and in every living room in the Kansas area!

On 20th December, we had a surprise visit from Tina and Denise from the Make a Wish foundation in Missouri. They had arranged a trip to Florida for Alex! We could stay at the Give Kids The World (G.K.T.W.) resort there and visit Disney World! We were both surprised and delighted. I made sure they were aware he was from England and not a native but they assured me that he was eligible because he was a patient in Missouri. We would fly out after his chemotherapy treatment before he had his first surgery. It was a small window of a week but it was so exciting. We would fly out on 30th December and return on the 8th January. We were staying at the G.K.T.W. resort from the 2nd for a week but we were able to supplement our visit with money we had raised so we would spend the first few days in Disney World itself!

We met Noni and her mum, Yvonne, for the first time the following day. They would visit several times during our stay in the U.S. and become part of the core group of friends who got heavily involved in fundraising for us. Noni's brother Chris would also come over and play games with Alex. Noni wished to help us fundraise using her fledgling fabric company 'Princess Pineapple' to make some "Alex" and "Sophia" pillow covers. Alex's had owls on them and Sophia's had flowers. She was clearly skilled in this area and wanted to help to raise funds. Noni had her own crosses to bear and despite being an articulate, kind and well-rounded human being she was afflicted with her own medical challenges. I admired her strength of character and her generosity of spirit. She was yet again another person, fighting their own battles who was inspired and motivated to step up and help my son; a complete stranger. We sold numerous pillow cases on our web site and everyone who purchased one helped to raise the funds we so desperately needed.

His first week of chemotherapy was complete and we headed back to the Wetzel's home. Our TV and newspaper appearance had reached the attention of two completely different people who would be impactive on Alex's life. Through the Kansas City Star and then K.C.K.P.D. we had messages from a lady called Kim Hess from the Lakeside Nature Centre and Audrey, an English woman who had moved to Kansas just after the Second world war.

Kim had noticed that Alex had a passion for birds of prey and extended an invitation for Alex to visit the nature centre where she was director. So much was happening at the time so I made a brief call to her thanking her for the kind offer and asked if we could take her up on that offer when Alex was feeling stronger and we could plan our time. She agreed and would await our call. I am so glad that I did contact her some time later as she became a powerful force in Alex's well-being and someone whom Alex would come to adore along with a group of owls: Hootie, Darwin and Legacy that she looked after.

Audrey had written to Alex and informed us that she had seen the news and watched him arrive in Kansas City. She was not a user of social media so everything she had heard about Alex was from the TV and newspaper. I read her letter out to Alex and he listened as I relayed her recount of her own journey after the second world war from England to Kansas. She hoped to meet us while we were in the U.S. but it would be several more letters and cards later before that would come to fruition.

We had received dozens of well wishes and prayers through Alex's social media and Chief Terry informed us that literally hundreds of cards and letters were arriving at his police department for Alex. This attention was still surprising but also gratifying. Support for our son continued to grow and that could never be a bad thing. I knew social media was a double-edged sword but for the most it had been a powerful force for good when it came to Alexander's Journey. One thing was for certain, Alex's popularity was growing...

I remember coming downstairs the following morning after we had returned from hospital to the Wetzel's house. As I made a cup of tea I observed the latest edition of the Kansas City Star on the kitchen side. Donna McGuire's article about Alex was on the front page. The front page! It amazed me and astounded me as to how or why that would happen. I remember reading the captions that occupied the front page "Islamic State claims attack on market" and "Alex is amazed by KC's kindness". Unbelievable!

Officers from numerous police departments visited us throughout our stay and many came around Christmas time. K.C.K.P.D. officers would regularly drop in cards and parcels periodically and particularly in those first few weeks of our arrival. I also remember Major Reece and a number of deputies from the Johnson County Sheriff's Office (J.C.S.O.) visited on the 22nd December bearing a great many gifts, cards and messages of support for Alex. K.C.K.P.D. and J.C.S.O. had both, very kindly, offered to take in cards, gifts and presents for Alex to avoid us giving Dr. Wetzel's home address to the numerous well-wishers who were supporting us.

Alex received, via J.C.S.O. and K.C.K.P.D., lots of cards and drawings from local elementary schools in both Wyandotte and Johnson County as well as letters and drawings from a local prison! Chief Terry had 'thank you' letters typed up for Alex to sign for the hundreds of well-wishers who had made the effort to send him something.

Our overnight stays had finished for a week or so but we still had daily visits to Children's Mercy Hospital for blood tests and booster injections just like in the U.K.

Tim from the Kansas City Chiefs visited the house on 23rd December with some gifts for Alex and Sophia. Rather marvellously, he offered us tickets to the playoffs match but Alex was in hospital. I meekly proffered that I could go but that didn't seem to cut the mustard. It would appear that Alex was the celebrity they wanted, not his old dad. Not even a cup of English tea would win that battle for me!

At home back in the U.K. we would have spent Christmas Eve with Maruška's family and enjoyed a traditional Slovakian meal as well as opened up a present each (as is the Slavic custom). Alas this year, the two weeks of treatment and then numerous visits caught up with Alex and he spent the whole of Christmas Eve resting. We did have a visit from one of the cops from Roeland Park PD and his wife and daughter. Don, Kim and Dakota would be part of the core of friends that worked so tirelessly to support us through fundraising while we were there. Don was on the escort the night we arrived and he and his wife came back to the Wetzel's with us that first night. Now when I look back at the photos and video footage I can see them there. They had brought some extra special Christmas presents for Alex and Sophia. Sophia loved the Princess Castle dolls house that they brought her. It made the journey home with us as a priority and now has pride of place in her new butterfly bedroom.

Don and I formed a friendship, I wouldn't say that we were very close but we seemed to get each other. I respected him as a man who had walked the walk and he put his advice rather well. He had retired from one police department and then joined another part time! He was one of the few people who even after a beer or two actually listened to what you were saying instead of just waiting for his time to talk. When I was considering a possible future in the U.S. a few months later he was one of a handful of cops that I debated the finer points with over a beers.

Christmas morning was a real experience! We woke early and went downstairs into a room full of presents! Alex and Sophia opened up some of their gifts at the Wetzel's house but they decided they would wait with the rest because Jane and Lou had gone to church and we were going out for the day. We were then picked up by Chief Terry and went to his house for Christmas lunch and spent time with him and his wife. We also met Kramer! Kramer was an old Cockatoo that Chief Terry had adopted by accident. Kramer had appeared in his yard one day and he had stayed there ever since! Despite Chief Terry's prior attempts to return him to the wild he kept coming back.

I remember Terry recounting a story where he had homed Kramer in his study temporarily and had then decided to return him whence he came. He cast Kramer out into the big wide world and watched him fly off into the distance. He then retold how he could just make out this tiny speck in the sky appear to circle round and start heading back. That speck in the sky, became Kramer, clearly visible back in his yard and at his porch. Alex and Kramer seemed to have a rapport and he was an old bird content with perching on Alex and enjoying the moment. I swear at times they seemed to watch TV or the Ipad together. Months later Kramer joined us at the Mariott where we would stay and became Alex's pet in residence during our stay there.

That Christmas day morning whilst at Chief Terry's house we were visited by Scott from the Fraternal Order of Policing (like the Police Federation in the U.K.) for K.C.K.P.D. who wished us well and brought even more presents. He also brought along with him a gift and a short note for Alex and Sophia from the family of Captain Melton. This was touching. I felt I have so much to say to the families of both Captain Melton and Detective Lancaster but, for now, I don't have the words. Maruška would meet his sister at a bake sale fundraiser for Alex at the end of January.

I enjoyed the afternoon relaxing with Terry and we talked of the coming months and the obstacles that lay ahead. We also talked of battling them together.

Boxing Day was spent at the Wetzel's and the family was around. We watched the Chiefs game and played Top Trumps (a card game from the U.K. that was unheard of by everyone we met in the U.S.). We enjoyed goose and wild duck (thanks to Troy). All the Wetzel family were there and we had a wonderful festive meal photo taken. They were good people and they made an effort to spend time with Alex and Sophia. I remember, later in the year at Alex's birthday party, Alex playing some of his favourite Rock songs to some of the family during one of their regular Top Trump tournaments. After a few minutes, the music was turned up, the speakers in both the inside and outside of the house were blasting out AC/DC and Dr. Wetzel and several of his off-spring and their partners were rocking out with Alex. That was a wonderful, albeit strange sight. One that will remain etched and cherished in my mind's eye.

On the 28th December, Chief Terry had arranged a reception for us at his force headquarters where so many of his officers and staff had come to see us. I attended in my police tunic and that went down well with the majority of officers who wanted a photo with me in this rather archaic uniform and traditional police hat that personified the British Bobby across the world.

Later that day we, following an invite to appear on his show, met DJ Nightmare at the Black Sky Radio studios in Kansas City. DJ Nightmare was a bear of a man: the stereotypical Rock DJ. It took all of a few minutes for Alex to get under this tough exterior and he came to visit us a few times in the months ahead. He made Alex a raptor whistle from antler horn for his birthday in May and Alex would cherish that gift from that day onward. At our first visit to DJ Nightmare's studio we were joined by two of the Kansas City Chief's Cheerleaders who, after just ten minutes with Alex, had become the latest victims of his adolescent charms. They were as kind as they were attractive and I even managed to get a photo with them. They gave me a few calendars including a rather splendid one which had been autographed by the whole cheerleader team. I neglected to raffle that one in particular and decided to keep it. I felt it was a reasonable consolation prize for failing to secure the playoff tickets in Alex's absence!

That week after Christmas Sophia got her Cowgirl boots from Cavender's, the self-proclaimed Western Outfitter in Kansas City. Alex received, as a gift, a Cowboy hat from them too which, to be honest, was actually rather awesome and very well made. Photos of him in that hat and his Wyandotte County Sheriff's top made the evening news that week. What a celebrity he was!

However, in the middle of this we had to go back to Children's Mercy on the 29th for blood tests and checks. As a treat, we went to

Chief Terry's house and we were visited there by the Make a Wish Missouri ladies Tina and Denise who gave us the tickets for our flight to Give Kids The World (G.K.T.W.) and Disney! The following day we were flying out! Once again, we were given an amazing reception, this time by Florida Highway Patrol (F.H.P.) and Orlando Police as we arrived at airport. It had been arranged by Trooper Steve of the F.H.P. who had been following Alex for some time. He was there with several other officers. Lining up alongside them was Phil Cooper who was a retired police officer from Warwickshire, I couldn't believe my eyes when I saw this British Bobby standing with the Florida Cops resplendent in his tunic. He had worked with my Inspector when she was young in service and now he had retired out in the sunshine and volunteered with his wife Joanne at G.K.T.W. What a small world we live in!

The trip had come at the right time. We had finished chemotherapy for now and the tremendous obstacle of the surgery was the next step. We had a window to take stock. The trip was one of both highs and lows for Alex. We arrived for a few days stay at the Animal Kingdom and Alex loved it. He fought back his fatigue and was completely enraptured with the place. It was natural for him to love it and I wouldn't have expected anything else really. After those few days his exhaustion caught up with him and he spent a long time recovering. We spent the rest of the week staying at the G.K.T.W. resort in Kissimmee, just 12 miles or so from Disney World. Give Kids The World Village is a non-profit resort for children with life threatening illnesses and their families. The staff at G.K.T.W., mostly volunteers, were passionate about what they did. It was a strange time for Alex, he still had his Hickman Line and couldn't play in the swimming pools as he wanted, he was also exhausted much of the time. Another thing that was difficult for him was seeing so many other children who were so ill at the resort. He was inquisitive and was burning with questions and concern about the welfare of the other children there, particularly those who were in wheelchairs or who were without limbs. He was clearly anxious about it. He would ask "Is that what will happen to me?" "Are they alright?" "Did their surgery hurt?"

This was my son, who, despite wrestling with his own fears, cared more for others than for himself. This was Alex the compassionate, Alex the considerate, Alex the thoughtful.

We returned from warm and sunny Florida in the second week of January to snow in Kansas and the kids were playing in the back garden at the Wetzel's building snowmen. Strange how just a few days before we had been in the beautiful sunshine and had travelled for just over two hours by airplane. The contrast was really difficult to get our heads around – shorts to scarves in a couple of timezones.

Twenty

Alex was back at hospital on the 10th January and met his favourite nursing assistant David. I liked David, we all liked him. He was an easy going, soft spoken but rough looking kind of guy. He, like me, had refused to let go of some of the passions he had as a child and teenager and he and Alex would often debate who was the strongest superhero, who would win in a fight, what colour lightsabres were the coolest and other random distractions that would lead Alex away from the routine of medicine and tests and into a more appealing realm in his mind. We were so pleased it was David who did the final checks before the surgery the following day. Alex was terrified and this helped calm him and see that everything would be ok.

David became a friend to Alex and I recall that when I had returned to the U.K. and Alex was very emotional he had turned to David for comfort and consolation. Maruška told me that Alex had said to David that he was fond of him because he reminded him of me.

David, many months later in April 2017, invited us to the Kansas City Comi-con, a huge annual event celebrating comic book culture and science fiction. Alex, dressed as Iron Man, and I, dressed as myself, went as VIP guests. We were taken around by a gang of superheroes and Star Wars and Manga cosplayers who were, frankly, superb companions for the day. Dressed up as Spiderman, David was also part of that group. Alex hadn't recognised David who, to be fair, had gone to great lengths to mask his real voice as well as donning the costume all day. Another David was with us on that day, better known to Alex as Wolverine. Alex had met this cosplayer in March at Kansas City Zoo but on that occasion, he was Captain America. David (Wolverine) contacted us after the event at Kansas City Zoo praising Alex's courage and character. He would also attend Alex's party the following month as Wolverine. As we reached the end of our time at Comi-con David (Spiderman) revealed himself to Alex by removing his mask. Alex cried and hugged him so tightly. I was so proud of him. He had been so ill over the days prior to us going and I didn't know if he would make it there.

Despite ulcers, chronic crippling fatigue and pain we went because Alex insisted we did. He endured and smiled and was happy. Alex the resilient. Alex the irrepressible. Alex the superhero.

11th January was the big day. Day of the surgery. We had woken Alex early and he had become accustomed to the ritual of feeling ill and tired and aching and having to gather his strength for another day of tests, treatment and checks. Today he seemed very nervous but extremely focussed. I had mentioned that we needed to post a video that morning before he went into surgery to put on Social Media as all his supporters would be thinking about him… After a moment to think, he said he wanted to do the video there and then. So, in the early morning of his bedroom, with the curtains closed, he did a quick video. The video started off as normal and then he said, *"today is the day I defeat this cancer."* He then explained how the surgery would remove the majority, some 90% of the cancer and then repeated what I had told him was happening for the benefit of the social media viewers. Then after asking for positive thoughts he spoke for himself, unrehearsed unprepared or predetermined.

"So guys, this is the most important day of my life, so please keep those positive thoughts higher than you've ever done before".

He looked pensive, worried and meek. He gave a thin smile as he said his goodbye to my mobile phone lens. The response that day on social media was amazing. The video had over 40,000 views and he received well wishes and prayers from hundreds of people on Twitter and Facebook. He received a wonderful video message from Peter, Lou and Jane's son, who is an elementary school teacher, standing with his school class, wishing Alex well. Sophia had been preoccupied that day with Jane taking her to nursery. Sophia loved it and felt very welcome. It was the right place for her to be. She didn't need to know what Alex had to face and the more normal we could make the day for her the better.

Alex was very nervous and physically upset. We had Chief Terry and his wife with us and Dr. Lou and Jane were never far away. The surgery lasted over six hours and was agonising for us as his parents. We sat, waiting in a small side room, at the hospital as our son went through such challenging surgery. We had placed the care, the very life of our son into the hands of one man, Dr. Rosenthal. We waited hoping for the best outcome. We felt that thousands of people were with us on that day. Local media were there in force as well, and Jill Chadwick, the K.U. press and media person, was around managing that whole media circus. Jill was a very useful person to know. She had previously worked in the media industry at the sharp end and clearly had a good grasp of how to handle the media and the flow of information to and from them. Cliff, another all-round decent chap from Jill's team, had captured the footage from the surgery on camera.

The surgery was a success but Alex was drained. The long and painful process of recovery, healing and rehabilitation would now begin. He spent his first 24 hours in Paediatric Intensive Care until being transferred onto regular paediatric ward. He had lots of tubes in him and looked exhausted. He had an epidural. He always seemed to have visitors - not necessarily friends - but medical professionals in some guise or another. A constant flow of experts, consultants, checking on him from their medical perspective. Physiotherapists began the long process of getting him out and using the leg, despite his fears and anxieties. We were told that he needed to use it as quickly as possible and start to put weight on it in a managed progressive way. We were presented with photos of the surgery taking place and we received a rather unsettling but informative close up of the diseased femur that they had removed. I couldn't believe that had been taken from my son. I can't deny it still haunts me to think what could have happened if it had been allowed to remain in his leg… It was painful and upsetting to see but we had drawn comfort that Alex was alive and this was now about healing and recovering not fighting or trying to stop the cancer from winning. This was Alex's battle with himself, for himself. The nurses that looked after him immediately after his surgery have a special place in my heart. They were so patient, attentive, kind and warm spirited with him. Some of them now continue on the journey with us on social media. They know who they are and I thank them.

Alex continued to heal, recover and had daily intensive and demanding physio. He needed to manipulate the leg and on top of it all, his prosthetic femur was slightly longer than his original one. It was an adult prosthesis that provided him with a gap for his growth before he could have the second surgery.

Dr. Rosenthal invited Maruska and I in to share the good news that the surgery had been a great success. Not only had the primary tumour been completely resected but necrosis (kill rate) of the tumour was 100%. 100%! That was a statistic I liked! The entire tumour was dead. Furthermore, he had managed to complete the elements of the second surgery that had been planned on the acetabulum during the first procedure. The spread of disease hadn't been as bad as he had anticipated and he had also managed to retain the shape and structure of the cup area of the acetabulum in the pelvic bone as well as remove the diseased area. The acetabulum had retained it shape sufficiently to allow the ball joint of the prosthetic femur head to still fit correctly there. Three planned surgeries had become two, which meant that only one remained.

Dr. Rosenthal came to see Alex at the hospital on Sunday 16th of January. It was unusual because he came in casuals! He had a shirt and jeans on and was clearly not at work that day. It was nice and it made me like him more for it. He spoke in a more relaxed manner and more openly to Alex as well as checking his leg. He also changed the dressing on Alex's leg. This was an eye opener for me as I couldn't imagine for one second one of the doctors doing such a thing in the U.K. - either to come in on their day off to check up on a patient in a more relaxed situation or to change the dressing of a patient. He spoke of when he was a small boy of Alex's age, his parent's family business and his favourite foods!

The leg was healing well but the process was slower than normally because he was still dealing with the remnants of the chemotherapy in his body. This slows down the healing process. Physio continued with the same vigour and Alex disliked it immensely. When his leg had healed sufficiently he was discharged from the hospital to rest and heal at the Wetzel's but he had to continue with the physio. The physio was essential, the team at KU managed this at first whilst he an inpatient there but after his discharge Dr. Rosenthal chose the Physiotherapy department at Children's Mercy to continue with the program to make sure his leg was strengthened and would bend and straighten correctly. It was also used to bring the feeling back to his nerves that had to repair following the surgery where muscles and tendons had been severed and nerves manipulated. Physical therapy and medication were part of the treatment plan.

However, the cancer treatment plan remained and not only would Alex have to have limited consolidation chemotherapy but radiation therapy also. This was in addition to the intensive and sometimes brutal physiotherapy. The leg needed to be straightened to stop it seizing up. The plan had always been to get him out of the wheelchair and the aspiration was to one day have him walking; perhaps with the aid of a walking cane but walking all the same. This was a long way from a "significant loss of functionality" as predicted with the surgery proposed back in the UK.

I remember him having regular sessions that he feared. Chris, his usual physiotherapist, had the patience of a saint as Alex tried every aspect of creative thinking he could to get out of the more intense elements of the treatment plan. The physio was a mixture of dry manipulation and treatment in the pool. The leg straightening involved weights but also direct pressure and this was painful and frightening for Alex. I remember him screaming out in pain as direct pressure was applied to the prosthetic knee to straighten it. But it was necessary. He had to leave the wheel chair behind. He had to walk.

The gifts and presents continued to roll in to both the hospital and to home via K.C.K.P.D. and other police departments. We tried to take photos with them all and thank the people on social media, but it was difficult keeping up especially when he was in hospital so often. We found ourselves having piles of letters and parcels that needed opening. We felt awful because people had gone to the effort of sending it, caring enough, and we wanted them to know we were grateful for the effort and it was appreciated. As the backlog grew we would get the occasional contact via email or social media messaging with people enquiring as to whether we had actually received the letter, gift, parcel they had sent weeks earlier! I would like to take this opportunity to thank everyone who sent in gifts for Alex at this time. It was great for his morale and recovery. Thank you.

Alex was healing and exercising and enjoying the company of his family and our extended family at the Wetzel's house. He was using his walker and received regular physio at the hospital and daily physio from Maruška or myself that had been outlined to us by the hospital. He was still very sore and taking a tremendous amount of pain relief.

The support we were receiving was phenomenal. From the start of our journey months earlier back in the U.K. we were receiving police patches, t-shirts and other items of memorabilia including from the U.S. challenge coins. Challenge coins are something that were unfamiliar to us before we came to America and are coins or medallions usually associated with the military but also, in the U.S., with the police services. Alex and I would spend hours sorting through our police patches and challenge coins. We decided that when we were both home, we would select our favourite coins and put them in a presentation case. I remember putting out a request on social media for challenge coins and receiving an amazing response. We now have literally hundreds of them! Some are beautiful in their design, some are emotive, some are interesting because of who they came from. All of them were gratefully received.

Whilst we were occupied with getting Alex recovered from such major surgery, a group of women, the wives of Kansas police officers, were busy raising money for Alex through bake sales. They were connected to the Sheriff's Office's in Johnson County and neighbouring Miami County as well as Roeland Park. This was at a scale I had never seen before and they had laboured at it with such vigour it left me humbled by their commitment. These women included Kim (Don's wife) and her daughter Dakota as well as Laura, Bridget, Teri, Keri and Katy. They were baking pies, cakes and pastries on an almost industrial scale and had also sought the support of local catering and baking companies to acquire donations of their products to sell for Alex too. They had travelled across the police forces in that region selling their wares and raising money for Alex. In a stroke of fundraising excellence, they had also got the support of the local Olathe branch of a national outdoor pursuits chain of shops called Bass Pro who would allow us to have a bake sale event at their store on the 20th and 21st January 2017.

Thanks, primarily to Teri (the husband of Scott, a retired detective from Johnson County Sheriff's Office) the bake sale had received lots of press attention and several of the local TV stations would be there covering the event. We had to be there and Alex wanted to be there to show his support - if he was strong enough. He had just undergone major surgery a week previously, so that gave us little time. There was a huge turnout and lots of support. Noni and Yvonne were there too and set up a stall to sell pillowcases for Alex. Mariette and her family came aswell.

In addition to the hundreds of off-duty cops that were there over those two days, dozens of officers in uniform from the forces in the surrounding area stopped by to show their support. The Sheriff's from Johnson County and Miami County also attended to show their support. It was surreal as I sipped tea and talked about Alex's journey with Sheriff Hayden, Chief Terry Zeigler and Sheriff Kelly (some of the most powerful and respected men in the room) and the differences and similarities of the job one country to another.

We would attend on the 21st January. Chief Terry picked us up and we travelled with him. Alex was sore that day but was keen to make an appearance. I remember foolishly catching his foot when I was getting him out of the car and into his wheelchair. That made him terribly sore and he left after staying as long as he could possibly endure. You could not tell from the photos taken on that day that he was in so much pain and discomfort. He wanted to stay to make sure everyone that had helped knew how happy he was to see them and how grateful he was that they were helping him.

The event at Bass Pro Shop was an epiphany for Maruška and I. We had arrived in Kansas to a tremendous fanfare of support that had, truthfully, been overwhelming. We had focussed our attention on Alex and his important yet challenging treatment, almost failing to notice the support that was there with us, every step of the way. We weren't aware of the massive effort people were going to for Alex, for our son, whom they had never met, to help him live and thrive. That was truly chastening. These people cared about him, were inspired and motivated by him. They were moved by him to do what they could for him.

The bake sale sowed the seed for us to move ahead with the next piece of merchandise to raise money for Alex. The people that were running the bake sale wore special "Alexander's Journey" t-shirts that had the U.S. flag and the Warwickshire Police Queen's crown and crest. As well as the thin blue line, it proudly proclaimed that "In this family, no one fights alone". We were given them too and we wore them with pride during the day. Several people attending the bake sale asked if they could buy the t-shirts but they were not for sale. The demand however did prompt us to move ahead with a specific Alexander's Journey t-shirt that could be sold to raise funds for Alex. The bake sale not only made me realise that we had so much perpetual and constant support but also connected me to so many people who became close friends and would walk side by side with us throughout Alex's journey.

Teri and Scott were introduced to us on that day. I had communicated with Teri on social media in the weeks prior to the event but this was when I finally put a face to the name. Teri is an exceptional woman. Whilst not a cop, I suspect she probably was in a former life! She is a petite woman but what she lacked in size she completely makes up for in personality, strength of character and

193

generosity of spirit. She is also a skilled markswoman who also bakes one of the tastiest cherry pies I have ever tasted and one of just a few people that was able to compete with Jane Wetzel in the dessert making department!

Scott, her husband and retired detective from J.C.S.O. was a man of hidden depths. He had a wicked sense of humour and was quite happy to ruffle the occasional feather or two to deliver a propitious and killer punchline. He often wore a cowboy hat and boots. We talked about American history and he shared interesting stories with me on some of the people I had read about as a child including Wyatt Earp and the James and Younger Brothers. I liked Scott and so did Alex: he was an outdoors man like Troy and he and Teri would often, much to Maruška's delight, bring organic home-grown vegetables for her and Alex to enjoy. Teri and Scott were such a support for Alex and Maruška particularly when I was back in the U.K. It is thanks to them that Alex finally, a few months after the bake sale, would go to the Lakeside Nature Centre on the 9th March 2017.

I also met Frank Kelly, the Sheriff of Miami County, whose wife Laura had worked so tirelessly to help make the bake sale a success. Sheriff Kelly was a good man and I was immediately drawn to his strong but gracious personality. We also met his son, Matt, who was a Sergeant and Sheriff's Deputy. I liked Matt, they say the apple never falls far the tree and it hadn't with Frank and his son.

These people spent time with us. We would go to their homes and as the Americans would say "visit" with them. Their kindness was genuine and their friendship real. Alex and Sophia created bonds of friendship with their children. Keri and her husband Brandon (a J.C.S.O. deputy) spent time with us and Alex spent time with their daughter Addy. He became rather fond of that girl. Sophia loved to play with Matt's daughter Preslei and was happy when Dakota or Noni gave her attention too.

We were surrounded by friendship in the U.S. and all these people became part of Alex's journey. At the centre was Lou Wetzel, Jane and Chief Terry as well as the officers from the motorcycle unit. Mariette would be part of that as we spent time together and a few other people that we were yet to meet would be included. All were cherished. These were bonds of friendship that we hoped would endure even when we returned to England.

Twenty-One

Now, at the end of January and the following months ahead, Alex was riding the crest of a wave of popularity and had appeared on television and radio so many times. He was gaining Twitter and Facebook supporters from a new group of supporters in the U.S. as well as keeping the support back in the U.K.

We had been running the social media accounts since June 2016 and some 15 months later, until he left the U.S. to return to England in August 2017 we had been fortunate really to have only had a handful of negative experiences on Twitter and Facebook.

Trolls! I always knew them as a cave dwelling creature but now it describes in the age of electronic communication, "a person who sows discord on the internet by starting quarrels or by upsetting people". Unfortunately, we had contact with at least four people over the course of this journey who met that criteria and a few other people who, whilst not Trolls, were certainly unpleasant, insensitive or simply seeking "conflict" or as they would probably put it "debate". Fortunately, as I filter most of the messages prior to Alex seeing them he didn't see the majority of them. He never checks them alone.

The first was when we were back in the U.K. in July 2016, on the same day we had reached 2,000 followers on Twitter as well as so many other memorable things around that time. Alex had commented that it was great that he had so many followers and he hoped to get more. A comment that could have been construed as attention seeking perhaps? But for a 9-year-old boy with cancer hardly a justifiable target for criticism. We received a tweet from someone based in England saying that "he has got more to worry about than getting more followers" or words to that effect. I didn't share this with Alex.

The second, while we were still in the U.K. was a comment to a photo I had put on of Alex and Sophia hugging each other and saying goodnight as Sophia left for home and Alex stayed with me in hospital overnight. It was thick with sarcasm and offensive stating that we were posting the standard "disabled child hugs sibling" photo or words to that effect. I was stunned and immediate to anger. I sent a message from my own account to this man asking if I had misconstrued his comments thinking surely that no one would say such inappropriate things. I was wrong. This man replied with what he assumed was some clever articulate riposte. Fortunately, as with the other Trolls our followers took all the action required and he shrivelled away into obscurity. This was a common theme and worked on all occasions to one degree or the other. Our supporters took the mantle and frankly hammered the miscreant into submission invoking either an apology or a cowardly shuffle aside with a cowed deletion of the post and usually a move to make their account private.

The other two Troll incidents occurred whilst we were in America with American posts. The third was from a woman who was staunchly defending her political position but then decided to bring Alex into the conversation. Stating that we (presumably British people) were criticising her President but we had the nerve to send 'this kid' to "our country". It was a little more colourful than that but this was the essence of it. I on this occasion replied directly from my personal account to her publicly. As did several hundred other Alex's journey supporters. She never replied to me but she almost immediately closed her account to private settings.

The final Troll was the most impactive. Alex had managed to get out onto Wyandotte County Lake and fish and a photo was taken of him in a lifejacket on the boat holding fish. A woman sent a scathing post from out of nowhere saying Alex was fat and that the poor fish was suffocating! Aside from the fact that Alex was skin and bone having just finished chemotherapy (albeit wearing a life jacket which could have given the impression of being fat) he was recovering from major surgery. He also loves and respects nature and the fish was returned to the water whence it came. She couldn't have been so wrong and if she bothered to just spend five minutes on his page she would have surely re-evaluated her post. On this occasion, we were looking at the feed together and this one slipped by: Alex had seen the post but was confused rather than upset. He assumed naively that the lady had made a mistake as he loved animals including fish and he wasn't fat.

I decided to place her post on our main page with Alex's reply as he had said it. The response was something I was ill prepared for. The woman was literally torn to shreds and, if I'm honest, I felt a little sorry for her (not too much though: you live by the sword, you die by the sword). The messages she received cut across the whole spectrum of Twitter users and covered a myriad of possible responses from death threats to pity. I could imagine her waking up the following morning to check her several hundred notifications and frankly wanting to get back into bed!

I believe that she could not ignore the tidal wave of responses as well as the media attention the post had received. She, reluctantly in my opinion, posted a message to us apologising for the post and offering to close her account. She blamed her ill health. This time it was slightly different however. Alex knew about it and like the deep reflector he is, he thought long about her comment and about her. He wanted to know more about her and I decided to show him her Twitter page. He immediately began a narrative to me as we looked at her profile and her posts: Alex picked up on the fact that she was an old lady and "looked nice" and that she "cared for animals especially dogs". I told Alex that she had said sorry and that she would close her account. He immediately replied distraught saying that she couldn't close her account because she is helping dogs. He asked to send her a video message. Cautiously I agreed. The message was completely unrehearsed like so many of his speeches and messages but I consoled myself with the fact that I could simply not send it if it wasn't appropriate. His message was wonderful, enchanting and supremely kind and gracious. He told her that he had forgiven her and she should keep her account open. He wished her well and smiled at her. It didn't come across as patronising as I suspect an adult sending that same message may have done. It was sincere. That message went viral and the episode was picked up by many TV stations and newspapers in both the U.K. and the U.S. All praising the response of my son who, despite the pain and suffering he had endured, wasn't bitter or wanting to strike out and punish anyone (and this would have been an ideal opportunity). He was the opposite. My son, Alex the gracious, Alex the forgiving, Alex the humane.

I realise, and so does Maruška, that when you open yourself up to the public, regardless of what you are doing, you open yourself up to public scrutiny. Everyone has an opinion and people love sharing that opinion with anyone that is prepared to listen. We had a few other people who shared the kind of opinion that we didn't appreciate, some on social media, others in the circle of colleagues that Maruška associated with where she had worked previously. These kinds of people frequent and scan social media often looking for a place to put their opinions and crush others. What I find amusing about social media is that everyone screams about their right to free speech and to say what they want, regardless of who it impacts upon, yet, ironically, they don't allow other people the same courtesy.

I recall one of Alex's followers who, despite following him would occasionally put in a slightly obtrusive tweet that whilst not overtly antagonistic was negative and likely to stir up some response. They could type and send the message from the safety of their own homes and then act all shocked when their message was "misunderstood" or was sent as a remark usually including the word "but".

This was also the case with Facebook. We had a comment asking "why we were fundraising when the NHS was free etc". I sent a detailed public reply which was then deleted by them as it clearly wasn't conducive to the debate they were trying to stoke.

I remember one Kansas City resident asking quite "innocently" why is Alex getting all this attention and others aren't? He was advised.

But these comments stood out so starkly like a black stain in a pool of white amidst the relentless flow of love, positivity and kindness.

Maruška had informed me on a few occasions that some former work colleagues who she had considered friends had spoken quite brutally about Alex and our situation. She had been informed by a number of her friends who still visited the centre where this group of people worked about what was being said.

i.   They had spoken cruelly saying that it was wrong that we had forced Alex to make videos or be photographed when he was so upset and in pain to invoke sympathy.
ii. They commented that it was inappropriate that we were travelling first class to the U.S. when we had raised money for Alex's treatment.
iii. They commented that as soon as we would return from the U.S. we would be "ripping" money out of the NHS because of the organisations shortcomings when it would just take more money out of the public purse.

If true, they had made harsh comments like so many people with only a fraction of the information or indeed the truth. But that didn't stop them. I could see them in my mind's eye like witches over a cauldron with nothing better to do than spit venom and bile at a situation they knew sadly little about other than to make broad assumptions.

Alex has made hundreds of messages and literally just a handful showed him upset or in pain. There were dozens of messages that never made it to social media because he broke down whilst recording them or was in pain or discomfort. We made the decision right from the start that this wasn't going to be a platform to curry sympathy and invoke totally emotional responses based on pity. Alex's journey was about positivity. The few occasions Alex did show emotion on public videos it had been put on at Alex's request and carefully gauged by us. Cancer is a horrible evil thing and sometimes, just once in every hundred posts, we wanted to gently remind people of that.

As previously mentioned, Virgin Atlantic had been so very supportive and they had upgraded us for free on occasion and heavily subsidised Alex's flight and his sister's. Alex had to fly with sufficient leg room otherwise he could not make the journey without being in agony. We had to sit with him as opposed to being half way down the plane: too far away to help him or hear his cries for us.

The situation with the NHS is one I am currently seeking to resolve. I have commenced a dialogue with the three hospitals and with our local doctors practice. Some meetings have taken place, some admissions of failings have been made. We are seeking a mutually satisfactory resolution to the situation and hope and pray that nothing like this ever happens to another child who may not be as lucky and blessed as Alex. We hope, in some way, get some honest dialogue with the NHS to draw a line under this and get on with our lives.

Twenty-Two

It was now a few weeks since the big surgery and Alex continued to heal. Aside from his regular physiotherapy sessions with Chris his visits outside of the house were short because he was still very frail. Lou and Jane spent precious time with Alex and the rest of us when they were at home, time which we look back on warmly. It was here one evening that we have sat with Lou and went through the medical scans and files in tremendous detail right from the outset back in the U.K. We had also received feedback from Dr. Chastain on the historic issues that she considered to be the pitfalls in Alex's overall care and attention from his first contact with the hospitals and G.P a year earlier. We would have the information we needed to move this forward when the time was right.

Alex, whilst loving the time he was spending with his family and extended family, was missing the outdoors and was keen to get back to nature and wild things. He had taken to bird watching from the Wetzel's kitchen and dining room. On the 24th and 25th January he spent hours with his binoculars at the large windows in the house that overlooked the beautiful garden. Sadly, as January came to an end so did our time at the Wetzel's. We would see them every week but the time had come for us to live elsewhere for the rest of our time in Kansas City. The day we moved from that wonderful home, and it was a home to us, was a tearful one. We loved and still love that family and they are so dear to us. Jane was clearly upset as she helped us move the many trappings we had accumulated in the weeks we were there, but we still spent quality time together as I hoped we would one day in our home when they would come to visit. We had moved to the Residence Inn Marriott Hotel in the Legends area of Kansas City.

We now had our own apartment with disabled access, two bedrooms and a small kitchen area and living room. It was basic but it was somewhere we could settle. The staff were pleasant and friendly and we built up close friendships with several of them especially with Emlee, one of the housekeepers, in particular. She was a very kind and she and her family became part of the army of supporters walking with us. We had budgeted for the costs of accommodation but also received support from donations as we stayed there until August. The hotel had a pool and Sophia loved to spend time there. Alex was still unable to use the water due to his Hickman Line but that was soon to change and he would enjoy it too.

Alex had a busy week ahead of him. The 30th January saw activity back in the U.K. where we still had so much support and people were still fundraising. Some of my old colleagues Matt, Tom and Tim (with some logistical support from Stephen) from the C.N.C. had endured a coast to coast cycle ride in appealing weather conditions. Those appalling weather conditions also affected Inspector Paul from my force who was doing a sponsored walk for Alex. He sent video updates to Alex during his trek which usually involved him getting drenched.

This U.K. support still included hundreds of messages every day and we would, due to the time difference, wake every morning to many messages and posts of support and love. If you add the number of supporters particularly in Australia, we had pretty much every time zone covered and that meant Alex's social media was a 24-hour concern. I recall around this time we had received a touching poem from a U.K. Police Inspector who went by the pseudonym 'Policey McPoliceface' called 'Brave Journey'. It struck a chord with me and we have it printed out at home.

Brave Journey

There's joy in the curl of feather
as a raptor's wingtip
skirts grass to reach
gloved safety and food
in thanks from watching people

There's wonder in the scale of dinosaur
finds from archaeopteryx

to megalosaurus and who knows
what tales they tell
through crocodiles today

There's warmth in family
Spread across countries
All wearing sorts of blue
so all fight together
And hands link over oceans

There's wisdom in the grace
of a young warrior
who taught an old cop
how to be brave and wear
a smile of tough days

There's gratitude from thousands
For your messages of hope
With wishes for us all,
So keep that spirit shining
And we'll stand with you

Alex went to K.U. Sarcoma Centre for a check up on the 31st January
and all was going well. We were back at Children's Mercy for tests
that afternoon. In light of Alex's disappointment in not being able to
enjoy swimming pools and a nice bath we had managed persuade him
to change the Hickman Line to a more modern access port system.
This would allow him to be fully immersed in water with no
problems. He was nervous because of the need for the use of
needles to access the port but one the boys at the hospital called
Noah spent time with Alex and reassured him. We were going ahead
with the minor surgery for the Hickman Line removal and it was
agreed and it would take place on the 2nd February.

This was the day we received the message from Stephen Walters and
the song "Hold On". We are still considering releasing that song to
raise money for Alex with perhaps HOMM on the other side and a

piece from a young lady called Maite who has a beautiful haunting voice. Maite is the daughter of Michaela (Maruška's friend). When the dust has settled back home I shall talk with Stephen, Ross, David Jones Senior and Junior and Michaela and Maite! And we shall see what happens.

Alex was getting stronger and was able to endure longer journeys. On the 1st February we managed to get to the Sea Life Centre in Kansas City and it was here we met Amy Anderson of KCTV5. Alex loved his time spent close to animals and he talked about the sea life to the staff and other visitors with his usual knowledge. I could see he missed being with animals and nature as this visit, like the birdwatching, ignited a fire within him again. We were interviewed by Amy of KCTV5 who did a piece for her TV station. She was clearly very fond of Alex and they seemed to build a rapport very easily. Amy and her team back at KCTV5 would become a positive force for Alex in the months to come.

The 2nd February arrived and Alex had his port put in and had the Hickman Line removed. He would be able to enjoy the water again and we talked of getting him out to Disney World one more time before we left for home. We had funds available that had been raised for that specific purpose. It was funny now how we had started to look to the future more. We talked of things we wanted to do before Alex left the U.S. Alex and I also spoke of getting him a garden and a place to spend time with hopefully an owl of his very own. Grow flowers and vegetables. Things you wouldn't expect a normal boy of his age to want and to desire. But Alex is no normal boy.

Very soon he would enjoy the pool and he and Sophia would spend time there often. It was good for him as he was exercising the leg in the weightlessness of water and having fun. Mariette would bring her daughters to play with Sophia and Alex and the friendship and connection grew closer. Mariette and Maruška became close friends and Sophia and her girls went to gymnastics together. Mariette was an important strand in the net of support we had in the U.S. and she would play an important role in the progression of this book and DVD in a few short months' time.

On the 8th February, we had been invited to Lenexa Police Department by a Captain Mendoza. She was part of a fundraising group called Guns n' Hoses which supported needy people in the local police and fire service family and they had decided they wished to support Alex too. Captain Diana Mendoza had reached out to us weeks previously and I had, just like Kim at the Lakeside Nature Centre extended our thanks and promised to be in touch. Again, like Kim, I am so relieved that I remembered to make sure that this meeting happened. Diana and her husband Kevin were to become as close to us as Chief Terry and the Wetzel's. Their friendship and kindness is something we all hold dear.

Lenexa Police Department are tasked with the well-being of the City of Lenexa (named after a native American Indian princess who lived there many years before). It has a population of around 50,000 people and lays just outside of Kansas City. We arrived and were met by Captain Diana and her husband Kevin who was the Deputy-Chief of neighbouring Leawood Police Department.

Diana and Kevin, at face value, seemed like chalk and cheese: she was of Hispanic decent and Kevin Irish but you couldn't be more wrong. They were tight and seemed to have perfectly balanced success in a demanding career and fun and fulfilment together at home. They were also lovely, kind people who, like everyone who came across him, were touched and inspired by Alex. Alex became very close to Diana and Kevin as did we all. Maruška and Diana shared a love of Margaritas and Mexican food and Kevin and I shared a passion for the job that was underpinned by the ability to let it go sometimes and talk about beer and other manly topics! I liked Kevin. I felt relaxed in his company and he along with a handful of others would become a surrogate father to Alex whilst I was back in the U.K.

We enjoyed a tour of Lenexa Police Station and met several officers including Sergeant Jason who would also follow us for the rest of our time in the U.S. We also met the members of Guns n' Hoses who had donated money to us. They were good people who thanks to the communications of Chief Terry, had been made aware of Alex's plight and were on board. It was a happy moment laced with a small degree of sadness as one of the members had recently lost her husband to cancer. She was very nice and we held hands tightly. We had been riding the crest of a wave with Alex and his successes. He had become a celebrity and this moment, literally a few seconds, anchored me again to the steely fact that we were still in a battle with a deadly disease that took too many people away from their loved ones. Despite this moment, the night was an enjoyable one and we would spend time with the Guns n' Hoses people again (and spend a huge amount of time with Diana and Kevin!).

On the 13th February we had another visitor: Sergeant Josh from Portland P.D. in Indiana made the 580 mile trip to visit us. He was one of the first U.S. cops to follow us on Twitter and we had spoke in messages about meeting one day. Our trip to Kansas City had afforded Josh that opportunity. His wife, Jen couldn't make it but we were assured she would come next time. It was great to see him and Alex enjoyed the time too. Josh and I had about the same length of service in the police and we shared war stories as all cops do. He spoke openly about how finding Alex had changed his life and inspired him. We would keep in touch and he became another advocate of Alex spreading the word in his home town. He spent just one day with us but when he left, promising to bring his wife with him next time, the world seemed a smaller place.

The plans laid at the bake sale had become a reality and we advertised Alexander's Journey t-shirts for sale to raise funds that same week. They were on a shield bearing the four flags of the four major countries where our support was: U.K., U.S., Canada and Australia with the thin blue line across them and the words "In this family, no one fights alone". A crown adorned the top and an eagle underneath, its wings unfurled carrying the shield. They were a success and again were covered by the TV stations. Keleigh from KMBC9 came to visit us at the hotel and covered the story which such gusto! She had also been drawn to Alex's story and pledged to support us how she could. She was very nice and, just the fact that she had a photo taken wearing the t-shirt, probably boosted sales! Maruška and the "L.E.O. wives" managed to get the help of the Bass Pro Shop one more time and did a t-shirt sale event there. I remember several of them posing for the camera in their t-shirts and proudly displaying their bespoke love-heart forearm tattoos for the occasion.

I recall, just after the t-shirts were out, we met one of the K.C.K.P.D. cops Kellee and her son Wyatt at Legends and went to the T-Rex restaurant there. When we arrived, we noticed them straight away proudly wearing their Alexander's Journey t-shirts! Wyatt and Alex shared a love for Pokémon and dinosaurs so it was always going to be a good visit! The restaurant itself was very impressive with amazing dinosaur decorations. If the food was as good as the dinosaurs we would've been back every day!

We embraced the opportunity to get Alex outdoors and involved with his passions: nature and wildlife. Troy arranged for us to visit the F.L. Schlagle Environmental Library and The Ernie Miller Park and Nature Center.

The F.L. Schlagle Library is an educational centre at the Wyandotte County Park and Lake and we visited a few times over a short period. It was a small wooden building set at the lakes edge surrounded by woodland and contained many hidden treasures. Alex spent time with the staff there who were very kind. One of Troy's old school friends, Jessica, ran the centre and she and Alex spent considerable time together. Alex loved his time there enjoying the snakes and turtles as well as an extremely impressive collection of fossils that Alex poured over with much excitement. Alex also did some birdwatching there and Alex and Troy talked of fishing in the Lake when it was warmer.

The Ernie Miller Park in Johnson County was also a place Alex, Troy and I visited. Bill and the rest of the team there gave him a tour of the centre. They had several birds of prey and lots of reptiles. He loved seeing the owls as well as a rather impressive Red-tailed Hawk. We met a man there that inspired both Alex and I: a Cherokee Indian called Billie "Womp Ni Womp" Thompson. His native name 'Womp Ni Womp' translated as 'Loud Foot/Walker' was due to his large foot size. What was impressive about him, aside from the fact he was an Indian, a cop and a zoologist, was that he spoke with such calmness and passion about his role and the world around him. Alex and I talked about him for hours that evening. We spoke on the telephone a few times after that meeting as he was helping me with my own book. I hoped to meet him again. Alex would before he left for the U.K. and home.

The third nature centre Alex would visit and frequent often was the Lakeside Nature Center in Kansas City, Missouri. It became his refuge and place to find his peace and contentment. The director, Kim, became a close family friend and such an important person in Alex's life. He would not go there until the beginning of March while I was in the U.K.

Our original treatment plan in the U.S. was for Alex to have the first two parts of his surgery, recover from them and then return to the U.K. at the end of February for consolidation chemotherapy and radiotherapy. He would then return next year to the U.S. for the final part of the surgery, which was the removal of the oversized titanium femur and to replace it with the telescopic one that would grow with him into adulthood. The success of the first surgery and the skill of Dr. Rosenthal had resulted in the second scheduled surgery being completed alongside the first.

We were getting ready to return to the U.K. but something would happen which would change all that.

Twenty-Three

"At this time, Alex's chances of survival over the next five years are still twenty to thirty percent"

Dr. Chastain's words rang inside my head like a bell. I asked her to repeat what she had said as I genuinely thought I had misheard her. We were at Children's Mercy Hospital and Maruška and I were having a meeting with Dr. Chastain and Lindsey. It had begun as a discussion on where we were and how Alex's treatment was going. They were impressed just how quickly his leg was healing and how the scans all indicated that we were in the best place we could be.

On this occasion Maruška and I had met them without Alex being around so we seized a chance to talk about the reality of what Alex was fighting. We had been made aware previously of the weight of the challenge that we faced but for some reason I assumed, after so many successes, we would be in a much stronger and more positive position. We knew that it was a statistic and just as I had assured myself before, the number of people in that sample meant that it was only indicative. Dr. Chastain assured us too that it was a statistic and Alex had responded so well to treatment.

This brought home just how fragile our apparent position remained. Tears filled my eyes. I was upset, shaken and shocked and so was Maruška. We needed to do everything we could to maximise his chances of life. I would not allow him to leave me. I had not suffered the feelings of fear or desperation for weeks but now they had returned. Being in the U.S. had allowed me to hope: to dare to hope.

Dr. Chastain continued to explain that once the five-year mark had passed the statistics indicated his chances of survival increased significantly. He would require detailed checks every three months for the next five years so that any indication of a reoccurrence could be dealt with swiftly. I was gripped by anxiety at the thought of me placing my trust in the same people who I felt had failed us in the

U.K. hospitals. I know it may have been unreasonable, but I had lost confidence and I was filled with dread. I had already shared my reservations with Maruška about our return to the U.K. and placing Alex back into the care of our local medical facilities. I had an overwhelming need to keep Alex here. I even considered the realistic prospect of moving to the U.S. for the next five years or longer. My brain processed so many scenarios and possibilities in a matter of a few seconds. The doctors here were doing a tremendous job and Alex would survive, I knew he would, if the care was sustained. We had already discussed previously the potential for us to stay here somehow and for Alex to have the final surgery this year instead of waiting for the next. That would mean that he wouldn't return to the U.K. and a degree of normality and school to then have it taken from him again. I wanted and needed to stay here and have the rest of the treatment done in Kansas City for the sake of my own mental health. We needed all of it to be done here: the consolidation chemotherapy, the radiation therapy and the final surgery. We also needed to come back as often as it would take for the scans and femur lengthening to be done.

We discussed the scenario at length with Dr. Chastain and she agreed to draw up a treatment plan and contact the finance department. The costs would be remarkably similar to the projected costs we already had for him to return next year and we would just have to find the difference. And we would find the difference, if I had my way.

We left that meeting with a myriad of tasks and enquiries to conduct including the thorny issue of our permission to stay in the U.S. I had no choice but to return home and get back to work, but the matter would still be a problem for Maruška and the children as their entry stamps, based on the ESTA visa-waiver, would only allow them to stay until March 13th and that was less than one month away.

We discussed the issue with Chief Terry, Dr. Lou and Mariette and between us we researched our options- which were limited. The rules allowed us to readily obtain a one-month extension whilst still in the country but after that we had no choice but to leave. Alex's new treatment plan would necessitate him remaining in the country until August or September to ensure the treatment was completed and he was sufficiently healed to endure the flight back to England. We decided to share our predicament with our circle of friends and on social media. The response was surprising.

With hindsight, it may have been prudent for us to delay or withhold the information from social media altogether. By sharing it with our network of friends several of them had already reached out to their elected representatives and to government officials to assist us. We had also spoken with the British Embassy in the U.S. and our own Member of Parliament for the constituency where we lived. Pam, the International Services Director at Children's Mercy Hospital also gave us a steer on how to progress things.

It was unfortunate that a great many people on social media attempted to use our situation as a political weapon: blaming individuals and policies from one side of the political spectrum to the other. The social media 'experts' came out in droves, telling us what to do. The predominant piece of advice was to 'simply' fly home and fly back again, and this time with the correct visa. They seemed to have forgotten that Alex would find the journey excruciating and that he needed to begin his consolidation chemotherapy in his treatment plan immediately. Any delay would create further problems and once it commenced, travel would potentially be very dangerous to his health. The TV stations covered the issue as we sought a suitable and workable solution.

Luckily, as a result of the TV media provision, we received support and advice from elected officials across the political spectrum in the U.S. who were all kind and most helpful and considerate of our plight. We had a meeting at Congressman Yoder's office in Kansas and received sound advice and support that allowed us to meet with officials from the U.S. Citizenship and Immigration Services at their Kansas City office. Thankfully, due to the unique circumstances of the case we were allowed to stay until Alex's treatment was concluded. Thus, the whole event was resolved in a matter of weeks thanks to some well-placed telephone calls, some sound advice and a modicum of common sense. Thank you to Congressman Yoder, The Secretary of State for Kansas and the elected officials and civil servants on both sides of the pond who helped not make a drama out of a possible crisis.

With immigration issues resolved and behind us, Alex began his consolidation chemotherapy and we tried to find a routine. I remember a few days before I had to return home to the U.K. talking with Chief Terry and Dr. Lou about the journey we were on and how no one would ever believe the things that had happened to us. That was where we hit on the idea of writing a book about our experiences. After some thought and the much earlier comments from Damian at Into Productions I agreed and began to set my thoughts down to paper. We shared the decision with several of our closest friends and they were very supportive and excited! Mariette was a great help right from the outset at progressing things and over the coming months changing a brilliant thought into a stunning reality. She had an energy and optimism that was infectious. She was always smiling and always ahead of the curve. The kind of person I needed to push me along.

The time had come for me to make a decision about work. I was expected back as I had exhausted all my generous leave time away from the police force back home. I deliberated our options and considered what was best for Alex. In the words of a famous Clash song, "should I stay or should I go?". Yes, it was should 'we' stay or go, but in essence I was the key variable. I had received offers of employment from three law enforcement agencies in the state of Kansas as a police officer and Sheriff's deputy. Ironically the offers from the Sheriff's departments recognised my experience and service and I would, when certified, start as a Class A deputy. The issue was, of course, getting certified. I would need to obtain citizenship and that, short of divorcing Maruška and marrying an American woman, would take several years! (And I'm not sure how Maruska would've taken that!). As an interim, I could undertake a civilian job. I also discussed the situation with several of the cops with whom I had become close over a beer in the nearby Yard House. I remained undecided for so many reasons. I had found a fondness for America, particularly Kansas and the friends I had made were treasured by me, that was for sure. I could see myself living there for sure but it was a gamble and one that I wasn't sure I was prepared to take (I had a lot of my gambling chips invested in another game that was far more important). I love my country and I also had so many strong links to home as well as a loyalty to Warwickshire Police who had stood with me through all this.

I wouldn't make my decision now, so on Wednesday 1st March, I flew back to the U.K. leaving my family behind. I was racked with guilt and worry but had no choice. I had to start the process of returning to normality here: back to work, back to routine, back to normal life. I was also beginning to pave the way for the three of them to come home too. We had to find a new home as well and that was also on my "to do" list.

Before I left, Maruška and I had arranged a trip to Disney World for when I returned, in-between his chemotherapy and radiation therapy, so we all had that to look forward to. For the next seven weeks, I would receive updates and news by telephone and live video calls. Maruška and the children received so much support while I was away and Alex continued with the chemotherapy. On the 9th March Alex, enjoying a few days of respite from his treatment, finally visited Lakeside Nature Center and that visit would change his life.

The Lakeside Nature Center is home to birds of prey, reptiles, fish, small mammals and a coyote! It is primarily a rehabilitation centre for injured or orphaned animals but also provides wildlife education. Maruška told me that Alex had fallen in love with the place within minutes of arriving. I, during later visits, had witnessed his joy first hand.

Over the following months as he endured chemotherapy, radiation therapy and the healing and physiotherapy after his final surgery, Lakeside was his "go to" place. He felt peace there and had so very easily built up the trust needed with the owls as well as the reassurance required with Kim, the director. He had shown to her after several visits that he was both equally competent and caring with the birds, beyond his years and thus she allowed him to become involved in caring and handling some of them. This was exactly what he needed. He missed Anita and the solace he felt when handling her owls, Murray in particular and this was a welcome substitute. He had his favourites: Hootie the Barred Owl and Darwin the Eastern Screech Owl.

Hootie, an older owl, had cataracts and had become a permanent resident at the centre due to his inability to survive in his natural habitat. Alex would hold him and simply speak softly and gently to him as he perched comfortably on Alex's glove. They both seemed so at ease with each other and content to share that moment.

Darwin had suffered from the West Nile Virus whilst in the egg and as he grew his feathers didn't develop properly. Despite the center's best efforts to rectify the deficiency he was deemed unsuitable for release so he too was kept as an education bird. Alex would always talk about the events of the day after every visit to Lakeside before he went to sleep, just as he had done with Anita. He always reminded me how much he would love a garden of his own and to have his own owl to look after in it. He deliberated for hours on what type of owl he would have: finally, he chose an Eastern Screech Owl and planned to name it Darwin just like his, not so feathered, friend at the centre.

I had returned to work and undertaken weeks of tests and assessments to get 'match fit' for my role. It was mid-April before I could get back to visit them and I did so with my Mum. We flew out on the 16th April and arrived on 17th. Alex had endured chemotherapy throughout my absence and had continued to have his physiotherapy. The children were so happy to see my Mum and she was so happy to see them. It was just the tonic Alex needed as he was exhausted. The week my mum was there Alex was so ill and we didn't go anywhere, she had come all the way to the U.S. but had seen very little except for the Marriott hotel. When I apologised to her for it she dismissed me straight away telling me that she was happy because she had seen the children and that was the most important thing for her. It had been his final week of chemotherapy and his body had endured enough. For about seven days his mouth ulcers had broken through. He was the most ill from the side effects that we had ever seen him, even in the UK. He was still recovering when we were hoping to get to Comi-con, but he was determined to fight through it and we made it there... he had a great time. He deserved to have a great time as he was really pushing himself at this stage of his treatment.

On the 28th April went to the KU Cancer Center for our first meeting with Dr. Massey for checks. Dr. Massey's name had been mentioned in conversations previously and I had seen her on email lists prior to leaving the U.K. but this was the first time we had met. Dr. Massey was the oldest in the team of experts that were part of his treatment plan. Dr. Massey was impressed by Alex's courtesy and kindness and often remarked about how polite and well-mannered he was. She outlined the plan to give Alex conventional radiation therapy which consisted of 30 sessions over six weeks with each one lasting, after setting up the process and positioning Alex, just a few minutes. He would adopt a pattern of having five sessions and then have two rest days before resuming the treatment again.

As we approached the end of the meeting Dr. Massey mentioned a possible alternative treatment if Alex was deemed suitable and that was called stereo-tactic radiation therapy. This was a more specialised form of radiotherapy and involved just five sessions over the significantly shorter period of only six weeks. It was because it used specialist scans and equipment to allow it to deliver precisely targeted, higher doses that minimised collateral exposure to nearby organs and tissue. That was such a shorter period of treatment! Eagerly, if at all possible, we voiced our desire for the latter method. We would have to wait for the decision. When we returned from Disney World Alex would commence the radiation therapy treatment, whichever one it would be.

Alex's health had improved but he still struggled to raise his blood levels after so much chemotherapy and we were unsure, even up to the day before our flight, if he would be strong enough to fly to Disney. I took him to hospital the day before we were to depart and he had the blood test. He was in good spirits and spent the time, whilst we waited for the results, painting pictures again. We sat in the playroom and I watched him interact with the other children there. A boy slightly older than Alex kept coming in and out of the room on crutches and seemed angry and upset. About what, I did not know, but what I observed during my time there was that he was mean and spiteful to the nurses and other children there. I noticed that he was the only child that did not have a parent close by. Some were in their child's rooms or snatching an opportunity, whilst their child was engrossed in play, to grab refreshments or visit the rest room. He sat slightly apart from the other kids including Alex and drew his own picture. As he came into the room for the fourth time we were there, Alex again said hello: nothing overt or blatant but sufficient to have been noticed by this boy, yet he didn't reply. He was, it appeared, satisfied to dwell in his own sphere and only interacted with the other children to scold them as he passed them or commented on how they had the colour paint he needed. Alex began to exchange a few words with him about sharks and he had noticed, as I did later, that the boy had painted sharks on his water scene. Over the period of about 40 minutes Alex had engaged with him and as we left that day they hugged and said goodbye. Such was Alex's superpower: Alex the inspirited, Alex the patient, Alex the persistent.

My mum then left for home and the children were sad and would miss her. We did however get some good news: the blood test results and Alex was able to fly to Disney World!

On the 1st May we flew out to Florida and Disney's Polynesian resort. This time no one was waiting for us besides the glorious sunshine, but that's all we needed. It was nice to get away and the resort was marvellous. Alex and Sophia spent most of the time enjoying the amazing water features and pools there. Now with a port, Alex could truly enjoy the water and he was often in the pool. Sophia, meanwhile, was often seen, flowers in her hair, twirling and swaying around in hula skirt and frequently treated us to a rendition on her newly acquired ukulele. Both children rested and recharged their batteries, as did Maruška and I. We visited the Disney parks and Sophia loved meeting the princesses and Lilo and Stitch. We visited Epcot and I remember we spent time at the 'World Showcase' attraction. Alex enjoyed the fish and chips at the United Kingdom pavilion (designed to look like a stereotypical British village, complete with English gardens and eateries). They tasted as good as home.

The staff at Disney and at our resort in particular, were so friendly and Alex left his mark on many of them also. Several of them keep in touch via social media, including Andrea who has promised to visit us in the U.K. We also spent time with some of his followers including Liz who visited us at the Polynesian resort, Valori who shared a magical day at Universal studios with us and Symberley a life guard at Animal Kingdom whom we met at Epcot.

The holiday allowed Alex to become a child again for a short time and I remember recording him on my phone at the resort. He was in a dancing procession being pushed in his wheelchair by Mickey Mouse as he and Sophia shook maracas.

Whilst in Florida I received a call from Dr. Chastain. We had agreed that she would update us on a recent scan taken of Alex days before we left for Disney. She was calling whilst on a conference in Canada. Her news wasn't good. The scans had indicated a 'mark' on his pelvic bone that needed investigation. He would have a scan when we returned to Kansas City. I shared the news with Maruška and we pushed it to the back of our minds and enjoyed the rest of our time in such a magical place. We returned on the 14th May- with heavy hearts for what was waiting for us in Alex's next biomedical investigation.

Alex had a biopsy on the 15th May in order to investigate the mark indicated on the scan: no weeks of agonising wait here. We had the results the following day, it was identified as a slow burn infection resulting from the biopsy Alex had undergone in the U.K. prior to us arriving in the U.S. Their comments on the U.K. biopsy and the resulting infection are best left out of this book!

With the worry of the scan and the biopsy behind us we moved forward towards Alex commencing radiation therapy. On the 16th May we visited Dr. Massey at her clinic. Alex was fitted for his mould that would keep him in the exact position for each session of radiation therapy. We were still waiting on a decision as to whether Alex could have stereo-tactic radiation therapy but preparation continued regardless! Things happened here, we were always working towards the objective: no waiting, no delays, no frustration.

The following day was an important one. During the time I was back in the U.K. and indeed when I had returned to the U.S., I had begun to pen the book. As was always the case, I never walked alone. Kevin's close friend J.P was a cop in the Fairway Police Service. He was good friends with Roger and Vivien, the owners of an independent book store in Fairway, Kansas that enjoyed a national platform: Rainy Day Books. A meeting was arranged and I was keen to obtain their support to give us a huge springboard for the book and documentary of Alexander's story: Alexander's Journey – Dum Spiro Spero.

Twenty-Four

I visited Rainy Day Books and met with Roger Doeren, the Chief Operations Officer and husband of the owner Vivien Jennings. I attended with officer J.P. and Mariette, who had very kindly agreed to travel there with me. It was a meeting full of energy and enterprise. Roger had a boldness and passion about him and we connected so very readily and so easily. I retold Alex's story to him and why we had decided to write the book and have the DVD produced. Why? Because it was a tale of enormous courage and triumph over adversity. A story of good people coming together in a bad situation and of enormous positivity against a backdrop of fear, pain and darkness. How had one small British boy captured the hearts of so many and inspired so many to be better people? A boy with a life-threatening illness who battled daily? A boy who loved animals and despite his frailty, cared more for others than himself? I told Roger of Alex the brave, Alex the inspirational, the kind, the inspirited, the passionate, the daring, the gentle, the warrior.

Roger was on board: physically, mentally and spiritually. They would support the book and we were grateful.

Rainy Day Books are a small book shop with a big presence: enjoying a strong mail order market as well lots of local loyal customers. Everyone- and I mean everyone- we knew in Kansas had shopped there! They punched way above their weight. Vivien was a respected book critic and notable entrepreneur within the industry. The company had been around for decades and was an influential member of a consortium of independent book stores in the United States.

On the 17th May Alex met Roger and Vivien at Rainy Day Books and this cemented our alliance! We confirmed that we would have a book event in Kansas City on the 27th July where we would celebrate the publication of his book and premiere of the DVD. During our visit Roger and Alex talked about books, nature and science. They spoke for hours until Alex was exhausted and I had to drag him away to rest.

Other preparations were being put into place too and we had met with AlphaGraphics K.C. who would print the book for us! It was again, like Rainy Day Books, a seemingly small concern that punched above its weight. Allison became our key contact there and she was to endure so many up and downs in the writing of the book as I navigated potential legal pitfalls and contentious litigation issues. What was important was that they were on board and Allison, like Roger, had an emotional attachment to Alex. She would do us proud in the months to come.

Thursday 25th May was a very important day! We were so worried that we would never see it, hidden as it was in a forest of our fears... It was my son's tenth birthday. A day to celebrate for very obvious reasons. Chris and John from the Traffic Unit arrived in the morning with hundreds of cards and gifts that had been sent to K.C.K.P.D. KCTV5 were there to cover the story and we met another TV anchor from that station called Joe Chioda. It wasn't long before Joe became yet another one of Alex's supporters and he covered another story with Alex just a month later in the city of Mission, Kansas. I watched Alex open his cards and drew enormous pleasure from it. Here he was, my son, refusing to give into cancer, refusing to let Death take him from us. Fighting. Winning. Alex the warrior, Alex the resilient, Alex the defiant. Alex the birthday boy!

We all received a present that day: a telephone call from Dr. Massey informing us that Alex was able to have the stereo-tactic radiation therapy and that was one of the best presents I had received for a while. We enjoyed a birthday meal that evening at the Wetzel's. It was nice to spend time with them. Lou and I spoke of the news of Alex's radiation therapy. I owed this man and his family so much. He is an amazing man who had, despite working so hard and forever being a work, retained the valiance of youth. I believed that was down to his mind set and his steadfast faith. I admired him and Jane and I hope we will spend time with them for many years to come.

That weekend we had Alex's official birthday party at the Lakeside Nature Center. Weeks in the planning had finally come to fruition and I hoped for everyone sake, especially my son's, that it went without hitch. It was a BBQ at the centre using their outside cook out facilities. Bad weather had been forecast and I remember setting up with some trepidation. We prepared the tables and food thanks to Troy, his wife Kim and their children Jake and Megan. Two of the K.C.K.P.D. cadets, Jordan and Ken, also came and gave us a hand. As we laboured we watched the black clouds roll over and within an hour the heavens opened and the wind howled. We had a storm too and the thunder boomed overhead. We were huddled around the BBQ with Troy and the cadets hoping for a change in the weather before everyone arrived. Mercifully, the storm abated and the Sun managed to get through for a few hours and that's all we needed to have a superb day. His party was well attended and it was so pleasing to see so many people from different walks of life who had come into our lives there. DJ Nightmare and his wife (Mrs. Nightmare as Alex had called her), several Nurses from K.U. Hospital, Roger from Rainy Day Books, Keleigh from KMBC9, Donna from the Kansas City Star and lots and lots of cops and their families!

K.C.K.P.D.'s S.W.A.T team also made an appearance. They were a good bunch and had previously spent time with us at the reception held shortly after we arrived. They had presented Alex with a beautifully framed presentation case containing their unit and department patch and challenge coins. It remains one of Alex's favourites.

Chief Terry and the Wetzel's were there too as was Diana and Kevin and our favourite motorcycle unit officers and their families. We also met Brian from Kansas City Missouri police and his family. Brian and I had exchanged many messages on Alex's Facebook account and it was good to finally meet him properly. He seemed a good man and easy to get along with. Brian had offered to arrange for us to visit the K.C.M.O. mounted unit and we firmed that visit up at the party. That was something that Sophia would really enjoy.

Wolverine from the Comi-con also attended and put his claws to good use at the BBQ!

Alex and Kim, when things had calmed down a little, presented a few of the birds of prey to everyone. Alex introduced them one at a time and answered questions from his assembled crowd. Maruška and I watched from the corner of the room beaming with pride as our son spoke confidently and with passion about a subject so close to his heart. Anita would have been proud!

Alex slipped into bed that night exhausted but so very happy. It was so warming to see him fall into sleep wearing a smile. Those times had been so rare for the last year but I hoped to see them more and more.

I had, whilst back in the U.K. been making preparations with Damien of Into Productions with regards to the production of the DVD. They had been extremely busy interviewing so many people there and putting together hours of footage. The time had come for them to make the trip across the pond and film here in Kansas City!

On Sunday 28th May, Damian and Aaron of Into productions arrived! Chris from the motorcycle unit and I met them at the airport on a very hot and stifling day. I had approached KJO Media at Westwood, Kansas for their help and they readily agreed. T.J. at KJO Media and his team were a tremendously kind and giving group of guys and we spent time with them as well as Damian and Aaron over the following week that they spent in the U.S. filming. Thanks to T.J. and Damian, a huge amount of time effort and expertise had been given by them freely to help Alex and I was truly humbled and grateful.

With Mariette's help as "Production Assistant" and Troy's as "Key Grip" an extremely hectic itinerary was arranged for that week as they walked the path that Alex had walked. Filming locations, people we had met and were indebted to, people who had become friends and the special few whom we had brought into our extended family circle. They worked hard and played little. With help from Jill at K.U. and Lisa, the Media Relations Manager and her team at Children's Mercy, they managed to spend quality time at the hospital interviewing some of the people that had helped us so very much. The doctors involved in Alex's care were obviously interviewed but so were many of nurses. All had a personal perspective on their relationship with this little boy from England. Some had been more profoundly affected by him than others: but all had been left with a positive and emotive experience.

On the 30th May Alex started radiation therapy. He was very nervous at first particularly because it was an unknown. The procedure took just minutes but there was a considerable preparation time in setting up the mould and placing Alex correctly and precisely on the machine. He experienced little ill effects from the procedure and was able to enjoy some recreation time which involved more visits to Lakeside Nature Centre and he visited some of the people that had reached out to him over the time we were there.

Another person we met several months after we had first become connected was Audrey. We finally met Audrey after she had sent more cards and letters to us. She was an expatriate living in Kansas City having made it her new home after the Second World War. She had an interesting story herself and one that I hoped would be told one day. Despite being in her late eighties or nineties (you never ask a lady her age) she still managed to get around and visited us at the Marriott hotel. It was interesting to listen to her talk. She had a Kansan accent that would occasionally reveal her English roots with a slight word difference or inflection. She was very nice and very loving with Alex. It was obvious she had left a piece of her heart in England and we talked of British things and of the relationship between the U.K. and the U.S. We also spoke of how our undeniable cultural and historical connections were portrayed slightly differently in each country. I enjoyed similar conversations with Mariette who, as a history teacher, was naturally passionate about her subject. It was interesting that Sophia had also developed inflections in her accent but the other way to Audrey and much more prominent. She was at the age where she was a sponge to the environment around her. She had been attending nursery in Kansas and was surrounded, as often as we could manage it, by children her own age. I only noticed how prominent her accent had become when she returned home to the U.K.

We took Brian up on his kind offer and visited K.C.M.O's Mounted Unit on the 1st of June - and that meant horses! Troy, Mariette and the Into Productions crew came with us. Sophia loved it. The officers were so kind and made the day such an amazing experience for her. Into Productions captured some superb footage of her that always brings a smile to my face whenever I watch it. As the filming continued we were able to meet trooper Ben again who came down to make his contribution to the DVD. It was good to see him again and we had English tea! As the interviews continued it was apparent just how much of an impact Alex has had on their lives. Sometimes in small ways- other times huge- but each comment, each testimony was enriching, inspiring and left me so proud of this British boy battling cancer.

We also managed to attend the annual Guns n' Hoses motorcycle event and the footage Damian got from there was amazing. Hundreds of motorcycles following a predetermined route that reminded me of our arrival in Kansas City in December. KJO Media filmed using a drone as they had done at our arrival. Filming continued as Alex had his next radiation therapy and Into Productions were able to attend the clinic with him and capture some of it taking place.

However, this was not Alex's only dalliance with film crews at this time! We visited KCTV5 and spent time with Amy Anderson. Alex sat in the studio with her and I posted a video clip on social media of him hosting the news at KCTV5. We met Amy's news team who were all following and supporting Alex too. We also went to KMBC9's studio and met Keleigh Gibbs there as well as one of the other weather presenters Jennifer McDermed. I watched Alex deliver a weather report in front of a live green screen and on the nearby monitor in front of the map of Kansas complete with sun, wind and rain CGI. All these events were timely and would, I hope, make the DVD a remarkable, memorable and emotive experience.

As Alex got stronger, we arranged the fishing trip that he had spoken about so many times. He had gone fishing with Scott and with Troy prior to this trip and enjoyed the experience so much. Into Productions came along and captured some magical moments. It was the 4th June when we ventured to Wyandotte County Lake with Troy and Troy's dad. Chief Terry came too and Damian and Aaron of course. Alex was bubbling with enthusiasm as we prepared for the day out and during our journey to the lake. He was so excited and talked continuously. Troy had made the arrangements and we took out a boat and a pontoon with Troy piloting one and his Dad the other. Alex hooked and netted a few fish and was very happy with the outcome of the day. We vowed to return again.

As we said goodbye to Damian and Aaron I was also preparing to return to England myself. They had obtained so much footage and I was excited to see the fruit of their labours. Days later, I left for the UK and home as well but this time with one very important addition: Sophia. Maruška and I had discussed it many times and finally decided that she needed to come back with me. Sophia's life was moving on and she was starting school in September back in our village. The new starts were having induction classes in June and July and it was essential that Sophia went to those so that when September and her first full day at school arrived she was prepared and had met her classmates and already forged some friendships. We knew it would be hard for her but my Mum would be living with us and take care of her while I was at work.

Alex had some important milestones ahead before, finally, he could return back to the U.K. himself. His radiation therapy treatment, much shortened by the use of the specialist method, would be over soon. He would then have his last surgery and then very important scans which would be the first of his three-monthly checks after his final chemotherapy. I wouldn't be around for any of them and

Maruska would manage them without me. I tried to console myself by drawing comfort from the fact that she wouldn't be alone: we had so many friends, close, dear friends that would be there for her and for my son.

As we made the flight home, I was sitting on the Kansas City to Atlanta flight with a woman called Kelly who was the boss at a company called Unify Health Services. The company, based in Jacksonville, had a portfolio that covered the country and she had been in Kansas City to meet with one of her major clients that was based there. We began to talk about my reasons for being in the U.S. and the conversation, as with every other conversation I had with strangers during my travels, got onto the subject of Alexander and his inspirational journey. She was amazed at the hurdles we had faced and she explained how her company would have shortened the agonising wait and made the connections immediately. It seemed like the company was a more connected and more accessible version of Red Arc who had helped me so much back in the U.K. She promised to keep up with Alex's story and wished us well.

My time spent at home was full with work, writing the book and commencing the mammoth task of attempting to create a dialogue with the hospitals back here in the U.K. This was a very taxing time and fortunately I had the support of friends. Shona and Jason visited when we could all find the time and I enjoyed my Aikido training and their company as well as integrating back into the team at work.

On the 12th June Alex had completed the course of radiation therapy and I watched the video of him ringing the bell at Dr. Massey's clinic. KCTV 5 was there as well as Jill, Cliff and Logan from K.U. Hospital media relations and the news made several local TV stations and local newspapers. You rang the bell at the end of your treatment and it was the same in the U.K. This was such a huge milestone for a young boy who had come so far during his time in Kansas. He would ring one more bell and that would be after his surgery. That would be the last one but this one signified that his cancer treatment was finally over. Alex was winning his fight. I can't tell you how emotional the sight of him ringing that bell made me. I had seen it rang twice before in the U.K. The first time was by a boy who we met briefly on the ward in Leicester and he rang it in July 2016 and remained cancer free. The second boy rang it at the end of last year but, so very sadly, he relapsed immediately and is now struggling in the fight. I knew Alex was different, he was victorious and would remain so.

The last element of the treatment plan was surgery to remove the titanium femur and replace it with the bespoke telescopic one. Dr. Rosenthal had explained that the surgery this time would be much easier and much shorter and most importantly less impactive on his body than the previous one. The surgery would be completed quicker and his healing time shorter. The physiotherapy was still required and would be for the following three months at least. I would try and seek assistance from the NHS for this when we were home but until then, and if we couldn't get that support, we would have to pay privately. The surgery was scheduled for the 5th July if, and only if, the specially made femur was complete and had arrived in Kansas from Essex, England in time.

That gave Alex four weeks of waiting but that time would be filled with visits and quality time with our close friends. On the 16th June, Spring Hill Police P.D. visited Alex and brought with them a beautifully made quilt with 90 police patches! Anna, a staff member at the force, had kept in touch with us and after months of waiting was finally able to meet Alex and Maruška and bring such a wonderful gift over. The patches covered mainly the police forces that surrounded Kansas City but also a few choice ones that were further afield. It was a fine-looking and unique present that its creators, Debbie and Leslie, must have spent an eternity working on. I was so touched to discover that it had an embroided message to Alex on the back of it. 'To Alex, from your family in Blue'. Spring Hill P.D's Chief Richard and Deputy Chief Brian were with Anna and they had been at the Wetzel's as part of the arrival convoy and also spent time with us at Alex's party at Lakeside.

Just before I had left we had been contacted by a Mr. David Block. I spoke initially with one of his assistants before speaking to him directly via telephone. I had naturally never heard of him before but our friends in Kansas City had: David Block was a very successful real estate developer and a supporter of local causes as well as being both a follower of Alex and an avid fan of the local baseball team the Kansas City Royals. I recall nearly being lynched by several of our friends in Kansas after telling them that I was particularly bothered about baseball. We English prefer cricket and baseball just hadn't gained any popularity in the U.K. as it wasn't played over here. I remember, rather amusingly, attempting to compare it to a game we used to play at school called rounders much to Kevin and Troy's disdain. Alex on the other hand, following some highlights of a game being shown whilst we were in hospital, became interested and was keen to go and watch a game first hand. Coincidentally Mr. Block very kindly offered us tickets to watch one of the big KC Royals games whilst we were there. Mr. Block and I spoke for some time on the telphone and he seemed a very friendly and genuine man. He asked after Alex and enquired if we were being looked after while we were here. Our conversation ended with him wishing me well and informing me that he would arrange for the tickets to be sorted for us. On the 21st June Alex and Maruška went to watch the game with Troy and his family courtesy of Mr. Block. They had VIP seats and he had also arranged for Alex to enjoy some KC Royals clothing and memorabilia. Alex enjoyed the game and the VIP treatment as did Maruška who recounted the day to me on more than one occasion.

People continued, both in the U.S. and the U.K. to support us through special acts of kindness and fundraising. Whilst I was away Kevin and Diana had arranged fundraisers at their local Mexican restaurant Sombrero's. We had eaten there several times and the food was very good. Our friend Teri and, one of the other women who had helped at the bake sale, Bridget had set up a fundraising account in the U.S to help with accommodation and living expenses. We also received generous support from a Kansas charity called Helping Hands. Whilst I was back in the U.K. I attended a fundraising event in Doncaster with my close friend Stuart and a group of his friends

229

and relatives affectionately known as 'team Alex'. I was aware of them on Facebook but we had never met. These people: Shyvonne, Tracey, Jasmine, Alison, Claire and Dannii were strangers when I arrived at the event but when I left, after enjoying some classic Yorkshire hospitality and big-heartedness, they were friends.

This was commonplace throughout the myriad of fundraising that had taken place: Skydiving, bake and cake sales, choir and singing events, sponsored walks, runs, cycling. Pennants were sewn and sold, boxing matches fought, collections made and raffles and auctions took place.

The money raised was being spent and I made further payments to the hospitals whilst I was there. Money had been spent on accommodation, food, clothing and transport too. When you live somewhere for well over half a year you need to buy clothes for the changing of seasons as well as ensuring you have enough to wear as there are only a finite number of suitcases you can bring over. We were making plans to ensure we had enough for the continued physiotherapy he would need back in the U.K. and for future visits to the U.S. and the scans and checks he would have there.

Twenty-Five

"First Order of Business: Honorary Mission Police Chief Alex Goodwin declares 'Big Monster Day'" read the headline. The photo alongside the article posted on KCTV 5's website was of Alex thrusting his newly awarded Mission P.D badge towards the camera! He had received his promotion from Deputy Chief of K.C.K.P.D. to the Chief of Police in the city of Mission, Kansas. KCTV 5 had also covered the event on their evening news with our friend and veteran of Alex related coverage Joe Chioda reporting.

I remember my surprise when I received the videos and photos Maruška sent me from their visit to Mission, Kansas and Mission Police Department on the 22nd June. It was here in Mission he received his promotion and was embraced by an entire city who would set Friday's aside for him.

Mission, Kansas began its days as an Indian mission in 1829 and grew from its origins as a trading centre and resting stop for wagons when moving west in the 19th century. It is now a city of just under 10,000 people with the cops of Mission P.D. being led by Chief of Police Ben Hadley. What was unusual about this invitation was that it came from the Unified Government of Mission, Kansas and not just the Police Department as had usually been the case elsewhere.

Chief Hadley had not met with Alex before this date because of the personal battles he was facing, but that delay made the eventual meeting with Alex all the more poignant. Alex was guest of honour at an event in the City and he was sworn in as honorary Chief of Police.

I watched the ceremony via a video recording Maruška had made. I watched intently as Alex, hand raised at a podium, recited the oath read out to him by the City's judiciary clerk. When he finished the whole room burst into applause. Another profound moment for me. I remember, as if it was yesterday, the day I took my oath and swore solemnly and sincerely to serve the Queen in the office of Constable.

I had, on several occasions over the years, wondered if Alex would follow in my footsteps as a policeman. This illness and the life changing treatment had most certainly put a stop to that now. He would get out of the wheelchair, I would make sure of it, but would he be a police officer? Probably not.

As Alex spent the day at Mission amongst new friends. The cops sought out his first command and his thoughts: he said that whilst they worked hard, it was important for them to have fun and he thought the best way to achieve that would be a special day. Thus, Alex, newly appointed to his role, gave out his first order of business: the institution of 'big monster' Friday. Much to everyone's surprise this would take place in just a few days!

Ironically and somewhat amusing, no one initially actually knew what that would entail but it involved a celebration of the monsters of classic cinema: Godzilla, King Kong, Frankenstein and the other greats from the golden age of film. Alex said that he wanted the officers to think of their childhood and enjoy the day. All the cops were given homework to study in preparation for a monster movie quiz. They, like every good police officer, took their responsibilities seriously and earnestly prepared for the challenge.

Alex and Maruška spent several days at Mission: enjoying the city's outdoor swimming pool with one of the cops Danny and his family in the glorious sunshine of that week. Mariette and her daughters Bella and Alex were there too. Alex got to spend time with Chief Hadley and the Deputy Chief Kevin and his family at their home: enjoying fishing, having a BBQ and good company.

Chief Hadley made sure it would be a memorable event and rallying the people of Mission managed amongst other things to acquire a giant Kong inflatable. The local bakery got on board and created special cakes in the shape of monsters and provided refreshments for the day. Monster movies were played in the conference room and posters of all the greats adorned the walls. Alex also gave a lecture, utilising power-point and projector, on the greatest battles that had taken place and as a final showpiece the officers, already in their assigned groups would do the imaginary battle of monsters to determine who would be triumphant. Officer J.P from Fairway P.D. was there too. It was a magical memorable day. Maruška told me that Alex could not actually believe that so many people have got together and did all that, just for him.

I only met Chief Hadley when I flew out briefly to Kansas City in August as Alex's time there drew to a close. I admire him greatly and we spoke about his own fight and how Alex had inspired and encouraged him on his own journey.

Chief Hadley declared it was going to be an annual event: every year, at the time when Alex comes back to Kansas for his checks the city of Mission will have 'Big Monster Friday'. I looked forward to the next one next year when, on that occasion, I would be with him.

Big Monster Friday 2017 had come to an end. This was another day that he fell asleep with a smile on his face. My son, Alex the contented, Alex the grateful, Alex the concordial.

I would marvel at Alex and how he could be so confident yet unassuming at the same time, how he could be such a source of inspiration for people that face the same adversity that he did. They turned to him for courage and furtherance. He was spectacular.

Did it really matter that he wouldn't be a policeman and not follow in my footsteps? Probably not.

Twenty-Six

Now Independence Day was always going to be an interesting one for Brits living in the U.S on that day. The war of independence is actually referred to over here as the American Revolutionary War. The day and the events causing it to come into being had been debated, discussed, disputed and argued over by me and so many U.S. cops and residents during my time in Kansas that I have lost count. The fanfare and celebrations were a welcome distraction for Alex as it was the day before his final surgery.

The 5th July was here. The day of the second and final surgery had arrived. Regular, intensive and sometimes brutal physiotherapy remained but, in essence, this was the final milestone before he returned home.

The telescopic bespoke prosthetic femur had been held by U.S. customs and had only arrived the week before the surgery. The cancellation and rearrangement of the surgery had been a real possibility but, thankfully, it was still going to take place.

Alex was just as nervous and anxious about this surgery as he had been the first time. I had hoped that it may have been easier for him the second time around, but it wasn't. Should we have been surprised? he was still only ten years old. A little boy who had grown wise and mature beyond his years because of the experiences he has had and the predicaments he has faced, but still needed the comfort of his mum or dad and still could not rationalise what was before him. He was unsettled just prior to it beginning but wanted to make a video for his supporters and for me as I was thousands of miles away. As Maruška made that video he looked visibly troubled and ill at ease and told everyone he was nervous. But he also wanted everyone to be okay.

Just like the first surgery Maruška had our close friends with her as she waited for news. We knew it would be a shorter procedure but she, as did I, wanted it done quickly. I couldn't settle until I received that call from Maruška that he was back with her and she could watch over him, because I could not. Local TV stations and newspapers were there and footage of Alex just prior to the procedure was on the evening news on several different channels.

After some 4 hours Maruška was informed that the surgery was done and Alex was in recovery. That news was passed to me and I felt the same palpable relief I had experienced in January. Dr. Rosenthal shared the good news with Maruška shortly after that it had been a success. The titanium femur was removed and the bespoke telescopic prosthetic was in its place.

Now he needed to heal and to endure the intensive physiotherapy that was so essential to his rehabilitation. Chris would continue to lead on his physio once he was discharged from K.U. Hospital but while he was there the team of professionals there would get him out of bed and moving as quickly as possible.

There was a balance to be found between rest, healing and the immediate manipulation of the leg. The femur needed to move, the muscles and sinew needed exercise. In addition to this the nerves, damaged from two sets of surgery, needed proper stimulation which would be managed through medication as well as massage.

The first few days would be agonising for Alex as he wrestled with the post-operative pain again and the psychological fear of damaging or tearing open the wound during his physiotherapy. But he did it. He cried, shouted and whimpered, but he did it. I remember the look of his face that I had seen with my own eye and also had been captured on the occasional photo and video footage. That look of pain at times but mostly the look of determination as he gritted his teeth. He was tough. He was my son. Alex the resilient, Alex the driven, Alex the indomitable.

Just a few days after he sent a video to his supporters on social media. He was brighter, more jovial and settled.....

"Hi everybody, it's Alex. This is a very fantastic day for me because I've worked really hard with this leg, my epidural has been taken out and my tube has been taken out that's been getting all the bad stuff out. And, if I do really really well today, and the doctors are really proud, which they are. I'll be going home, back to the hotel, tomorrow! Have a nice day and keep those ultra and powerful thoughts of me in your head and make sure you do fine aswell. Bye!"

He was discharged the following day. Over a week earlier than previously, such was his healing capability without the remnant toxicity of chemotherapy in his body. His hair had started to grow back too. It was finer and much lighter than previously. His original titanium femur was returned to him as a memento. We did own it and it was, aside from a house, the most expensive single item I had ever purchased at 90,000 U.S. dollars. It was also very heavy and I was bewildered how Alex had coped with it. I had joked about selling it so we could pay for the future visits but he got upset saying that we couldn't because it was important to him and had been a part of him.

It was time for him to ring the bell. The moment was captured on video and I watched it time and time again. It chimed so sweetly and Alex smiled to warmly to a backdrop of rapturous applause.

Dr. Wetzel was with him that day. All day. He pushed Alex out of the hospital in his wheelchair into the sunshine and warmth of a Kansas City summers day. He would get out of the chair and back on crutches soon after. He would start walking on his own weight aswell: a few steps only but they were bold ones.

He had defeated his cancer, the next set of scans confirmed no activity. We needed to keep it away now. Positive thoughts and love would fortify him. So would faith in himself, in goodness and the power of life.

Epilogue

This journey of Alex's hasn't been simply a medical one. It's been geographical – in that we have travelled globally to secure a cure and hope for the future; had conversations and made connections with other people from all over the world via the internet and social media, bringing worldwide experts electronically into our home to find out more about Ewing Sarcoma and how to battle it; trying to seek possibilities to move forward. It's been spiritual, religious, supportive, emotive and exhausting/exhaustive. It's not over yet, but Alex will be returning home, in remission, from Kansas as this book is sent to print. When we had the devastating diagnosis, I dare not dream of thinking up a sentence like that. I dare not hope of a future as a family. A future where I could hold my son and watch him grow into a man. A future where he would fall in love and experience joy with friends.

We have been loved by so many people who have dragged and cajoled us to this moment. We couldn't have done it without each and every one of them – no matter how big or small their financial or emotional contribution. As I discovered, comradeship got me through my darkest moments so I could be there for my Alex and my family. That was as valuable as any monetary commitment.

Maybe the longest journey has been mine. I have chastised myself and tortured myself over how Alex's illness began and deteriorated while I buried my head in the sand of policing and everyday things in my world. That will never happen again. I now appreciate every moment with them – my son, my daughter, my family. I feel so disappointed with myself that I haven't always felt like that.

Martial arts have taught me that a fighting spirit and mental and spiritual attitudes to discipline are equally as important as the physical ones. This has been true in our battle with cancer. I say *ours* because it consumed us as a family. Alex had to physically fight it alone – but we were the spirituality and strength behind him, supporting him through his gruelling treatment. This has led me to question my faith in humanity and in religion. I am religious. However, Alex's illness shook that to the core. It would any parent. Why my son? Why my family? Why me? I do believe in a force for good and that it exists. Some may argue it dwells within us. That we can naturally demonstrate resilience against demanding odds. Others may say that God infuses us with that strength. What I do believe is that no one came down and placed healing hands on Alex, but they may have enthused good people to do excellent and inspiring things. I believe that we are gifted the potential to do super heroic things – and what we do with that potential is up to us. Therefore, I have to thank every person for taking their God given gifts and talents and turning them towards Alex in order to give him the chance of a fulfilling life.

Although seldom referencing God, Alex has been touched by religion but also the goodness in people. He always asked for 'positive thoughts' and for him that included prayers. He finds peace, solace and comfort in a church. As do I. But he has also found peace in the company of good, kind, giving people because of who they are.

When faced with such a life threatening or life changing set of circumstances, it must affect you both mentally and physically, not to mention spiritually. I'm not just talking about religion here as so many of our followers are Atheists – including the brilliant Adam and Sara who stood with us on our journey and Creamy, my crewmate. The central characters in Kansas had all faced such traumas and difficulties – Chief Terry had gone from a devastated officer who had lost two colleagues, to a leader who saw others through such a terrible ordeal. Lou had made his own journey after examining his strength of character to cross the line from doctor to personal carer and friend when others in his profession wouldn't just when we needed them. Chief Hadley gained strength in his own battle that I pray he will win. I had travelled the road from distraction to being the best dad I could be. I felt a degree of redemption. I know others did too.

Sadly, throughout his journey and sharing it on social media, he had, as written about earlier in the book, come into contact with internet trolls. He has harnessed the good in himself and has tackled these troubled people with nothing but kindness and innocence. He has disarmed their words by using his inner good and peace against them. Some say 'fight fire with fire.' I say fight fire with water. Alex is the same. He took all his challenges the same way and turned something malevolent into something beautiful. I couldn't be more proud of how he handled that. Alex the Brave. Alex the Strong. Alex the Wise.

On this voyage, I have been repeatedly moved by how good people have come together in such a bad situation. This triumph over adversity led me, quite coincidentally, to the door of Chief Terry Zeigler in Kansas. Had it not been for the needless deaths of two Kansas City police officers, he would not have led me to the path of Dr. Lou Wetzel who has done so much for my family. It was kind of like a jigsaw or a mosaic coming together to show the full picture in the splintered pieces. So many people came together and helped. They invested in Alex because he inspired and motivated them; he invested in them, never thinking of himself, only in everyone having 'a great day,' with a thumbs up no matter how much pain he was feeling or how terrified he was of the treatment to come. I recall reading an article in the Kansas City Star newspaper which was based on an interview I had given in December 2016 at Children's Mercy Hospital. I was quoted as saying "He wants the best for everyone else. When he is frail himself". That speaks volumes as to who my son is.

He inspired people and had such an impact on them that they became supporters of his and wanted to do so much for him. Meanwhile, I built up friendships, deep enduring friendships, with people I didn't know because we had a commitment to the same cause… getting Alex well again.

There is one benefactor, who wishes to remain anonymous, who I really must thank - especially as I nearly ignored them thinking they were a hoax! However, this offer came at a time when we were being approached by manipulative and unscrupulous people who claimed they could help and attached themselves to our desperation to get Alex well and find an answer to his treatment. Luckily, we were rescued by genuinely compassionate folk, like our benefactor, who ultimately acted as a shield to these people, helping us through with their good words and deeds. See? Good does defeat evil.

Perhaps I have slightly missed the mark in this book when I said we were searching for a miracle and that we eventually found it through three people: the main benefactor, Chief Terry Zeigler and Dr. Lou Wetzel. Perhaps the miracle was Alex. And he had always been there.

He had certainly left his mark on the people that he had met on the journey. So many people had gone to see him off at the airport in Kansas City: Chief Terry, Dr. Wetzel, Diana, Kevin, Troy and John of course. But there were also others: Brian from K.C.M.O. P.D and his daughters plus Cherokee Indian Billie. I am sure had we extended the invite further several hundred Kansas and Missouri residents would have been there. That's what Alex had done to citizens in that area of the US. They were all part of Alex's Army and would support him however they could. They'd loved his story and many still follow him on social media. Alex is an internet sensation after all!

You may have noticed that there is a DVD of Alexander's Journey. The book doesn't exist in isolation to the film and they complement each other. We decided to make both to bring you the full story. This is because more than two thirds of the journey in the book takes place in the U.K. and less than one third in the U.S. It's the opposite way around on the DVD. This is purely because a lot of the narrative in the U.K. took place before we did any filming. The significant majority of the trials and tribulation took place in the U.K. and the emotions and obstacles were there but needed telling. Writing about them became cathartic to me. We were too emotionally raw to make a video diary or vlog at that time. These were the moments that put Alex in the position he found himself in. I was also chasing up leads for treatment so much and so often, I didn't have time or physical and mental strength to think about it. But we persevered and got answers. The success of Alex's online clips gave us the impetus to put together a film. The film completes our story to this point.

And what of the flower? When we left for the United States in December it had finally succumbed to Winter and was gone. I drove over to our old house a few days ago just before Alex was flying home and it had sprung out from the stone cracks again. It looked like it was lost, but it has returned. Perhaps I just needed to have some faith.

When I wrote the book I noted the number of coincidences and twists of fate. What if I told you that Mike, from the charity in Derbyshire was arrested last month on suspicion of fraud? What if I told you that we moved weeks before Alex fell ill and the only reason we moved was that I was experiencing a single recurring dream that I needed to return to mainstream policing? The only police Force that was transferring Authorised Firearms officers at that time was Warwickshire. I leave that to your thoughts.

As this is Alexander's Journey, I want to leave the final words of this book to Alex. Well, about Alex. Two years ago, no one had heard of him. To many he was a lad just getting on with the daily and ordinary job of growing up. Then cancer came along and made him extraordinary. He has always been kind, polite, gentle and a lover of nature. I may also be being biased. He's my son. But he has become extraordinary. He's faced his 'parasite' and repelled it. When he becomes older, he will pull up tree trunks. It became apparent that he could more than hold his own with fellow cancer victims. He sent messages to others enduring their own treatment, to 'be brave,' and they comforted and inspired each other. How could a nine-year-old be so level headed? He held it together so much better than I did. How did this boy who cares more for others and animals than for himself win the hearts of thousands across the world? By being open. Caring. Inspiring. Honest. He has only asked once or maybe twice- why? He fully remained committed to defeating it. He accepted what was happening but wasn't changed by it in any way other than a positive one. He has never got angry or miserable about it. He talked about God but never blamed Him. He never blamed anyone. It was one of those things and he had to conquer it. So, he just got on with it.

I remember he wept, just once or twice, saying that he had enough and wished it would stop. Wished he could be normal. Sorry my boy, you will never be anything other than extraordinary.

He is so excited about coming home. His first job will be to see his new garden and drink deeply in everything it is and can be. A place to find peace, cultivate flora and have his owl. Yes, during all this, we've moved to a new house with a garden.

I genuinely couldn't have managed that and everything else without the support of Warwickshire Police. I cannot believe there is a more supportive and committed group anywhere else in the world. I owe them a huge debt of gratitude.

We shall visit Cheshire falconry and both the Natural History Museum and Chatsworth again but before that and, after dwelling in his garden for a short while, the thing Alex will want to do is go for a Chinese meal in Dunton Bassett. Such a simple thing to do after such a complex couple of years… and I can't wait to take him.